You Love Your Daddy, Don't You?

A True Tragedy About Sexual Abuse

Sarah Harrison

CCB Publishing
British Columbia, Canada

You Love Your Daddy, Don't You?: A true tragedy about sexual abuse

Copyright ©2008 by Sarah Harrison
ISBN-13   978-0-9809191-4-1
First Edition

Library and Archives Canada Cataloguing in Publication

Harrison, Sarah, 1943-
You Love Your Daddy, Don't You?: A true tragedy about sexual abuse / written
by Sarah Harrison.
ISBN 978-0-9809191-4-1
1. Harrison, Sarah, 1943-. 2. Multiple personality--Patients--United States--
Biography. 3. Adult child sexual abuse victims--Rehabilitation. 4. Adult child
sexual abuse victims--United States--Biography. 5. Incest victims--United
States--Biography. I. Title.
HV6570.2.H37 2008   362.76'4092   C2008-901443-X

Publisher: CCB Publishing
             British Columbia, Canada
             www.ccbpublishing.com

This book is dedicated to the millions of victimized children whose innocence is stolen away and destroyed through sexual abuse and incest.

It is also dedicated to the United Methodist Children's Home of the North Georgia Conference in Decatur, Georgia, which helps in the monumental task of putting back together the shattered pieces of these broken lives.

Contents

You Love Your Daddy, Don't You?

Author's Note

This story is based on true events. I changed the names of some of the characters and locations to protect the innocent, as well as the guilty parties.

The purpose of this work is to tell the story of my life by sharing the most horrific nightmare that millions of children face around the world--namely sexual abuse by a trusted relative. I hope it will enlighten others who may be living in abusive situations and give them the strength and courage to do whatever it takes to separate themselves from their abuser, for only then can healing begin.

As Andy Stanley says in his book, *It Came from Within*, anger gains its strength from secrecy. Exposing the secret is both painful and powerful at the same time. You know intuitively that bringing it into the light will cause it to lose its potency, which means you will be able to stop your anger from becoming bitterness which only hurts you, the victim, even more.

In writing the book, I do drag out family secrets that hovered over me for many years. One of the benefits I have gained from writing this book is the ability to forgive—the kind of forgiveness Paul was writing about to the Christians in Ephesians 4:32: "Be kind and compassionate to one another, forgiving each other, just as in Christ God forgave you."

Ten percent of the book sales from the story of my life's journey will benefit the United Methodist Children's Home of the North Georgia Conference in Decatur, Georgia. My past church in Alpharetta, Georgia, Birmingham United Methodist, with John and Judy Wolfe as pastors, always send donations to this Methodist Home.

Reluctantly, in March 2007, I left that church and moved near Charlotte, North Carolina to be near my grandchildren. I searched for months before I found Harrison United Methodist Church, the most wonderful church. I am already involved with the Youth Group, Emmaus, Epiphany, and Faith Partners, a group for supporting others with substance abuse problems.

You can find me on **www.experts.com** in the parenting of teen's section. I receive questions from troubled parents and as well as teens. My dream is to help prevent abuse in children, especially by parents, by helping people who have been abused to cope with it and to understand those feelings they are encountering. After you read my book, your life will move to a better place because you will forgive yourself by realizing you were a victim of sexual abuse--rather than a participant. You will be able to look forward to the future, and you will love the Lord, as you learn all things are possible through Him.

Endorsements for
You Love Your Daddy, Don't You?

"Sarah's journey is a story that describes the courageousness and plight of a child faced with constant traumatic pain. Sarah's story is just one of millions that go untold and hidden in the shadows of shame and loyalty. *You Love Your Daddy, Don't You?* dares to break old secrets and chronicles the hope and journey to recovery.

The development of 'alters' like Sarah's Susie in response to childhood trauma is a beautiful innate process. It is a protective reaction much like a caterpillar constructs a cocoon for protection from the elements and prey while the core remains safe enough to grow when the time is right. This book provides light to a veiled population who remains in the dark."
- William B. Tollefson, Ph.D., CHT, CRT, NCP, Director
  Women's Institute for Incorporation Therapy, Hollywood,
  Florida

❖

"It takes courage and fortitude to share your story with the world, and Sarah Harrison has done that. For both professionals and survivors, this book offers insight and hope."
- Pat I. Richards, LCSW, CHT, Clinical Director
  Women's Institute for Incorporation Therapy, Hollywood,
  Florida

❖

"Sarah demonstrates a wonderful ability to touch people without seeking pity. Considering that any children were ever raised this

way is intolerable. To think she has emerged as an adult with so much talent speaks to the strength of the human spirit to survive."
- Michaela M. Whitfield, MS, LPC, MAC
  Counseling Services, Atlanta, Georgia

"When we read Sarah's material, our minds went immediately to the horrors of the Holocaust. The depth of her insight and the bravery she demonstrated in "going there" exceeds the valor attributed to the Silver Star. Her intellect is exceptional and her authenticity gives courage to others who know what she speaks and yearn to seek healing. What a woman!"
- Reverend John L. Wolfe, MDiv., Sr. Pastor
  Birmingham United Methodist Church
- Reverend Judy C. Wolfe, Mdiv., CT, BCC,
  Grief Counselor and Assoc. Pastor
  Birmingham United Methodist Church

"The material presented in *You Love Your Daddy, Don't You?* is disturbing, to say the least. This book presents childhood memories of parental abuse and neglect that would presently subject the parents to criminal prosecution, and would result in the removal of all the children in the Mahoney household. The implied conclusions reached by this writer seems to also blame the Primitive Baptist religion of the parents, and the doctrine of predestination, as a medium which allowed the parental abuse to thrive and continue. What the work does not explain is that God's holy ordinances as decreed in the Bible were routinely disobeyed by the parents, and at times by the children, as they reached their adult years.

On a personal note, after reviewing this work, I got down on

my knees, and asked God to take control of my household, so that I would always obey God's holy ordinances in the raising of my own children. I prayed that I would never put my own selfish behavior ahead of my children's welfare or interests. This is a powerful message that is implicitly conveyed in this work, and should be primarily directed to a Christian audience."
- Steven Harrell, Attorney-at-Law, Perry, Georgia
  Author of *The Unionist* and *The Rifle Captain*

"It was painful for me to read *You Love Your Daddy, Don't You?* because Sarah Harrison, the author, is my sister. I was writing my life story at the same time she was writing her memoir. We agreed we would not read each other's manuscript until they were complete. We did not want our books to read like the *same* story. For that reason, we didn't share our memories before completing our individual manuscripts. Another concern was that our siblings would dispute our version of events as recorded in our books; therefore, each of us would be responsible for the contents of our own book if we did not collaborate before finalizing them.

Sarah has recorded the events of our family life in an accurate, straight-forward, and heart-felt manner. Because Sarah's work covers a sixty-three-year period in her life, I believe her work will offer great insight into the dynamics of abuse victim survivors both for the professional and any reader interested in understanding those around us impacted by such a traumatic history."
- Mary Faulkner, author of a memoir, *No Room for Me*, which was placed on iUniverse Publishing Company's Editor's Choice List, and two novels, *Elana's Dream*, and *My Parents Betrayed Me*.

Acknowledgments

There are many to thank. I honestly believe the treatment I received at the Women's Institute for Incorporation Therapy at Hollywood, Florida, saved my life. I owe much to the entire staff at WIIT from the director, to all the therapists, nurses, technicians, intake staff, cafeteria workers, and shuttle bus drivers. Thank you for your support throughout my inpatient and outpatient stay in your hospital.

I never would have learned about the Women's Institute for Incorporation Therapy had it not been for my dear sister Mary. She made the arrangement with my insurance for my admission. She encouraged me to write this book as a healing therapy. She also did most of the editing of this book. Mary has written her own memoir, *No Room for Me*, by Mary E. Faulkner.

Third, I want to thank Joe, our cousin, for his kindness and his hospitality. He invited my two sisters and I to stay in his home after our long drive from middle Georgia to West Palm, Florida. Then he went with us the following morning to the hospital in Hollywood, Florida. Over the next month he visited me many times while I was an inpatient and then an outpatient at WIIT.

I want my son Allen to know how much it meant to me that he arranged his work schedule to travel from North Carolina to do an audit in Miami, Florida. He scheduled extra time into his trip so he could stop by and visit with me while I was an outpatient. Thank you Allen for all the encouragement and support you gave me during my recovery.

And last I owe Jerry, whom I met and married just as I was finishing the writing of this book. He helped me with the healing process by encouraging me to talk. I had become discouraged and I had stopped working on the book. With his encouragement, I came to understand that, because of my life experiences, this book may help someone else live a fuller life. If that someone is you, I hope you will not suffer as long as I did with sexual abuse, self-inflicted abuse, and multiple personalities.

Jerry died before I published the book. If it had not been for Judy Wolfe, assistant pastor to her husband at my church, who helped me through the grief and suffering of my loss and encouraging me to go on with finishing my book, I probably would not have completed it. I sat in her office crying one day asking her "Why? Why do I need to finish it?"

She said, "Just do me one favor. Read Andy Stanley's book, 'It Came From Within!' When you complete his book, you will know if you are supposed to publish your book or not."

I did as I was told and knew immediately that I had to publish my book.

I am eternally grateful to all these people and others too numerous to mention, and I thank you for your help, encouragement and support. And readers, I hope you will find new knowledge, quiet solitude, and a fuller understanding of yourself and your own self-worth. You deserve to live your life with dignity and self-respect.

Credit for the angel photo (Figure 2.6) goes to photographer: Linda Bucklin | Agency: Dreamstime.com

You Love Your Daddy, Don't You?

Introduction

The mind is incredible. The subconscious can protect and save us from some of the worst pain and guilt we may experience. Our minds can alter itself into other personalities as a mechanism to cope with real life situations and tragedies.

Throughout my personal life I have experienced many life changing situations. My family support system was very weak. From the time I was born I have always been used and manipulated to the desires and wants of others, from my own father, to my brother, to other men I have encountered.

Until one goes through a truly life-altering event one does not come face-to-face with one's life as it truly was and begins to deal with the facts. It was not until I was in my fifties that I began to recognize and understand more of my childhood, my relationships with all members of my family, my inner self. Through hospitalization and therapy I have begun to grow as an individual and recognize the past has already happened. I can't change that. I can only live in the present and be better prepared to meet the future as it becomes the present.

As you read *You Love Your Daddy, Don't You?*, you will learn of my years of sexual and emotional abuse by my father and brother, the double standard of sexual involvement among the sons and daughters in my family that was accepted by my parents: you will read of the drive, determination, and fortitude I had in seeking accepted outlets to run from my terrible family life. Also, you will learn the coping tactics I used to remain a surviving person, from creating alter personalities to smoking and drinking to acceptable outlets of acquiring a teacher scholarship to graduating with a four-year college degree in three years. Continuing, you will learn how my extreme low self-esteem and self-worth led me into marriages and family relationships where I was gullible and controlled by others.

Consequently, you will also read that there is always hope for everyone. Through reading, and seeking professional help, I have discovered and learned so much about life as I never before knew existed. Now, I will spend the rest of my life working with the "new" me.

My desire is the reader will work through my life trials, tribulations and experiences as you read this book and find that, you too, have hope for overcoming the baggage that has held you down for such a long time and learn you can begin a new, fruitful life in the future.

Family Tree

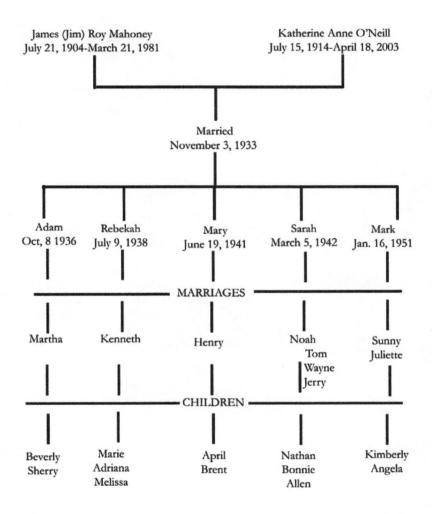

James (Jim) Roy Mahoney
July 21, 1904-March 21, 1981

Katherine Anne O'Neill
July 15, 1914-April 18, 2003

Married
November 3, 1933

Adam	Rebekah	Mary	Sarah	Mark
Oct, 8 1936	July 9, 1938	June 19, 1941	March 5, 1942	Jan. 16, 1951

MARRIAGES

Martha	Kenneth	Henry	Noah Tom Wayne Jerry	Sunny Juliette

CHILDREN

Beverly Sherry	Marie Adriana Melissa	April Brent	Nathan Bonnie Allen	Kimberly Angela

You Love Your Daddy, Don't You?

Part I
Just Call Me Susie

*"There is nothing quite so darling as a baby, sweet and small,
and the love that she is bringing is the loveliest gift of all."*
- Author unknown

You Love Your Daddy, Don't You?

Chapter One

Escaping Death

My mother, Katherine Anne O'Neill, was born July 15, 1914, into a genteel Southern family, who lived near Buena Vista, Georgia. The O'Neill family owned a dairy and a general merchandise store that also included a pharmacy. My maternal grandmother was a strong, competent woman, who oversaw the operation of the dairy and the vegetable gardens. My grandfather had pneumonia frequently and was often sick. For that reason, he managed the store and pharmacy. My mother loved her father dearly and many years later, even shortage of funds did not stop her from making an annual trip from Tennessee to Columbus, Georgia, to visit him.

My father, James (Jim) Mark Mahoney, came from a family less economically advantaged. My paternal grandmother married when she was fourteen and gave birth to fourteen children. Only nine of their children lived to be adults—six boys and three girls. My father's family lived on a rocky plot of land on the Tallapoosa River near Tallassee, Alabama. They raised sorghum cane, and made and sold sugarcane syrup from the cane for their income.

My father was stationed in the Army at Fort Benning near Columbus, Georgia, when he met my mother. Both of my parents came from Primitive Baptist backgrounds. They met when my father visited in the church where my mother's family attended regularly. My father knew immediately my mother was the young woman he wanted to marry and he began calling on her in her home when he could get time away from the base.

Mama's father did not approve of his daughter's choice for a mate. This soldier was discourteous enough to come to his home smelling of alcohol; he had also learned that the man was ten years older than his daughter.

Of his four daughters, Katherine was his favorite. Thinking back, he remembered the deep melancholy his wife had sunk into after their little eighteen-month-old daughter, Olene, had died of pneumonia. And then eighteen months later Katherine had come. She was a good baby who rarely cried. Katherine had chased the grief away and brought sunshine back into their lives.

Jim Mahoney chain-smoked, he drank, and he was not the man Leonadus O'Neill wanted his daughter to marry, so he sent her to West Georgia College at Carrolton, Georgia, to get her away from him. He was devastated when he received word that his daughter had run away from college. He waited for the word that came soon enough. Katherine called him and told him she and Jim had gotten married. The date was November 3, 1933.

*   *   *   *

The year is 1943 and Daddy, who is working for the Tennessee Valley Authority on the dam at Oak Ridge, Tennessee, calls to his mother's home in Tallassee, Alabama, when I am two weeks old. My mother, my two older sisters, and an older brother have been living with my grandparents for about a year and a half.

With a demanding voice, my father tells Mama, "If you don't get your butt up here I am going to get in trouble. I've done without sex long enough." Daddy had called three days earlier asking Mama to come, but she had delayed because I was sick.

Mama's reply lacks a ring of finality. "Jim, your new baby has double pneumonia. The doctor advised me not to travel until her fever goes down."

"Katherine," Daddy says in a hardened voice. "I'm ready to see you and the kids. Traveling is not going to hurt the baby."

Grandmother Mahoney, my father's mother, warns Mama, "Katherine, if you leave with the baby running 103 degrees fever, she might be dead before you get to Tennessee."

Mama ignores her; Mama ignores everyone when Daddy tells

4

her to do something. She packs our clothes, buys the bus tickets, and sets out for Knoxville, Tennessee, with her four children. The Mahoney children are six-year-old Adam, four-year-old Rebekah, twenty-one-month-old Mary, and me—two-week-old Sarah.

Now Mama is angry with Daddy for leaving her and her children with his parents for so long. She knows this has been an imposition on his parents. Daddy's demand that Mama leave and come to Tennessee while I am running a high fever almost results in my death. Mama does not have the bath water and medication she needs on the bus to get my fever to come down.

So many stories have survived the years...also many lies and secrets. Daddy takes Mama to one of their parents' homes when she gets pregnant. He has said he does not want sex with a pregnant woman. After the birth of the baby, he wants Mama back. Upon arrival in Tennessee, there is an immediate crisis to find a doctor when my fever skyrockets. I come closer to death than any of Mama's other three children have ever come.

My family lives in a rented apartment for a short time until Mama finds an old frame house she buys for $800. A fire has destroyed most of the main floor. It does have an attic and a basement where we can stay while Daddy rebuilds the main floor. Mama works hard to help Daddy, as she is ecstatic now that they have the first house of their own. She wants Daddy to hurry and make the house a real home.

Daddy is a carpenter, and in the first few years of my parents' marriage Mama followed him as he moved from job to job all up and down the eastern seaboard—from Georgia to Pennsylvania.

Finding work in the 1940s is challenging. Survival grows tough with the poverty we face when Daddy does not work. Mama is constantly trying to keep food on the table and clothes for us to wear, because she is too proud to apply for assistance. Her nerves are bad and she is often irritable. She screams at us and hits us. All her efforts and time goes into hand washing our clothes. Most of the laundry is bed sheets because all of us wet the bed until we are ten to twelve years old. Mama screams at us and whips us for wetting the bed, but it doesn't seem to help us stop. I later learn that Mary and I suck our thumbs and Rebekah sucks her two middle fingers until we are seven or eight years old. I understand now that bedwetting and thumb sucking were symptoms of the emotional turmoil present in our home life.

I remember little of my life on Bethel Avenue—from age two weeks to three years old—except for a bad plunge in the alley before I turn three years old. A sharp piece of glass cuts my knee so badly the scar remains today, measuring an inch and a half long and one-fourth inch wide. Because of the size of the cut, and because I lost so much blood, Mama should have taken me to a doctor to have stitches, but she didn't.

When I am three years old, Daddy finishes the house on Lay Avenue. It, too, is in Knoxville, not far from our house on Bethel Avenue. My whole family is overjoyed about the move to our new home. The only item I remember taking to the new house is Sally, the doll Santa Claus brought me when I was two years old.

Soon after moving, we are at the kitchen table. We have finished eating supper and are about to get up to leave when Mama yells at me, "Sarah, come here right this minute. Let me see your hands."

I feel nervous and shaky when Mama yells at me. She is a big woman, standing five feet, ten inches tall, weighing nearly two hundred pounds. Reluctantly, I turn my palms up, thinking she wants to hit me for something I have done, even though I have no idea what it could be or why she could be angry with me.

Her chilling voice cuts through my thoughts. "Turn your hands over. I want to see your fingernails," she says. "It's just like I thought. Go get the bottle of hot sauce. I have told you and told you…if I catch them bitten off to the quick and bleeding again, I would pour hot sauce on them again."

I have tried to stop biting my fingernails but I don't realize when I am biting them. The hot sauce burns where I have bitten them down into the quick where they are bleeding. When I am out of Mama's sight, I dash to the bathroom to run cold water over my hands.

Today I have memories, which begin about this age; however, I have relied on stories from Mary and others about what happened before I am three years old.

When I am about three and a half years old, I begin having spells; I turn blue and pass out. Rebekah and Mary tell others, "She passes out for the attention."

I don't pass out to get attention. I am sick, but I don't know how to tell Mama how sick I am. Mama believes my sisters and does not think too much about it until one day when Rebekah, Mary, and I are alone. We are playing outside. I guess I play too long and get too hot. One of the neighbor's boys lassos me with a rope and pulls me backwards off the front porch. My hip plunges onto a four-pronged rake. Two of the prongs poke holes deep into my flesh. I turn blue and pass out. I remain unconscious for a long time.

Rebekah and Mary think I might die, because they cannot revive me. When Mama gets home a few minutes later, they tell her, "Sarah is not faking. We cannot get her to wake up."

At first, Mama does nothing except check my hip and say, "The holes from the rake are deep." She decides I should have a tetanus shot but by then I have regained consciousness.

Daddy arrives then and yells at the neighbor boy, "Go home and don't ever come back to this house."

Mama says nothing more about the tetanus shot after Daddy gets home. Over the next few weeks my fainting spells begin happening more often. I turn blue and stay unconscious longer. Finally, Mama decides to take me to the doctor. The doctor asks Mama to describe the symptoms I have been having.

Mama is hesitant because she knows she should have brought me in earlier. "For about six weeks, she has occasionally been turning blue and passing out. She has hardly been eating anything."

The doctor touches my throat and I scream because it hurts. He gets a tongue depressor and asks me to open my mouth. I open my mouth and the doctor tries to hold down my tongue with the wooden stick. I gag and start to cry.

Dr. Morgan shakes his head and, when he speaks, he sounds as though he is angry. "Mrs. Mahoney, this child's tonsils are big, red, and infected. They are almost filling her entire throat area. That is why she is not eating. I will never be able to get her tonsils out without rupturing them and spilling poison down her throat. These tonsils have infected her entire bloodstream. That is the cause of her passing out. You should have brought this child in sooner. Her tonsils are infected, but we can't take time to give her antibiotics first. She will die if we don't get them out now."

Stunned by the doctor's diagnosis, in a barely audible voice Mama utters, "But I don't have insurance."

"Insurance or not, if you want your little girl to live, you will have her here in my office in the morning at eight o'clock sharp," the doctor answers with authority.

I survive the night, and the next morning we go back to the doctor's office. The doctor uses ether to put me to sleep. Although I am only three years old, I decide to stay awake so I can see what the doctor and his assistant do to me. They position a mask over my nose and mouth. The stuff smells terrible; I think I will vomit. The doctor's assistant takes the mask away and the doctor begins to cut.

"Ouch," I cry. "Where is my Mama? I want my Mama." I feel the mask when someone brings it down over my nose and mouth again. That is the last I remember.

When I wake up, I hear Mama telling Daddy about the doctor cutting my throat before I was asleep. When the doctor tried to cut my tonsils out,

Fig. 1.1 Sarah Holding Toy

they ruptured and spilled poison in my throat. Mama doesn't want me to vomit. She says I might break the stitches loose, and I might lose too much blood, but I can't stop vomiting. My fever skyrockets and Mama has to call the doctor at his home. He meets us at his office and gives Mama more medicine for my fever and infection. Later, Mama says the doctor gave me the toy I am holding in the picture because he said I was such a good patient. (See Figure 1.1)

This is the second "near death" experience in my childhood. For some reason, God has a purpose for me in this life. He is not allowing me to die.

Chapter Two

Come Sit on Daddy's Lap

At 6 PM Daddy goes into the living room to listen to the news on the big brown, round-top radio. One evening I go into the living room and I hear Daddy tell Mary, "Mary, come sit on my lap."

Mary starts backing up toward the door as she says, "I can't. I have to help Mama get supper ready."

Then Daddy smiles at me and his voice is oddly gentle but insistent. "Sarah, you come sit on Daddy's lap. You love your Daddy, don't you?"

Of course I love my Daddy, so I go to him. I begin sitting on his lap each evening when he listens to the news. My illness, which was caused by the infection from my tonsils getting into my bloodstream, causes me to be sick for several weeks. I have now become "Daddy's little girl." He lets me sit on his lap any time I want. Once, when no one is looking, he slips his finger under the edge of my panties, and he plays with my pee pee. I like it. It feels good. Daddy says he is giving me "special attention" but I worry because Mama may see him doing this to me. Daddy whispers with his finger over his mouth, "Sarah, this is our special secret."

Later, while sitting on Daddy's lap, I show him the change I have. "Look Daddy, I have three quarters, a dime, a nickel, and three pennies. If I had seven more pennies, I'd have a dollar."

"Do you want me to change it into a dollar bill?"

"Oh yes, I would be so happy. If it was a dollar bill, I wouldn't spend it; I would put it in my jar and save it forever."

"I think I can arrange that." Daddy takes my change and gives me a dollar bill. From that day on, he gives me "special attention" often when he is home, and he always exchanges my coins, no matter how small for a dollar bill.

When his carpenter jobs take him out of town I am glad, because I fear Mama will see him giving me special attention. Daddy tells me not to tell anyone. I think it must be bad if I have to keep it secret. I wonder how Mama will act if she catches him. Will she scream at him or will she whip me? I bite my fingernails while he is giving me special attention. I am nervous all the time. I wonder if other girls' Daddies give them special attention too.

When Daddy knows I am taking my bath he comes in the bathroom and watches me bathe. My sister Mary says Daddy watches her take her bath too. He pretends to be shaving, but he looks in the mirror to see us in the tub.

Then I have a frightening experience. I am sitting on Daddy's lap at the table while Mama is cooking supper. It is a cold evening, and Daddy has pulled his chair closer to the coal stove. Mama unexpectedly goes to the refrigerator for another egg. Daddy does not have time to move his hand. I believe I see her eyes gaze from his face to his hand and then to my face to see whether I am aware she saw Daddy's hand. Well, fortunately, she doesn't mention it, so maybe it was my imagination.

About this same time Susie, my first alter, begins appearing. (See Figure 2.1) Susie's older brother and her two older sisters continue to call her Sarah; however, she tells them, "I'm not Sarah; my name is Susie."

Figure 2.1 "Susie"

It makes her angry that her siblings won't try harder to remember to call her Susie. Sometimes Mary calls her Susie Queue. It causes Susie to become fighting mad and she says, "My name is not Susie Queue; my name is plain Susie."

After my fight with Mary, Mama says, "God will punish you when you are bad."

"When have I been bad, Mama? I don't remember."

"You shouldn't be fighting with your sister."

I walk away and go to my favorite place to cry—in the closet under the clothes. I cry for about an hour before anyone even misses me. I cry because I don't understand all the feelings I'm having lately.

Daddy comes into the kitchen and asks Mama, "Where is Sarah?"

"I don't know. I got on her for fussing with Mary. She's probably off sulking somewhere."

The room with the closet is just across the hall from the kitchen and I hear them talking. I decide I had better come out of the closet and show my face. I walk to the kitchen door and stop. My face is down; my chin resting on my chest.

Daddy feels sorry for me. He walks past me, reaching down to take my hand. "Come on, Sarah, you're my special girl. Sit on my lap a while."

I think, *"Don't go. Mary always tells him she has to help Mama and I can too."*

Susie talks in Sarah's head, "No, he said I was special. It feels good. I like it." A smile comes on Susie's face. Holding tight to Daddy's hand, she goes with him to his chair in the living room. Even though Susie doesn't have any change, Daddy later gives her a dollar.

Mary and I are so close to the same age, Mama makes us get into the bathtub together some nights. She leaves us there to bathe ourselves. As soon as we start bathing, I tell Mary, "It won't be five minutes before Daddy will be in here for something." Almost every time we take a bath, Daddy comes in to shave or wash his hands so he can see us in the mirror.

"I know," Mary tells me. "Look in the mirror when he stands before it. You can see his eyes and tell they are focused right on us. I'm not giving him the pleasure of seeing me. Soap up the wash cloth and shake it in the water to make a lot of bubbles."

"Yeah, and we can fold our arms over our chest, and just stop bathing until he leaves."

"That's what I do every time he comes in here."

That's what we started doing every time Daddy came in when we were bathing. Finally, his visits to the bathroom weren't so often, at least while we were little girls.

Mama continues to tell me God will punish me for my sins. I often cry because I think I am bad; however, I cannot remember being bad.

Daddy wants me to sit on his lap every evening when he listens to the six o'clock news. I don't know what happens. I get so nervous. I wish he would leave me alone. I don't remember what happens. Maybe I am bad. Maybe God will punish me. I don't remember putting all the nickels and dimes in my jar. I know Daddy gives me dollars for my change sometime, but I don't know where I got so many nickels and dimes.

At the age of five, I am nuts about my older brother Adam. He is seven years older than me, and my two sisters are older too. I am a tomboy and I follow Adam everywhere. He is building a boat to float in Williams Creek, which runs on the side of our third lot of land.

Near our house is a field of red clover. The creek has a huge oak tree, which grows at a slant over the creek and forks on the other side. Crawfish swim in the creek as if they own the world. Oh, what freedom. How can I manage to feel the freedom the crawfish delight in? The only way I know to arrive at such freedom is to take my little short legs and climb to the fork of the tree.

Maybe I will find out soon, I think. Being only five years old, I struggle up the tree with all kinds of weird emotions going through my brain.

What if I fall out and the crawfish get me with their pinchers? What if I can't get back down and I starve to death? Mama will never know where to look for me. That big brother I cherish so much told me the crawfish would not turn loose until it thundered.

I am frightened; I know for sure that freedom cannot possibly be worth the struggle I am facing. After reaching my destination, I realize I must now turn around before I can sit down. I continue to wonder if "freedom" is worth this fight.

Slowly, I turn around and look down at the crystal-clear waters below me. I say aloud to the crawfish, "Ha-ha, I'm free at last, free at last."

Wow, I think, *freedom is worth it after all. Daddy won't find me; Mama won't find me; nobody will find me now. I'm free!*

I feel good and close to heaven. A feeling of peacefulness like I have never known comes over me. I know Jesus has saved me from falling, and he has helped me make the journey up this tall, wide, dangerous tree so I can experience this freedom. I do not forget to thank him. Maybe his reason in saving me from dying those two times is for me to feel this freedom.

> Dear Jesus,
>   I know you helped me get to the fork of this tree without falling. I want you to know I thank you. If I had fallen, the crawfish would have pinched me. What would I have done then? It might not have rained for days, especially with thunder and lightning, to make the crawfish turn loose.
>   Oh yeah, thank you too, ahead of time, for helping me climb down. If I died, Mama might die too, because she loves me so much. I hear Mama calling now, so I must go.
>   But Jesus, I need to talk to you about something else important soon.
>   Thank you again, Jesus.
> Bye for now,
Sarah

My adventure to find a little peace has exhausted me, so I decide to find other ways to gain freedom. I never used the big oak tree again to be alone until first grade. My legs were much longer by then. If I need to be alone, I hide in the closet behind the clothes. If I want to find good luck, I go to the clover in the front yard, and I try my hardest to find a cloverleaf with four leaves.

As the days and months go by, I continue to have my conversations with Jesus.

Dear Jesus,

Do you remember I said I needed to talk to you again soon? I cannot understand Daddy. Do other little girls' Daddies bother them the way mine does? He told me not to tell anyone. It feels good when he does it, but I don't understand why. Now he is touching me on my butt and chest. He watches me when I bathe. What should I do?

I hope to hear from you soon.

Love from worried Susie

One day Mary and her best friend, Christy Hinson, are playing with their dolls in the living room where Daddy is reading the newspaper. I begin a fight with Mary because she will not let me play with them. I have no friends of my own. I hit her hard and she begins crying loudly. Mama comes in the living room to see what has happened.

Holding her arm and sniffling, Mary says, "Sarah hurt my arm."

Mama retorts, "Hush, you are a crybaby."

Then Mama turns to Christy and says, "Christy, you need to go home now."

Christy gets up and goes out the front door.

Daddy, feeling sympathy for Mary says, "Mary, come sit on Daddy's lap."

Mary says what she always tells Daddy, "I should go help Mama."

Daddy frowns at Mary as she and Mama leave the living room, but then he turns his gaze toward me and he smiles. "Sarah, you love your Daddy, don't you?" (Figure 2.2)

Figure 2.2
Sarah sitting on Daddy's lap

Just like Mary, I don't want to sit on his lap, but I close my eyes and I feel the smile as it appears on my face. Susie has come out and she runs quickly toward Daddy and jumps onto his lap. Daddy throws his left arm around Susie. He lays his left hand on her chest. There is no one in the living room now but Daddy and Susie. He wastes none of their time alone together. He puts his right hand under her dress and his finger enters the leg of her panties. Gently, he slides his finger back and forth over her tiny clitoris. His penis is erect, and he holds her by the waist and moves her back and forth over his penis, so she can feel it. His gaze at Susie is as soft as a caress and he tells her he loves her special. Susie feels a tingling in the pit of her stomach as her father enters his finger as far as he can into her vagina. Then a shudder runs through her body as her father pulls her close.

Susie leans her trembling body against her father's chest and she tells him, "Daddy, I love you so much."

"Oh baby, I love you too. Your hair smells so good." Jim's heart is hammering against his chest. He clutches Susie roughly, almost violently, to him.

"Daddy, you are squeezing me too tight."

Jim kisses her hair and says, "I'm sorry, baby, I just love you so much. Remember this is our special secret." He puts Susie down and goes to the bedroom for clean shorts; he has ejaculated and needs to change.

Even as a child of six, I feel sad and unlucky. I don't know how I would survive if it were not for this tree over the creek where I can come and get away from everyone.

Susie begins pinching her breasts and playing with her bottom. She begins sticking pencils, carrots and other objects into it. It feels good, but it also hurts.

I (Sarah) wonder why Daddy talks to me the way he does. I begin having feelings I am too young to describe. I hurt on the inside and yet I am too young to understand what is happening to me.

I start crying often but I don't let anyone know when I cry. I isolate myself and don't let anyone know where I am. I usually hide in one of the clothes closets and cry. If I hear someone coming or know someone is looking for me, I stand up and hide in the clothes. What would I tell them if they asked me why I am crying? I don't even know why I am crying.

Daddy hugs me, but it is Susie who turns in his lap to hug him in return. Susie feels his erection and Susie feels sexual sensations. Daddy puts his finger in the opening to Susie's pee pee and she squeezes her muscles around his finger. A shiver of delight passes through her.

I dearly love Ray. He is the little boy in the picture I am standing with against the chimney (Figure 2.3). He is my best friend. We crawl under the house to hide and be alone together. Without him to play with, I would be lonely. As an adult and looking back on childhood photos, I wonder why so many of the photos that include me

Figure 2.3 Sarah and Ray

showed my hands around or near my panties.

One day I decide I need to talk to Mama. I find her in the kitchen and I am nervous as I enter. My voice is low and unsteady as I begin, "Mama, something terrible is wrong with me."

Mama turns her frowning face toward me and, when she speaks, her voice sounds like she is irritated that I have interrupted her. "Why do you say that?"

My voice is fragile and shaking when I answer, "There's blood in my panties."

Now her voice sounded tired. "You must have fallen or something. Maybe you fell on your bicycle. It's normal. Don't worry about it."

I turn and leave the kitchen, discouraged because it has taken all the courage I could muster to get up the nerve to talk to her and she hardly even listened. Now my chance for help is gone.

I enter the first grade when I am still five years old and, about this same time, I begin sleepwalking at night. Instead of going to the toilet, I go to the kitchen and pee in the coal bucket. Mama catches me one night; however, she does not know I am walking in my sleep. When she yanks my arm, I wake up. It frightens me badly. She threatens to whip me if I ever pee in the coal bucket again, but I was unaware I was doing it.

My two sisters and I share a bedroom downstairs with only one bed. Since we are now getting older and the bed is getting crowded, Mama tells me I must now start sleeping upstairs with my fourteen-year-old brother, Adam. She says she picked me because I am the youngest of us three sisters. I love him but he is in the prime of puberty. Mama should have known better than to make us sleep together. I am seven now. On the first night, Adam does not leave the overhead light on because he says Mama might look up the stairs and see it. He doesn't want Mama to know what he plans to do. Adam hides a lamp under the cover so he can see what he is doing.

I think *Oh Lord, what should I do? Should I call Mama?*

Susie knows that Adam is planning something that Sarah cannot handle so she takes over. Adam and Susie both take off all their clothes on the first night. The lamp makes a tent of the sheet and Adam gets between Susie's legs. He begins playing with her pee pee. It feels good to Susie. A great feeling of excitement overcomes her. At first, she thinks Adam is doing her a favor. She simply lies on the bed with her eyes closed and the same sensations come over her that do when she sits on Daddy's lap. Her heart is hammering foolishly. A quiver surges through her and she rises up and looks downward toward the source of her pleasure.

Adam has a strange look on his face, which is tilted backwards.

He is shaking, and white stuff is coming out of his "thing" in spurts.

It frightens Susie badly, "Oh, Adam, what is wrong with you?"

"Nothing stupid, just go to sleep."

Susie still has flashbacks of that event today. She thought something was terribly wrong with Adam. Daddy had never taken his "thing" outside his pants when she sat on his lap, so she had never seen this happen.

The following night, in a small, troubled voice, Susie told Adam, "I'm keeping my head out from under the cover. I don't want to see the white stuff when it comes out of your 'thing.'"

I ask Mama to let me start sleeping with Rebekah and Mary again, or to let me sleep on the couch. She refuses, saying I will wet the couch and we girls are too big now for all three of us to sleep together.

Susie doesn't remember how many times this occurred after the first time Adam ejaculated. It became a regular occurrence because Adam insisted; however, going to bed held no more excitement for Susie—only a sense of dread.

When I am eight years old, a new baby is born into the family. Many visitors come to see our new baby. For eight long years, I have been the baby, but not anymore. The baby's name is Mark. No one can get to Mark's bed without me getting there first. They say I am jealous because I have been the baby for so long, but I am afraid they might steal Mark. I stay up as late as Mama will let me. I don't want to go upstairs with Adam. Unfortunately, most nights I embarrass myself by going to sleep, falling out of the straight chair, and hitting the floor with a bang. I hear everyone laughing at me. I excuse myself and go to bed.

Mark is only two months old when I get deathly sick again— too sick to go to school. I overhear Mama fussing at Daddy one day. She tells him she did not want another baby. She tells Daddy that five children are more than they can afford to raise. Then Mama comes to give me a teaspoon of sugar with a drop of turpentine on it. She rubs Vicks salve on my chest. My chest hurts.

I look at Mama's backside as she leaves my room and it is hard to describe the array of emotions I feel toward her. How could she not want our new baby? What if she decides she wants to keep Mark and I am the one she doesn't want?

Please, dear Jesus, don't let me be that one child too many.

This is my second day out of school. Why can't I begin feeling better? I feel so cold one minute and, when I pull all the covers around me, I feel hot. I have to go back to school or I will get behind with my work. I shiver every time I draw in a sharp breath.

That afternoon, when Mary comes in from school, I tell her what I heard Mama say to Daddy. She shares with me two stories that happened to her before I was born. When she was born, Mama and our older brother and sister were living in a tiny trailer in Jefferson City, Tennessee. Daddy was working in Ohio. Each day Mama put Mary outside in a screen-wire box. Eventually, someone called the Welfare Department, who told Mama she could not leave her baby outside in a screen-wire box unattended.

According to Mama's own stories, told years later, she told the social workers, "There is not enough room for Mary in this small trailer."

The social workers told Mama that her baby must be in the care of an adult at all times and they would return to check on her new arrangements. Mama called Daddy in Ohio. He came and took his family to his parents' home in Alabama where they lived until I was born.

Mary's second story is about the house on Bethel Avenue—the place we lived when we moved from Grandmother's house in Alabama. Mary says she was almost three years old when she began running away to a neighbor's house. She said the woman would hold her in her lap, rock her, and feed her. Mary tells me Mama began tying her to the clothesline each day until someone again called the Welfare Department. The social workers told Mama she couldn't tie Mary to the clothesline every day. Mama says no one can tell her what she can do with her own children.

Our parents are social, outgoing people and we often have

visitors. A favorite form of entertainment is telling stories. That is how we kids learn about many events that happened in our past. One evening I heard the story of Mama keeping Mary in the screen-wire box that Daddy built. Mama laughed and said, "No one can tell me how to raise my children."

Mary feels of my head and says, "I think you've got a temperature. Do you want some water?"

After many days, Mama comes in and takes my temperature. She does not tell me what my temperature is; however, she says, "Sarah, you have to go to the doctor."

Mama gets a washcloth and sponges the perspiration off my body. She gets out my clothes and tells me to get dressed. I feel so sick I don't feel like standing up to dress or go to the bathroom.

In a fragile, shaking voice, I say, "Mama, I am too sick. I can't get out of bed."

I'm remembering that she said she didn't want all us kids. I feel so terrible that I really don't care if I die.

I hear the irritation in Mama's voice as she says tersely, "You certainly *can* get up. You have to."

I push the covers back, stand up, and blink my eyes. I see spots before my eyes, and then I close me eyes and fall back down on the bed, because I feel like I am going to faint.

Mama comes over and yanks me up by the arm. "Now, get your clothes on like I told you."

Tears are blinding my eyes and choking my voice. The room is going round and round and it takes all my energy just to stand up. Finally, Mama takes off my nightgown and helps me put on my clothes.

At the doctor's office, someone takes an X-ray of my chest. Then the doctor tells Mama I am a sick little girl. He tells Mama I have double pneumonia again. He said I would be prone to developing pneumonia for the rest of my life. I run a temperature and it is a long time before the medication clears up the infection in my lungs. I have scar tissue from the time I had pneumonia when I was two weeks old. I finally get better and go on with my life, because again, I didn't die.

Hooray, school is out for spring break. Maybe I will have time to convince Mama I can be as responsible as Mary. On the way home on the last day before spring break, I talk with Joan, one of my school friends, and she tells me, "It will get better. I remember when my sister and I were in the same school at the same time. Teachers always wanted me to be like my sister. I told them, 'I'm Joan; I am not like my sister.'"

I thank her for sharing her experiences. When we cross the bridge toward our homes, we say good-bye and go our separate ways. I am not looking forward to being out of school. Mama expects the same from me that she gets from Mary.

I think, *I am not Mary and I never will be. I am myself. Maybe, if I talk to Mama the way Joan talked to her teacher, Mama will understand.* That night, when I went to bed, I prayed to God to help me communicate this need to Mama.

The following morning, I am awakened by birds singing on my windowsill. I jump up, run to the window, and peep around the edge of the blinds. On the ledge is a beautiful pair of sparrows. They are chirping to each other and I believe they are in love. In the distance are squirrels running around on the ground playing chase. New blooms on the shrubs and flowers are making their own rainbow across the yard. I cannot go back to sleep. I decide to sneak down the stairs and out the back door, not even taking time to dress.

Mary is already up too. She motions for me to be quiet so we will not awaken Mama. With a frown on her face, she says, "Go back to bed. I'm going outside."

I tell her, "No, it was my idea to go outside first." I don't know who was up first. Mary is angry because she doesn't want me to tag along with her, but she is not going to stop me from going outside.

Mary has already gotten cracked corn to feed the birds and squirrels. I ask her to share some with me. Much to my surprise, she does. I tell her I want to put some on my window ledge for the sparrows I saw. We go to the coal house where the ladder is stored. The ladder is heavy but, between the two of us, we manage to carry it to the side of the house where my bedroom is located on the second floor. Carefully, step-by-step, I make my way up to my window ledge. Then we spread the rest of the cracked corn in spots where we can watch them from my window.

We run back around the house to the open field of clover. The blooms of clover look like a red carpet spread for a king. I drop to my knees. Mary found a four-leaf clover last week and so many wonderful events have happened to her since. Her class won most of the field day events, and her boyfriend walked her home from school for the first time ever. She received a straight "A" report card this last grading period, and the physical education teacher asked her to help with some of the other grades field day events this year.

"I will find a four-leaf clover, and all those lucky things will begin happening to me too. You'll see," I tell Mary.

She answered quickly, with laughter in her voice, "You're right. All my luck was due to finding a four-leaf clover." Of course, Mary knew there was no truth to Sarah's statement; however, she said as she left, "Good luck."

I am short and chubby; Mary is tall and thin. Mary says she envies my blond, curly hair. Her hair is brown and our older brother, Adam, teases her by telling her that her hair is straight as a board. Mama plaits it and then pins the plaits on top of her head, even though Mary begs her not to pin the plaits on top of her head.

Mary races to the creek below the house. Ahead of her is the huge oak tree, at least thirty inches in diameter at the trunk. It has grown at an angle across the creek and forks at the other side. It makes a perfect seat for her escape. Throwing one leg over the trunk, Mary begins the climb to her place of seclusion.

When Mary reaches the place where the giant oak forks, she straddles the tree and leans forward on one huge limb looking down into the crystal clear water flowing over rocks below her. "Oh, how wonderful," Mary says, "Peace at last." There is no one to hear and Mary's voice is offered up to the natural plant and wildlife surrounding her.

Mary watches while crawfish float over rocks, and others seem to be playing with one another. Baby frogs are jumping to and fro as if they are dancing to music. Then, into Mary's awareness comes the sounds of wildlife nearby.

I continue to look for my special four-leaf clover, but I have no luck. When I stop to look for Mary, she is nowhere in sight. Time must have slipped away from me. Maybe she forgot about me and went back inside.

"Mary, Mary," I yell. She doesn't answer so I leave and go back to the house. Back in the house, I tell Mama that Mary and I left the house earlier this morning.

Mama scolds me and tells me I cannot leave home for the rest of the day. "Tell Mary she cannot leave home either. I must take Rebekah to an all-day Girl Scout camp meeting."

Mama writes down the telephone number where we can reach her if we need her. She reminds me Adam has a part-time job during spring break and tells me he has already left for his job. Then she and Rebekah leave for Rebekah's Girl Scout meeting.

I am worried about Mary so I go into the backyard screaming, "Mary, Mary, where are you? Why don't you answer me? This is no joke; Mama is mad with both of us. Mary, please answer me."

A long time passes and still I hear no word from Mary. *Should I disobey Mama and go looking for Mary? Should I call Mama at the number she gave me and tell her Mary still hasn't come home?* I decide to go look for her. Retracing our path from early morning, I neither see nor hear anything. I sit down in the middle of the clover field and begin crying so loudly that Missy, our little dog, hears me and comes running out of the brush near the old fishpond and begins licking my face.

I stop crying and ask, "Missy, what will I do? Mary has disappeared."

I close my eyes and it seems like I hear a voice from heaven speaking to me, "Fear not, follow me, and I will lead you to where

24

your sister lies."

Missy has been nudging me with her nose. Now, she turns and starts walking toward the old pond. I think about the words I have heard and I interpret them to mean, "Follow the dog." I follow Missy and she takes me straight to Mary. Missy had heard Mary's cries earlier and had stayed with her the entire time. When I see my sister, I cannot tell if she is dead or alive.

I look up toward heaven and say, "Thank you, God, for leading me to Mary. Now please let her be alive."

I jump down into the pond beside Mary and check to make sure she is breathing. I thank God her head is propped against the concrete in the corner. Even though several inches of water are in the pond, her head being propped against the concrete kept it out of the water and prevented her from drowning. Remembering the first aid and CPR I learned in my health class, I check her body and find that Mary's left arm is bent awkwardly. Obviously, it is broken. It has already swollen twice the normal size. I know I cannot move Mary by myself. I know Mary may be unconscious because of the pain, but it could also mean she has a concussion or internal bleeding.

Looking at Missy I say, "Stay here with Mary and I will be back soon." My hands are clammy when I pick up the telephone to call for an ambulance and the phone slips out of my hand. I pick it up and try again. I dial the number "zero."

Someone on the other end of the line answers, "Operator."

"Hello, I need for you to send an ambulance to my house as quickly as possible."

"What is your address?" the operator asks.

I stammer quickly, "Twenty-six, twenty-five Lay Avenue. Please hurry."

"Give me more information. Maybe we can help you while the ambulance is on the way to your house."

"No, I need to call my mother now, so she can be driving to the hospital to meet us. Thank you."

I hang up the phone and get the telephone number Mama left

for me and I call her. I try hard to keep my voice from shaking when I tell her, "Mama, I have some bad news. When Mary didn't come home, I went out looking for her. She had fallen in the old fishpond. Mama, Mary is unconscious, and I can tell her arm is broken."

Over the phone line I hear Mama draw in her breath. "What? I will be right home."

I tell her, "Mama, I have already called for an ambulance and it is on the way. I will ride with Mary in the ambulance to the hospital. Since you are so far from home, why don't you meet us at the hospital?"

Mama says, "I'll come home. Wait on me."

I say, "No, Mama. I can handle it. God told me how to find Mary and I remembered my first aid."

Later, Mama told me she could not believe how confident I sounded on the phone. The truth is, because Mary is smart and athletic, and is liked by everyone, I have a hard time not liking her too. I want to be like Mary.

While on the phone with Mama, the ambulance arrives and I tell Mama, "The ambulance is here and I have to go. We will see you at the hospital. Please hurry, Mama."

Mama is at the hospital waiting when the ambulance arrives. I run to her and the two of us hold each other tight for a brief moment.

The paramedics have brought Mary out of her unconscious state before reaching the hospital. They take her straight to the X-ray department. An emergency room doctor comes out and asks me some questions about Mary's accident.

While waiting for word on Mary's injuries, Mama asks me, "Sarah, how did you know to call the ambulance, and how did you keep from getting upset and crying? You handled it like a grown person."

Mama's compliment has special meaning to me. I am happy she noticed. I tell her, "Mama, God told Missy to show me right where Mary was. God gave me the strength to hold on until I could get the professional help to save my sister."

After a long time, an emergency room doctor returns to talk with Mama and me. He says, "Mrs. Mahoney, I believe your daughter will be fine, but it will take some time. According to what your other daughter said when you first arrived, Mary was unconscious for some time and that is not a good sign. She has a concussion on the left side of her head above her ear. We will watch her closely for the next twenty-four hours to be sure she does not have swelling of the brain or fluid buildup inside her skull. We need to ensure she will not have permanent damage from the concussion before we let her go home."

Mama says, "We don't have insurance. I need to take her home as soon as I can. What about her broken arm?"

The doctor says, "It will require surgery to set Mary's arm. I have already put a temporary cast on her arm. In the morning I'll ask a surgeon to examine her arm and he will schedule surgery. I hope he can do that tomorrow.

I will also call in an ophthalmology specialist in the morning to perform a neurological examination to see more about where we stand on Mary's concussion. After a concussion, it's common sometimes not to remember events right before, during or immediately after your injury. Don't be surprised if Mary doesn't remember her fall. After recovery, the memory almost always comes back.

If the neurological test checks out all right and the surgeon can set Mary's arm tomorrow, then you may be able to take her home tomorrow evening. However, I can't guarantee I can schedule both the appointments for tomorrow, and that the swelling in Mary's arm will have gone down enough to permit the surgery on her arm. We will have to wait and see how it goes.

"We have given Mary some heavy pain medication. You may find her to be disoriented. She is on the third floor. Ask the nurses at the nurses' station for her room number. Don't upset her; Mary needs to stay calm until we see the severity of the concussion. It must have been a nasty fall.

"Another thing we need to talk about is treatment for the concussion when you take Mary home. Healing will take time and rest is the best treatment. Before you leave, we will give you a prescription for headache pain. If it runs out and Mary is still complaining of headaches, call to have the prescription refilled. Do not give her any other medications, especially aspirin, without talking to the doctor. Aspirin can cause bleeding in her brain," the doctor tells Mama.

Mama sighs and irritation spills over in her voice, "I understand, doctor."

When Mama and I leave to find Mary's room, Mama says, "Sarah, I am aggravated with you and Mary for leaving the house this morning. My life is complicated enough without you and Mary causing me more problems. I'm a good mind to whip both of you when I get you home."

When Mama and I find Mary in her room, I am happy to learn Mary hasn't lost her memory. She tells me she is sorry for leaving me in the clover. Mary is so heavily sedated she is slurring her words, "By da way, did you find da four-leaf clov'r?"

Whispering in Mary's ear, I say, "No, I found something better. I found God."

"I can't vait to hear 'bout it," Mary says as she yawns and then lets sleep overtake her. She is still wearing her dirty pajamas. Mama and I leave and go to the nurses' station. Mama tells the nurse she has to go home because she has three other children to see about. The nurse tells Mama they will look in on Mary often.

The following day we learn Mary's concussion is not severe and she has surgery to set her broken arm. When Mary wakes up after her surgery, we take her home.

After supper I get in bed with Mary. Rebekah is still in the kitchen with Mama. Mary tells me she loved the time she was in the hospital. She says the nurse asked her if she wasn't lonely without her mother to spend the night with her. Mary tells me she told the nurse she wasn't lonely; she loved being in the hospital. She says she told the nurse it was quiet and peaceful in the

28

hospital—not noisy like at home. She says the nurse looked at her strange and asked her how she had gotten those scars on her legs. Mary says she told the nurse her mama whips her. She tells the nurse she wished she could stay longer in the hospital. She says she told the nurse she didn't get much to eat at home. The nurse let her order her favorite dinner—fried chicken, mashed potatoes with gravy, English peas, and apple cobbler. (Obviously, the nurse doesn't think Mary's plight is serious enough to alert authorities. No social services person comes to ask Mary questions.)

Tomorrow is Easter and I don't expect we kids will get Easter baskets or go to church for Easter services, though Easter is Mama's favorite holiday. The reason we don't go to church is there is not a Primitive Baptist Church nearby and Daddy doesn't want us to go to a church of another denomination. I have my own little talks with Jesus.

When spring break ends, Mama visits Mary's teacher and the principal, who had asked Mary to help with field day events for the younger children. She wants to let them know about Mary's accident and to apologize to the principal for the inconvenience it will cause by Mary not being there to help with field day.

Mama tells them she was not at home when the accident occurred but was away helping Rebekah with a Girl Scout event. She brags on how well I had handled the situation after the accident.

The principal asks, "Do you suppose Sarah would want to help us with field day events since Mary is unable to help? That is, if her teacher approves of her missing classes."

I'm sure Mama gave the principal one of her rare smiles, because she knew I would be excited when she told me. She later told me how she answered the principal, "I'm sure Sarah would love to help. It would be a wonderful reward for her, since she responded in such a grownup way on the day of the accident."

Mary's teacher adds, "If Sarah's teacher approves, I will be happy to take Sarah home after the field day events. Then I could work with Mary a while so she will not get behind with her classes."

Mama is surprised and grateful for her kindness. She tells her, "Thank you. I appreciate it." Then she looks at the principal and says, "Sarah is more outgoing than Mary. She will be excited about being able to help with the field day events. Will you ask Sarah's teacher if she can be excused from class?"

The principal ensures Mama he will ask my teacher. He also tells Mama he feels sure my teacher will agree.

When I get home from school that afternoon, Mama tells me I might get to help with field day events. I cannot believe what I heard. It proves to me Jesus does hear my prayers and answers them. I have to wait until he is ready.

The following day, I learn my teacher is happy for me to have the opportunity to help with the field day events for the lower grades. As promised, Mary's teacher brings me home after the events are over. She brings Mary's school assignments and stays for a short while to help Mary catch up with the work she has missed while being out with her concussion and broken arm.

I feel guilty for feeling this way; however, I feel more at home at the Michaels, our neighbor's next door, than at my own house since Mark was born. On Halloween, we carry large grocery bags to go "Trick or Treat," and we always get our sacks full of fruit and candy. We love the fruit because Mama doesn't buy much fruit because it is expensive. Our first stop is always the Michaels' house. We should go to their house last since our bags become overloaded with all the fruit they give us. We have the heavy bags to carry for the rest of the evening. The Michaels have no children, and they tell me they enjoy my visits. I know I extremely love my visits with them.

Christmas is about the only other time besides Halloween when we have fruit. Daddy buys us a sack of oranges and we kids love oranges. One day Rebekah goes to the store with Mama. When they are back home, Mama catches Rebekah eating an apple. She forces Rebekah to confess that she has stolen it. She whips Rebekah severely, and then takes her back to the store. Mama forces Rebekah to tell the store manager she stole the apple, and then Rebekah has to pay for it.

Monday morning arrives and it is good to go back to school. Tryouts for the May Day program are after school today. Mama says I can stay since I have been good lately. The Michaels are sitting in their yard when I arrive back home. I run to them to share the good news even before going in the door of my own house.

"Guess what? I was chosen to be in the May Day Dance," I say excitedly. My heart is beating like a little trip-hammer.

Mrs. Michaels asks, "Have you told your Mama?"

"No, I just finished tryouts and found out myself."

Mr. Michaels asks, "Don't you think you better go tell your Mama?"

"Yes," I reply, "but I saw you outside and I wanted you to know."

I tell them good-bye and run to share the good news with my family. Mark is crying when I enter the house and Mama and Daddy are quarreling. An hour passes before I can tell my parents I am going to be in the May Day Dance.

Mama says, "That's great, Sarah."

Daddy asks Mama, "And where are you going to get the money for her dress?"

Mama says, "I don't know, but I will get it from somewhere even if I have to rob a bank."

I begin to cry. I run out the back door and up the alley back to the Michaels. I am still crying when I arrive. I tell them Mama is going to jail.

"What will I do? I cannot live without her and neither can Mark," I cry, and tears run unchecked down my cheeks.

Mr. Michaels says in a tense, troubled voice, "Wait a minute, sit down. Your mama is not going to jail." (See Figure 2.4)

I blurt out, scarcely aware of my own voice, "Oh, but she is. You don't understand. She told Daddy she will rob a bank to get the money for my May Day dress."

Figure 2.4 Sarah sitting with the Michaels

Mrs. Michaels looks at Mr. Michaels and says, "Mark, remember all those weeds in our flower garden you were pulling the other day. You had to stop because of the pain in your back?"

Sarah's brow creased with worry as she says, "Oh, I will pull the weeds for you. I love pulling weeds."

Mr. Michaels smiles and says, "Yes, I remember well. Sarah, you can pull out the weeds for us, but not without pay."

I ask him, "What? I don't want any money for helping you. Being with you is enough for me."

The Michaels are so good to me. I often wish they would adopt me. Why wasn't I born to them? They tell me to go back home before Mama and Daddy become worried about me. They tell me we can talk again soon.

When I arrive home, Mama wants to know where I have been. I tell her I was talking to the Michaels. She has supper ready. Afterwards, Daddy calls us into the living room for a family talk. I never remember this happening before so I wonder what is wrong.

I think, *"Maybe Mama has already robbed a bank. Maybe Daddy is leaving, never to return. Maybe they are going to give away some of us children. I will volunteer to be Mr. and Mrs.*

Michaels' little girl."

When Daddy starts talking, his face looks troubled. He doesn't have a job now, and he and Mama have been fighting much of the time recently. Mama has been angry since Mark was born. She didn't want another baby.

Daddy finally begins by saying, "The niggers are moving into this area and I will not live near them. We are picking up our belongings and moving. When school is out, this house will be on the market for sale and we will be gone."

I look at Mary, and I can tell she is becoming upset. She hates it when Daddy says that nasty word to refer to Black people. She told me her teacher said people should not say that word.

"No, no, Daddy," I say in a loud voice. The outcry unleashes something inside me and I boldly look from Daddy to Mama. "I cannot leave Mr. and Mrs. Michaels. I will stay and be their little girl. They love me. They don't have any children, and they want me to be their little girl."

I see the anger in Daddy's face, but I meet his icy gaze straight on as I shout, "Mama won't have to rob a bank either. The Michaels are going to buy my dress for the May Day Program."

When I start walking toward the door, Mama says, "Little girl, sit your butt down until your daddy tells you that you can leave."

I continue walking toward the door as I say, "I hate you. I hate all of you."

I hear Daddy tell Mama to go spank me. She catches me by the arm and carries me out to the hedge by the alley. She gets a huge switch from the hedge bush and gives me one of the worst whippings of my life.

After I go to bed, I show Adam how badly Mama beat me. He has no sympathy for me. He says, "You should have kept your mouth shut."

I don't know why he doesn't understand how I felt, and it hurts my feelings that the brother I looked up to has no sympathy for me. I tell him, "I couldn't help it. I had to tell them how I felt."

The following morning my eyes are red and swollen. I dress in my long blue jeans so my teacher will not see the welts on my legs. Several places, where she hit hard and broke the skin, are still bloody and raw. I will have to wear blue jeans for a long time until the welts heal.

I don't even ask Mama if I can stay after school for practice for the May Day Dance, though I should have asked. When I get home from school, Mrs. Michaels comes down to ask Mama if she can see me. Mama is embarrassed and says she does not want them to buy my dress.

Mrs. Michaels answers, "Oh, she is going to work for the money."

"Oh, she didn't tell me that," Mama tells Mrs. Michaels, with some of the tension gone from her voice.

Mama calls me to the kitchen. I was standing by the door and heard them talking. I enter and sit down at the table with Mrs. Michaels and Mama. After Mrs. Michaels explains my jobs, I am excited and eager to begin work. Mama has obviously forgotten about me coming in late from school this afternoon.

The next afternoon I get my jobs completed for Mr. and Mrs. Michaels as quickly as possible. Mrs. Michaels says, "Sarah, we can go shop for your dress this evening if your mother doesn't have chores for you to do. If she does, we can shop another evening, but call me and let me know. If we are going shopping this evening, you need to take a quick bath because you are sweaty from working, but then come back as soon as you can."

I tell her, "Oh, I hope Mama doesn't have any chores for me to do. I want to find my dress today."

I feel blissfully happy when Mama says I can go shopping with Mrs. Michaels this evening. I hug her neck and say, "Thank you, thank you." I believe this is the fastest bath I have ever taken. I don't even wait to dry off my whole body. I jump into a dress that won't be hard to take off in the department store. Then I run back up the alley to Mrs. Michaels' house. Mr. Michaels' father is visiting from Ohio. I thought I had to wear a dress to make it easier to try on the new dress. I sure hope Mr. Michaels' father or anyone else doesn't notice the welt marks on my legs. I rush to find Mrs. Michaels to tell her I am ready to go. I am thankful that no one seems to notice the welt marks on my legs.

When we get to the department store, we find the dress, which I believe has been hanging there, waiting for me to come get it. I go to the dressing room to change. When I come out, I say, "It is just right, isn't it? We can buy it, can't we?"

While I am in the dressing room, Mrs. Michaels finds a hat to match my dress. She places the hat on my head and answers, "Well, it looks right to me."

I stare at my image in a mirror that is attached to the hat rack. Mrs. Michaels is standing behind me and she is looking over my shoulder into the mirror. She puts one hand on my shoulder and says, "Sarah, you look like a May Day Queen."

Mrs. Michaels buys me new shoes and socks too. (See Figure 2.5) I truly do feel like a queen. I take one last look at myself in the mirror, before disappearing into the dressing room to change back into my old dress. How beautiful and wonderful I feel, knowing I worked for these clothes, and knowing I was chosen as one of many girls to be in the May Day Dance. Jesus comes to my mind and I think of how he always helps me when I hurt the most.

Figure 2.5 May Day Dress

On the way home from the department store, I tell Mrs. Michaels about Daddy's plan to sell our house because Daddy said that Black people were moving into the area. At first, she appears upset, but then she explains we cannot change what our parents do.

At the same time, I think, *"Why don't you and Mr. Michaels keep me?"* However, after some thought, I decide I had better not tell her about my wish.

All the recent events in my life, both good and bad, are too much for me. I cannot cope with everything that is happening. My conversations with Jesus have gotten fewer and farther apart. I don't hear him talking back to me the same way he did when I was younger. Mama is constantly telling me God will punish me for my sins. I suppose God is not listening because of what Daddy and Adam are doing to me. Maybe it is because I still wet the bed sometimes. Maybe it is because I told Mama and Daddy I hate them. Maybe it is because, in my heart, I wish I belonged to the Michaels. I don't know. I know I don't like these feelings. Why do I feel all mixed up? Sometimes my throat hurts and it feels like someone is choking me. I go into the closet and cry, but I don't know why I'm crying.

Despite all my efforts to be good, I get into trouble at school the day before the May Day Parade. My teacher keeps me after school for one hour, which makes me get out of school the same time as my two sisters. When my teacher lets me leave, I run home as fast as I can. I fear Mary and Rebekah will see me on the street and tell Mama. When I arrive home, I have a red face.

Mama frowns at me from the place where she is standing in front of the kitchen counter. "Sarah, what is wrong with you?"

I stammer, "Nothing's wrong, Mama. I'm tired, but I'm excited about the May Day Dance and the parade tomorrow."

Raising her fine, arched eyebrows, she protests, "Little girl, you are not telling me the truth. Why are you late? Where have you been?"

I fear she can read right through my skin. Therefore, I tell her about my trouble at school today and how I ran all the way home. She sees little red spots on my face. She dries her hands and comes to pull up my shirt. She sees more little red spots. She pulls down my pants and sees still more spots.

Sighing, she looks at me and asks, "Do you know what these spots mean?"

"No, Mama, what do they mean?"

"They mean you have the measles, and your daddy has never had them. Get yourself upstairs. I will bring you some soup later."

A terrifying thought crosses my mind, and I ask, "The spots will be gone by tomorrow, won't they Mama? I still get to go to the May Day Dance, don't I? It won't work unless I am at my place at the pole."

Mama's voice rings with cold finality when she answers me. "It will *have* to work because you *can't* go. Maybe, if you had been good at school today, this wouldn't have happened to you. This is God's way of punishing you for your bad behavior. Now get yourself upstairs."

Mama doesn't even call the school to let them know I won't be there. I lay in bed thinking about Mama's words. *Is God punishing me for my bad behavior?* I can't swallow the lump in my throat and I feel the pain that is squeezing my heart. *How will I ever tell Mr. and Mrs. Michaels I can't wear my new dress?*

When Mary slips upstairs to see me, she finds me sitting on the bed, hugging my knees, rocking back and forth. "Sarah, I'm sorry. Mama said you have the measles."

I stop rocking and now turn my eyes, which had been unfocused, to Mary as I say, "Mary, I can't go to the May Day Dance. I can't wear my dress."

"I know, Sarah. I'm sorry." Mary knows how much I had looked forward to participating in the May Day Dance.

I pull my gaze from Mary and look straight ahead. "Mama says God is punishing me for being bad."

Mary moves close to me on the bed and puts her arm around me. "That's not true, Sarah. It was an accident that you got the measles now. I don't care what Mama said. God is not punishing you."

I look at Mary again and ask, "Will you go see the Michaels and tell them I can't go tomorrow? They had planned to go to the May Day Dance and Parade."

Mary goes to see the Michaels and then comes back and tells me it broke their hearts when she told them I was sick and could not go to take part in the May Day Dance.

I never intend to talk to Jesus again for a long time since Mama said he was punishing me. This is too much punishment; I wasn't *that* bad.

Shortly afterwards, Mary breaks out with the measles too. I guess Mary has been bad too. Several weeks go by and I have recovered from the measles. During these weeks, while we are finishing our school year, Daddy has been making trips to Heiskell, Tennessee, moving furniture to a small shack he found for us to rent for $15 a month. He is moving everything except the bare essentials, so we can leave as soon as school is out. I will complete second grade; Mary, the fourth grade; Rebekah, the seventh grade; and Adam, the ninth grade. Mark is now four months old. We children are all sad to be leaving Lay Avenue with its clover field, the fishpond with the quicksand, Williams Creek below the house, and the old oak tree.

This school year will end tomorrow. There is little left for us to pack. I cannot understand why we are leaving and the Michaels aren't leaving. It makes no sense to me. Mary is upset too. I see no Black people in our neighborhood or in surrounding neighborhoods. I think I will never be able to survive without the Michaels. I have given up on being able to talk to Jesus anymore.

I head for the creek, make one last round up and down the beautiful water all the way to the wooden bridge and back to the big oak tree. I stop to gaze at the fork and wonder if I should take time to go up and sit for a moment. I decide I must. I sit down and stare below at the crawfish.

My thoughts go back to the day Jesus spoke to me when I was four years old. It had taken much effort to get to this spot to have a moment of peace and freedom—freedom from those who were causing feelings in me that I didn't know how to cope with.

At seven years old, my vocabulary is limited and I don't have the words to describe how desolate and depressed I feel. I can't describe the anxiety that is present in my body when I wake up and when I go to sleep at night? I feel so alone sitting here in the tree, knowing I am leaving home and all that is familiar. I don't know where we are going and the house Daddy has described sounded terrible with no water or bathroom.

Too much has happened to me. The things Daddy and Adam did to me weren't right. Something is broken inside of me and I don't think it will ever get fixed because I can't even talk to Jesus anymore.

I am sitting in the fork of the tree with my head drooped forward, my arms dangling, and my eyes unfocused when, before my eyes, appears an angel dressed in a white robe. (See Figure 2.6) With gentle softness in her voice, the angel says, "My child, Jesus hears your prayers and knows your every need. Do not give up on him for he will never give up on you." Then, as quickly as she came, she is gone.

I feel a warm glow flow through me. I feel joy bubbling inside me.

Figure 2.6 The Angel

Dear Jesus,
　　Please let me keep this joy as a treasure in my heart. Let me remember it always. Forgive me for giving up on you. Thank you for not giving up on me.
　　I love you, Jesus. Amen.

I feel blissfully happy as a feeling of peace settles over me. I know I can make it now.

I climb down from the tree and run around singing, "Jesus

loves me, this I know, for the Bible tells me so. Little ones to him belong. They are weak, but he is strong. Yes, Jesus loves me, yes, Jesus loves me. Yes, Jesus loves me, for the Bible tells me so."

I learned this song in Bible School last summer when Mama let us attend Bible School at the Missionary Baptist church on Selma Avenue, which is near our home. I believe, after this spiritual experience, Jesus truly does love me. I will never doubt it again.

Part II
Personality for Faith Develops

"I have learned the secret of being well-fed and of going hungry,
and of having plenty and of being in need."
- Philippians 4:12

You Love Your Daddy, Don't You?

Chapter Three

This Old Shack

May 31, 1951—Mama, Mark, Mary, and I are with Daddy in the front of the pickup as we travel with the second load of furniture to the house we will move into near Heiskell, Tennessee. I feel butterflies in my stomach because I have already heard a description of the house and it sounds dilapidated. Adam and Rebekah came with Daddy on the first load this morning and Adam will travel back to Knoxville with Daddy to load boxes and small tables for the third load today.

We are on a dirt road when I see a stream of water up ahead that is running across the road. Daddy says we will have to "ford" three streams of water before we get to our new home.

"What does it mean to ford the streams of water?" I ask.

"It means there is no bridge," Mama answers. "Daddy will drive the truck through the water to the other side. The streams aren't deep."

The road goes on forever and it feels as if two huge monsters are rising and closing in on either side, shutting out the sunshine.

Later, I learn the shack sits in Raccoon Valley between two ridges. We have fewer than normal daylight hours, because it is late in the morning when the sun rises over the eastern ridge, and the sun sets early behind the western ridge.

Mary and I were adults when she told me she thought the fewer daylight hours may have been one of the factors contributing to the depressions Mama and she suffered with while living between those ridges. She told me it was a condition called seasonal affective disorder (SAD). After we were adults, being with Mary triggered flashbacks, and I felt a wild grief rip through me. I loved her and I knew she had her own pain about the past, but it

43

sometimes hurt to be with her. Often, I went through convoluted mental gymnastics to avoid memories of our past. That was before I went into the hospital. Now, I wish Mary and I lived closer so we could visit more often. We are not only sisters, we are friends and we are closer than we have ever been. We no longer feel the old sibling rivalry; we champion each other for each success. In our childhood, the secrets fostered a lack of trust among members of the family, and hugs were rare. Now, Mary and I never tire of hugging each other and saying, "I love you."

Shrinking back into the past, it is May 31, 1951, and Daddy is pulling the pickup into the front yard of the place where we will live for the next nine months. The shack is sitting about fourteen feet from the dirt road. The front yard is dirt and it is hard to tell where the road ends and the front yard begins. Daddy pulls in and backs up until the truck is backed up to the front porch. Mama opens the door and gets out. She is holding Mark. I jump out behind her. I run up on the steps as Adam begins to let the tailgate down. As I start to go into the house, Mama reminds me to carry a box with me.

When Mama gets busy in her bedroom, we kids cannot keep quiet any longer.

"This is idiotic," Mary says. "We have a good house in Knoxville that is paid for, and yet we're moving into this shack that we will have to pay rent to live in. Somebody tell me what kind of sense does that make?"

I chime in, "I can see outside through some of the cracks in the old rough boards on the walls that are covered in wallpaper that is mostly rotted and fallen down.

"Golly," Mary says. "I can see four different kinds of wallpaper. It seems they would have torn the old wallpaper down before putting up new."

As Daddy enters from the kitchen door, I add, "Under all the wallpaper is plain old newspapers. I guess they were poor and couldn't afford wallpaper the first time."

Daddy laughs and interjects, "The newspapers were for

insulation to help keep the house warm. That was also why they didn't tear down the old wallpaper when they added new. The old wallpaper added more insulation."

"I'm glad there is a fireplace. We are going to freeze this winter with these cracks in the walls," Mary says, looking at her father.

He shakes his head and says with force and authority. "I won't be here so y'all better remember this. You cannot build a fire in this fireplace. Don't you see how the bricks have crumbled? (See Figure 3.1) That's the way they are up in the chimney. As old as this house is, if you build a fire in the fireplace, the whole house will go up like a tinderbox."

Mary fires back, "This house is not fit to live in. Why did you bring us out here?"

Daddy ignores Mary and goes into the kitchen where Mama is organizing dishes and cookware in the cabinets and drawers.

Figure 3.1 Fireplace of the Old Shack

Mary and I begin exploring. There is no phone, no bathroom, and no running water. The kitchen opens onto a small stoop. The living room and Mama's bedroom are the other two rooms downstairs. In Mama's bedroom is a steep stairway with no handrails that goes straight up to a second floor. The second floor is one big opening with no finishing on the walls. I can see the sky through holes in the ceiling. I wonder if Daddy will fix the holes before it rains. Rebekah, Mary, and I will sleep on the second floor. Rebekah will have a bed, and Mary and I will share a second bed. Mark's baby bed will go in Mama's bedroom and Mama tells Adam he has to sleep on the back porch stoop. None of us know why Adam has to sleep on the stoop. Why can't he sleep on the living room couch or on the living room floor on quilts?

A wood stove in the kitchen serves two purposes—cooking and heating. Daddy builds a shelf with one-by-ten inch boards on the stoop off the kitchen. The purpose for the shelf is to sit a bucket for water. Daddy and Adam have prior approval from our landlord and now they go up the hill and pipe water from the landlord's pump downhill to a faucet attached to the shelf. We don't have hot water but at least we now have cold water on the stoop. For the nine months we live there, we take our baths by heating water and pouring it into a number two galvanized tub sitting by the wood stove in the kitchen.

When the task of getting water is complete, Daddy leaves and goes to Ohio to find work. Except for visits, he stays in Ohio the whole time we live in this rundown shack.

Mama isn't cooking well-balanced meals like she did in Knoxville. Maybe it is because it took all the money for Daddy to buy Mama the old car before he left. But he couldn't leave us out here with no transportation. When we have been living there approximately one month, Mama tells Mary and me to get in the car. She tells Mary to hold Mark. She cranks the car and then Mama tells us we are going to the post office at Heiskell because she is expecting some money from Daddy. Then we are going to buy groceries. When we get to the post office, the money is *not* there and Mama is angry with Daddy.

That evening Mama cooks biscuits, grits, and flour gravy for supper. We don't have any syrup or margarine to eat with our biscuits and we are all feeling sad. We do not talk while we eat.

Rebekah's bed is on the other side of the huge opening upstairs, and Mary's voice is low, but I can hear the barely controlled anger. "It's Daddy's fault that we have to live like this. He hasn't sent money as promised, and that's why we haven't had enough to eat for the last two weeks. Sometimes I hate him. It wasn't because a Black family moved into our community that we had to move away. It was for some other reason that Daddy

46

doesn't want us to know about. Mama is angry with him. Maybe it was because of the redheaded woman I saw Daddy with when Mama was in the hospital for the birth of Mark. Maybe it was because he shot the Black man, or maybe it was because Daddy was in the Ku Klux Klan."

Mary is scratching a red rash that has appeared on her neck. Clearly, she is angry with Daddy. She sat up in bed and continued, "It isn't fair that our family has to live like this because Daddy causes trouble. He does what he wants to and goes where he pleases regardless of how it affects the rest of the family. I will bet Daddy isn't living as poorly in Ohio as we are here. I bet he has plenty of money up there. Sarah, you can sit there rocking back and forth all you want to. It won't change our situation. I know what you're doing. You are trying to tune me out. You don't like to hear me talk negative about Mama and Daddy, but neither one of them treat us right. They put their own needs and wishes first. No matter what Daddy wants, we have a good house in Knoxville that is paid for. Sarah, Mama could move us back there without Daddy."

Continuing to rock, Mary's sister says, "I'm Faith and I know what I can do. I'll go get my money jar from my drawer and see if I have enough to help Mama buy some groceries. I'm tired of being hungry; I'm tired having only biscuits or cornbread, and homemade syrup that Mama made with sugar, water, and maple flavoring."

Faith slips away to go to Sarah's dresser where she keeps her money jar hidden. She opens the jar, takes out all the money, and then puts the jar back under her pajamas in the drawer. Faith goes back to Rebekah and Mary where they are waiting. She opens her hand, and then spreads out the money on the bed shared by Mary and her. Rebekah helps Faith count the money, and they discover she has twenty dollars and eighty-six cents.

"Mama can have it. Sarah will never know what happened to it."

Rebekah and Mary both look at Sarah and shake their heads.

Mary and Sarah are close in age—only twenty-one months between their births; they are also close emotionally. Mary has observed what she believes is Sarah pretending to be someone else. She ignores Sarah's previous statement and asks, "What will we tell Mama? You know she will ask where the money came from?"

Rebekah asks, "Where *did* the money come from?"

Faith answers, "I've been saving my money since before we left Knoxville. Daddy pays me to clean out his truck. I empty the ash tray and clean out all the cigarette boxes and food wrappers he throws on the floor. And he pays me to polish his shoes. We can tell Mama we all decided to pool our savings; tell her Adam even put in some of his money too."

When life gets too stressful for me, something has to happen. I can't take discord and hard feelings. First, I depend on my prayers to Jesus. As you saw on the last day before we left Knoxville, sometimes angels appear and talk to me. I couldn't cope with the pain I saw on Mama's face when she looked through the mail at the post office and found that Daddy hadn't sent the money he had promised. I can't bear it when my family doesn't have enough to eat. I can't bear to see Mama getting more and more depressed each day. I watch Mama stare off into space, and sometimes she doesn't hear us when we talk to her.

Mary asks, "Are you sure you want to give away all your money? You've always been so protective of it. You've never been willing to share a penny before now."

What Mary and Rebekah don't know, and what I don't know, is that my second alter, Faith, has just been born. (See Figure 3.2) It wasn't Sarah who was giving away her money. Sarah didn't know anything about it.

Faith tells Mary, "Of course, I'm sure."

It is Mary who is now looking off into space. Her voice is disconcerting. "A few

Figure 3.2 Faith is born

years back, you wanted us to call you Susie. A while ago, you said you were 'Faith.' I wish I could turn into somebody else, and not have to live with this crazy family in this old shack…. Well, I guess I better close my mouth before I blow a fuse."

Mama is still up when I go downstairs, so I go back upstairs and my sisters and I decide to give the money to Mama tonight.

Mary says, "Rebekah, you do the talking. Mama has always believed you more than she does Sarah and me."

Rebekah agrees. We tiptoe down the staircase and go to the kitchen where Mama is sitting at the kitchen table, looking through bills, which she had no money to pay. We three sit down at the table and Rebekah asks if we can talk with her.

When she agrees, Rebekah begins, "Mama, we saw how upset you were today when you didn't receive the check from Daddy, and we decided to put all of our money together and give it to you for our groceries."

Mama's brows draw together in an agonized expression. Her voice sounds tired when she says, "Oh, my children, I can't take your money. Rebekah, this is money you saved from you paper route in Knoxville. Mary and Sarah, this is money you earned from chores you did for our landlord. You worked hard for this money."

"We all agreed and we want you to have it."

Mama's blue eyes were full of pain and unquenchable warmth. "Well, only as a loan until I receive some money from your father. Tomorrow I will go buy some groceries. Thank you all so much."

We hug Mama and tell her goodnight; then we disappear up the stairs. My sisters tell me I was sweet to do that for Mama. We say goodnight to one another. When sleep came, Faith was temporarily gone too.

NOTE: Sarah's core personality was already split by the birth of Susie, and it is now further fragmented by the appearance of Faith. Sarah is a sensitive, compassionate eight-year-old child, and she can no longer stand the pain and uncertainty of not knowing if her Daddy will send money for groceries. She can no longer bear to see her mother sink lower into depression, because her father rarely comes home and, when he does, he shows little affection for her mother. Instead, they quarrel over money and his infrequent visits home. Faith is stronger than Sarah. She will empathize with Sarah's mother, and relieve Sarah of much of her stress related to her worries about groceries.

In this shack, I am scared and there is no place where I feel safe when I feel the need to hide. Sometimes Mama calls for me and wants to know where I have been. I tell her I went outside for a few minutes and she says I have been gone for two or more hours. Then I can't remember those hours. I don't know where I have been while I was gone. It scares me so badly. Sometimes I go upstairs to be alone a few minutes. Then Mama calls and says I'm trying to get out of work. She says I've been upstairs an hour, when I can only remember being upstairs for a few minutes.

I wet the bed much more than I did at Lay Avenue. Mama seems to think embarrassing us kids will cause us to stop; however, it makes it worse. An example of embarrassing us happened one day when Mary and I were upstairs reading. We heard footsteps on the stairs and looked up to see Mama and our neighbors, Mr. and Mrs. Nelson, standing in our door. We spoke to them as Mama led them to our bed. The covers were thrown back because one of us girls had wet the bed the previous night.

Mama pointed to the brown circle on the sheet and said, "These girls will be teenagers in a few years and yet they still wet the bed. I don't have a washing machine and I have to spend most of my days scrubbing their wet sheets in a tub, trying to rinse out the soap, and hanging them out to dry. You know we don't have many hours of sunshine here, so it's a fight every day to try to get the sheet dry before it is dark again."

I glanced up in time to see Mrs. Nelson shift her eyes toward me. My cheeks colored under the heat of her gaze. I lowered my head and shifted my eyes to Mary. Her eyebrows drew together in an angry expression.

Mama turned and the Nelson's followed her out the door.

Mary's voice was shaking, "Sometimes I hate her. A mother shouldn't embarrass their children like that."

I kept my mouth shut. By showing them the wet bed, she contradicted what she told them. She doesn't spend most of her days washing sheets, and she has no plan to wash the sheets today. Most days she lets the sheets dry right on the beds and we sleep on the soiled sheets after they have dried. I suspect the Nelson's figured that out after they left our home.

The worst accident happens outside when I go to the outdoor toilet. I go into the dark, stinky little outhouse, and a huge snake is coiled inside the hole where I have intensions of sitting. I scream, "Snake, snake, snake!" all the way back down the hill. I am mortified when I realize I am messing in my pants.

I think, *"How will I ever get clean without a bathroom and running water?"*

Rebekah and Adam both grab a hoe. Unfortunately, it is too late as the snake has escaped. I never want to go back to the outhouse again; however, I have no choice.

Dear Lord, we have moved into a $15 a month rented shack, way out in the country with no running water, in the middle of nowhere. How will we survive in this shack without Daddy's income if he doesn't send us more money? I know Mama doesn't have any money. Please help us, Jesus.
Love, Sarah

Back in Knoxville, Mama loved having company. Now she doesn't care that we rarely have any visitors. I believe she feels uncomfortable for anyone to see the way we live.

I dearly love my new baby brother (Figure 3.3); however, I don't get to see him much because Mama assigned Mary the job of taking care of him. Mama said my job was to help her with the garden. I didn't complain because I love the outdoors. Who wants to stay in this dreary old shack anyway?

Summer passes quickly because much of my time is spent in the garden. It is time for school to begin and I feel nervous. Mama

Figure 3.3 Sarah holding Mark

has made each of us girls a blouse and skirt from the twenty-five pound flour sacks she has been saving. This is my first opportunity to ride a big yellow school bus. It pulls up and stops on the road before our house and we get on—all except Mary. Mary stays hidden until after the bus has gone. I learn that evening that, after the bus left, Mary told Mama her job this summer was to take care of Mark. Therefore, now she will stay home and continue taking care of Mark. Mama told her she had to go to school and she had no choice.

The next day Mary gets sick and cannot go to school. On the third day Mama forces Mary to get on the bus. Mary becomes depressed and she isn't faking it. Mary does not excel in her schoolwork as she has always done before. Eventually, Mama has to go to school to talk to her teacher.

With Daddy gone, and Adam sleeping on the porch, I don't have to fear they will bother me anymore. However, the tension and anxiety that was a huge part of my life at Knoxville is still hanging on, even though I know Daddy and Adam can't bother me here. In the evening I feel my body grow tense. I feel my muscles tie in knots, and I feel a suffocating sensation in my throat. Then I realize it is time for the six o'clock news. Only when I remember that Daddy is *not* at home does my body begin the slow process of relaxing again.

I also have similar mind-body related problems when it nears the time to go upstairs to bed. Each night I have to go through the ritual of telling myself I will sleep with Mary—not Adam. Sometimes, however, I still have nightmares in which I see the white stuff coming out of Adam's penis. Often my screams wake

Mary, but I never told her what the nightmare is about. But, slowly, I am beginning to think more about what is happening in my life today, and less about what Daddy and Adam did to me in the past. It was terrible when my mind couldn't concentrate on anything but that. Now, other than nearly freezing when we try to wash without a bathroom or hot water, my life is beginning to get better. It is better having a school bus take us to school than walking a mile on city streets like we did in Knoxville.

Somehow, we learn about the church pictured in Figure 3.4. If Daddy were here, he wouldn't let us attend, because it is a Missionary Baptist Church—not a Primitive Baptist Church. However, Daddy isn't here and I believe Mama thinks it may help us feel better if we go to this church, even though it isn't the denomination we normally attend. She says we should meet our neighbors.

Figure 3.4 Church we attended

I learn that going to this church is fun because I meet new people. I like the young people and I *love* the old people. Everyone is friendly and they seem happy that we have started going to their church.

My alter Faith loves the beautiful music she hears each Sunday in this small church that sits in a wide sunlit valley.

This morning Faith closes her eyes as her family's new friends, Gerry, Donna, and their mom, Mrs. Bailey, sing "I'll Fly Away."

"Some glad morning when this life is o'er, I'll fly away; to a home on God's celestial shore, I'll fly away."

Faith feels the spiritual presence of the Lord almost every time she comes to be with the people in this church. She reaches over to hold her mother's hand. Tears fill Faith's eyes and pour down her cheeks, and she doesn't even notice.

I like my school and I love Mount Harmony Church but, oh, how I miss the Michaels, the clover field, the creek, and the big oak tree. When I think about Lay Avenue, I always remember the angel who appeared to tell me that Jesus never forgets about me.

Dear Jesus,
Thank you for sending Daddy to Ohio and thank you for letting me sleep so far away from Adam. Thank you for letting me not think about that so much anymore. I know moving here is what made them stop bothering me, but I wish I could see the Michaels. I miss them so much.

Thank you for leading my family to Mount Harmony Baptist Church. The people are so warm and friendly. Mama seems glad that we started going and many people always invite us to come again.

Jesus, please bless Mama and help her to feel better. I pray that Daddy sends some money this week.
Love,
Sarah

Since we have no phone, Daddy calls our property owner, Mr. Tillman, and asks him to tell Mama he will be home for Thanksgiving. We are at the supper table when Mr. Tillman knocks on the door. Adam goes to open the door and he asked Mr. Tillman to come in. Mr. Tillman comes through the living room to the kitchen and delivers his message.

I am startled by the thought of Daddy coming home, and I accidentally knock over my glass of milk. I jump up to get a dishcloth to wipe up the spilled milk. Mama starts shouting at me about the cost of milk, and she asks why I can't be more careful. It is embarrassing for her to shout at me while Mr. Tillman is standing by the table. I wipe up the milk and then run from the kitchen and go upstairs.

Lying on my bed I wonder how I will handle Daddy's aggravation. I decide that, somehow, I will avoid sitting on his lap.

Trying to think positive, I hope Mama will feel better with Daddy home. Maybe Daddy will help cut wood for the kitchen stove; however, for some reason, I doubt if he will because Daddy is lazy. When he is home, we kids have to wait on him almost hand and foot. Mama said children should wait on their elders. She said that is Primitive Baptist teaching.

Sure enough, on Thanksgiving Day we are out of wood and Adam and Mary have to go up on the ridge to cut more wood with only the ax. Daddy sits in his chair ignoring the conversation between Mama and Adam, and he doesn't offer to help cut wood but he does tell Adam he can use his pickup truck.

The ridges look like mountains to me. They are covered with rock boulders that look like and endless expanse of balding grey heads. Interspersed are green, shadowy groves of trees that become blue with the haze of distance nearer the summit of the ridge.

After Adam and Mary have gone to cut wood, Daddy goes into the living room while Mama and Rebekah are preparing Thanksgiving dinner. Then he goes to the bottom of the stairs in Mama's bedroom and calls for me. I stayed upstairs trying to avoid him. When I come down the stairs, Daddy says, "I've missed my special girl. Come sit on Daddy's lap."

My pulse begins to beat erratically, and the silence is tight with tension. My jaws ache and I fear I will break my teeth because my jaws are clenched so tight. My mind and body are locked in a battle. Daddy continues to grin at me until Susie ends the struggle in my mind. She smiles and runs forward to sit on her Daddy's lap. He tells her if she works hard, makes good grades in school, and behaves for Mama; he will take her to visit his family in Alabama for the Christmas holidays. That is where Susie's Aunt Sarah lives.

Daddy's infectious grin has set the tone, and Susie turns in his lap and hugs his neck. "You know I want to go see Aunt Sarah. I was named for her." Susie decides she will grant Daddy all his wishes.

NOTE: I recovered the memory of what happened on the following afternoon when I was fifty-nine years old and a patient at Women's Institute for Incorporation Therapy.

It is Friday, November 23, 1951, the day after Thanksgiving. Mama asks Daddy to drive to the store at Heiskell for a loaf of bread. Daddy calls out for me to ride with him. Thinking I might get an opportunity to buy something, I run to my dresser drawer and grab my jar, and find it is empty. Who stole my money? I am furious. I'll have to find out after I get home because I can't hold Daddy up. He's already waiting in the truck.

NOTE: Sarah has no memory of Faith giving her money to her mother.

On the way back from the store, Daddy pulls the truck down a little dirt road. He pulls me over close to him. I feel happy about this because all I have ever wanted was for Daddy to love me the way Daddies should love their little girls. I am eight years old.

I feel Daddy's heart beating against my chest and his face is buried in my hair. His voice is husky against my ear. "Darling, you are my special girl. Today we don't have to worry about Mama walking in and learning our secret."

I close my eyes and that causes the tears to spill over and run down my face. I had hoped Daddy wanted to hug me in a good way. But he is talking about Mama learning the secret. Now I wish I had stayed home.

I wipe away tears and then take a deep breath. Daddy lays me on my back on the seat and pulls off my panties. My heart is beating fast and I am afraid. Then Daddy pulls his penis out of his overalls and pulls my feet closer to him. I close my eyes and I can feel my whole body shaking. Why did Daddy take his "thing" out? I'm only a little girl—the littlest girl in the family. I am hurting inside. Daddy has betrayed me. He doesn't love me; he only wants to use my body to please himself. I feel my body growing numb—

like I am made of wood. I'm not breathing. I feel myself going away.

Susie gasps for air. Good Lord, Sarah was trying to kill them by holding her breath. She takes several deep breaths and then looks down. She cannot believe her eyes. Wow! Daddy has never shown her his penis before. He smiles at her, lifts her body and taking her hand, puts it around his penis, and squeezes. The shock of him runs through her body. Adam never asked her to touch his penis. Daddy puts his right arm around Susie's small shoulder and pulls her close, pressing her against his erect penis. Then his hand cups her cheek and he kisses her lightly on the forehead, then the nose, and then the mouth. His nearness is overwhelming her.

His hand makes a path down her body until it rests on her thigh. Then he lays her back down on the seat. He parts her legs and his steady gaze bores into her deep blue eyes as he parts her lips and touches her clitoris. Her reaction is immediate. Her small body arches, the pleasure obvious on her face. He gently massages her clitoris until currents of desire flow through her. He pauses to kiss her and to tell her she is special and he loves every part of her. With his finger he enters her vagina as far as he can until he feels her pulling back.

She trembles and says, "Don't, Daddy." He shudders, as he pushes his pelvis forward toward her, and his spasms come, spurting semen on his overalls. Susie raises her head and watches as the white stuff comes from her father's penis, the same as she had seen it come from Adam's penis upstairs on Lay Avenue. Pulling a handkerchief from his pocket, Jim tries to wipe the semen off his overalls, and he tells Susie to put her panties back on.

Before Jim cranks the truck to leave, he pulls Susie onto his lap and holds her tenderly. "Darling, I want to remind you that this has to be our secret. You can never tell anyone about our secret. Do you understand?"

Susie hugs her Daddy's neck and answers, "I remember. I won't tell anyone about our secret."

When we pull back into our yard, Susie goes away and I am Sarah. I am shaking all over and I enter the shack with my head held down. I head straight for the stairs and I lie down on my bed. I don't know if the thoughts in my head are real or if I just hear voices in my head. Within minutes I fall asleep. After that day, I do not think about the incident, talk about it, or tell anyone. It never enters my mind again until I am admitted to the hospital at WIIT, a hospital in South Florida.

Sunday comes and Daddy leaves again. Sunday evening, when Mary and I are putting on our pajamas, Mary says to me, "It isn't fair for Daddy to give you money and not give money to the rest of us."

I tell her, "Daddy doesn't give me money."

"Well, who gave it to you?" Mary asks. "I saw you put some more in your drawer. I know Mama doesn't have any money to give away, and besides you just gave all your money to her."

I am puzzled by what Mary is saying. I don't remember putting any money in a drawer. "I don't know what you are talking about. Somebody stole my money."

Mary goes to my drawer and pulls out two one dollar bills. I stare at the dollar bills and then I begin crying. "I don't know how it got there, Mary. Maybe Daddy *did* give me the money. I must have done a job for him."

"What job?"

"I don't know. I can't remember. Wait, I remember; I did two jobs for him Saturday evening. I polished his shoes and cleaned out the cab of his truck."

I really had done the jobs for Daddy, but I didn't remember him giving me the money, and I didn't remember putting it in the drawer. I add, "I will give the money to Mama. I can tell her I found the money down by the cushion in the chair where Daddy sits when he is home."

"That's sweet of you, Sarah," Mary says. "Mama needs all the money she can get for food."

Mary and Rebekah went to sleep hours ago, but I cannot go to sleep. It is a drizzling, ugly night and I cannot stop listening to the rain on the tin roof, and the sound of each drop of water as it drips into the five-gallon buckets placed all around the floor to catch the water from the leaks in the roof.

Mostly, my head is going round and round like a merry-go-round and I can't make it stop. I'm worried about so many things that sometimes I forget all the things I'm worried about. I feel nervous all the time. I wish Daddy would go away and stay. I'm afraid of him and I'm afraid to say anything to Mama. If Mama made him go away we wouldn't have any money, and Mama needs Daddy to give her money. Why can't I remember how the money got in my drawer? I am so tired. I am too tired to figure it out. I can't figure out the problems. I wish I could go to sleep.

When I think of Daddy's family, I think of Uncle Clayton, Daddy's brother, because he is my favorite of all my uncles in Alabama. It is his wife I love so much. When Mama named me for Aunt Sarah, she gave me a twenty-five dollar bond shortly after I was born.

The Christmas holidays seem slow in arriving, but finally they are here, and we are going to Alabama. Winter comes hard in the Smoky Mountains of Tennessee. Seven of us cannot fit into the cab of Daddy's pickup truck. Daddy, Rebekah, Mama, and Mark will ride in the cab and Adam, Mary and I will sit in the back of the pickup. Daddy has built a body over the back, which keeps the wind off, and he has painted it blue.

People comment when we go by, "There go the Mahoney kids in the 'Doghouse Blues'" (See truck body in the right side of the picture in Figure 3.2.)

The Primitive Baptist use the term "week's meeting" in the same way Missionary Baptist refer to their "revivals." The week's meeting for Daddy's church, Providence Primitive Baptist Church, is in progress while we are visiting in Alabama and we hear some good preaching. Rebekah and Mary join the church on Wednesday night. Mary had wanted to join Mount Harmony Missionary Baptist Church but Daddy had told her she couldn't. He had told her to wait and join his church over the Christmas holidays.

It is Friday night and the people are singing "Just as I Am" for the invitational hymn. Faith moves toward the aisle to join the church. Mama pulls her arm and tells her to be still.

Since Daddy was here for Thanksgiving, I have been going off alone where I could cry and no one would see. I was hurting on the inside—in my throat and in my heart. I felt like I was bad...like I wouldn't get to go to heaven. My mind has been in constant turmoil.

Faith wants to join this church like Rebekah and Mary did. She doesn't want Sarah to feel like she's bad. She wants Jesus to make us clean.

Faith pulls on Sarah's arm where Mama is holding it and she says, "Turn loose, Mama. Jesus is calling and we must go."

Mama looks at Daddy and they agree to let us go. Later, I hear them say they thought I went because Rebekah and Mary went on Wednesday, but that was not the reason. I don't remember my feelings at the time. I only know that Jesus called me, and I am so glad he did. Before, I felt so lost—so torn up inside—but now I feel cleansed from my sins. Jesus saved me, and I don't know what I would do without him in my life. He has never forgotten me and I will never forget him.

Aunt Sarah is the pianist for Providence Church. I persuade Mama and Daddy to let me go to her house and stay until the following Sunday. Aunt Sarah is part-owner of a jewelry store in downtown Tallassee, Alabama. She takes me to the store on Saturday and shows me several silver necklaces. Then she tells me to choose the one I want. She is giving me the necklace to wear when I get baptized. I choose a necklace with a cross. Jesus is on the cross, depicting the time of his crucifixion. I am happy when Aunt Sarah asked me to pick out necklaces for Rebekah and Mary too.

On Sunday my sisters and I are baptized. I am so happy that I cry because being baptized caused me to feel like I was washed clean. Getting saved and being baptized is a special thing. Jesus is now in my heart and I want to live for him.

I left my clothes at Aunt Sarah's on purpose so we would have to go back by her house on the way home. We stop by Aunt Sarah's and I get to hug her good-bye, then we start the long journey back to our shack in Raccoon Valley.

While we travel homeward, I sit on the bench close to the cab and hug myself. This old second-hand coat that someone gave to Mama does little to shut out the freezing cold. My thoughts are on the conversations Aunt Sarah and I had. I had told her what Mama and Daddy said about me wanting to join the church only because Rebekah and Mary had joined earlier. After telling her about the angel that had appeared to me before we moved from Lay Avenue, Aunt Sarah told me I was ready to join the church. She told me not to worry anymore.

The monotony of the winter wind whizzing by the "Old Blue" truck body lulls me until I can no longer hold up my head. It is dark and Daddy told us he would drive through the night. Mama brought along quilts and pillows.

"Mary," I ask. "Will you help me spread out the quilts? I'm tired."

"Sure," Mary tells me. Mary gives one of the pillows and quilts to Adam so he can sleep on the bench where we three have been sitting and she and I make a bed on the floor of the truck.

I snuggle as close as possible to Mary, trying to draw warmth from her body. Finally, I sleep and the rest of the trip passes quickly. When I awake, we are pulling into the yard of our shack in Raccoon Valley. Daddy spends one night at home and then he is gone again.

The winter in this shack is freezing cold. The wood-burning stove in the kitchen will not heat the whole shack because there are cracks in the walls, which let in the wind. Even if it wasn't for the cracks in the walls, we can't keep enough wood for the stove. We can't afford to buy and have someone deliver us a load of wood. We have to cut our own wood from up on the ridge and we only have an ax to cut the wood. Most days we keep on our coats and huddle around the stove, trying to keep warm. I see images of Daddy in Ohio, sitting in a warm room, talking and laughing with the woman he is boarding with.

When night comes, I beg Mama not to make me take a bath in the number two tub in the middle of the kitchen floor. There is not enough wood in the stove to get the bathwater hot and the air in the kitchen is freezing too. After I bathe in the icy water, I cannot stop shaking. I go up the steps and the air is cold upstairs too. I have never slept in such a cold house in all my life. How can I go to sleep when I can't stop shaking?

Some of my best childhood memories are of the times we spend at Auntie's house in Columbus, Georgia. Auntie is my maternal grandfather's sister. My maternal grandmother is dead and my grandfather, who we call Papaw, and Auntie live together. I love to take a bath in Auntie's old claw foot bathtub. I think one reason, besides the novelty of the tub, is Daddy is not with us on these visits. I can take my baths without worrying about Daddy coming in to watch me bathe.

I learned early that Daddy does not like Papaw, and somehow, I sense the feeling is mutual, though Papaw never talks about Daddy in the presence of us children. Even though money is scarce, Mama comes once a year on the bus to visit Papaw and Auntie, and Daddy never comes with us.

Figure 3.5 Auntie in her dining room

Auntie's kitchen is small— so small that, once you are in the kitchen, you can hardly turn around. Also, her dining area is small. Squeezed in the corner behind her dining table is a cabinet where she stores canned goods and other food items. On top of the cabinet is a huge cookie jar. (See Figure 3.5) I don't know if she always has it full of cookies, or if she only fills it with cookies when she knows we are coming.

Often, when no one is watching, I get in a chair, climb up on the table, and reach for the jar to get a cookie. Mama is the lucky niece who inherits Auntie's cookie jar when she dies and later, Mama passes it on to me. It has a number three on the bottom, so I doubt many were in circulation. One side of the cookie jar has a bear and the other side has a pig. Naturally, I still have it with its original paint, and I treasure it with all my heart.

Papaw has a black Model T Ford car. No one I know has a car as old as Papaw's car. Papaw takes good care of it. He tells Mama he has a man to service it regularly. On the inside, it is spotless. On the outside, it is shiny and I can see myself in the reflection.

Auntie's driveway runs right beside her house on a downward incline to the back of the house. A walnut tree grows on the line between Auntie's house and the next homeowner. I love walnuts. I had forgotten to go out and pick up the walnuts from the driveway. Papaw is driving his car up the driveway to the street. We are going to the pharmacy to get some medicine for him and to the grocery store. I hear the sound of the walnuts as the tires run over them.

"Pop, pop, pop."

"Stop, stop...STOP, Papaw," I cry.

"Why? What's wrong, Sarah?"

"The walnuts, I have to get the walnuts."

Papaw stops and I jump out of the Model-T Ford. I pull up my skirt to hold the nuts, and begin picking them up. Mary gets out and helps me. When we finish picking up the walnuts, we run into the house to leave the nuts. We are laughing and running down the long hall to the back where Auntie and Papaw lives. This is the first time we get into trouble at Auntie's house. Mama is furious with us for making noise in the hall because we have been told not to run or make noise in the front part of Auntie's house. The front part of Auntie's house is divided into apartments, which she rents to other people. The one closest to Auntie and Papaw is rented by a

63

registered nurse who is a dear friend to them. She often takes care of them. When we returned to Papaw and the Model-T Ford, he was patiently waiting for us.

Mama and her sister, Aunt Karen, write letters to each other every week. Aunt Karen has written to Mama about a house and 100 acres of farmland her husband's family is planning to sell through a closed-bid auction.

Mama has been angry with Daddy for a long time. She tells us that she wants to move closer to some of her own people. Aunt Karen persuades the bank president to finance the farm for Mama if her bid is the highest. The bank president tells Aunt Karen that Mama will have to get the down payment from another lending source. Mama's brother owns a plumbing company in Columbus, Georgia. He agrees to lend Mama the down payment.

Mama is excited when she takes her bid for $5,000 to the post office. Two weeks pass before Mama learns that her bid was the highest. We are all excited. Mama bakes a pound cake and we celebrate. Daddy comes home and begins making trips to Georgia. The first load includes Rebekah's piano, a cow, a pig (who will make the trip under the cow), and Adam, so he can start working on the fences. Daddy has to make four trips of moving essential furniture and appliances before the trip when Mama and the rest of us four children go to Georgia. It is wonderful to leave this uninhabitable shack in Raccoon Valley. It takes many more trips to get all our nonessential belongings moved.

After we move to Georgia, Mama receives a letter from Papaw telling her Auntie is "very low." Mary asks Mama what "very low" means, and Mama explains that it means Auntie might not live much longer. Mama tells Daddy she is taking Mary, Mark, and me with her to go see Auntie. I can tell by the tone of Mama's voice she is going regardless of what Daddy says.

Auntie is in the bed in her bedroom when we get to her house. I can tell she is weak, but she knows who we are and calls all of us by name. She squeezes my hand a little when I hold her hand. Mama is cooking and I am in the room with her when she takes her last breath. It scares me. Papaw comes running when I call and tell him she is dead. He gets the registered nurse to come and she confirms that Auntie has passed on.

The nurse slips Auntie's false teeth into her mouth before her face gets cold. At that moment, I feel so lonely. Auntie meant so much to me. I will miss my visits with her more than any words can express. I walk backwards so Mama and Mary can get to Auntie's bedside. Still walking backwards, I bump into Auntie's dresser.

A comparison is waging in my mind and I am hurt and angry. I want so much for Daddy to hold me and love me. But, somehow, I know he doesn't. Somehow, I know it is bad to love Daddy. But, Auntie was a good person. She was so sweet. She made me feel good on the inside. She gave me cookies and potato candy. Afterwards, I felt good about myself and about her. I didn't feel bad like I do when Daddy holds me on his lap. *Why, Jesus, did you let Auntie die instead of Daddy?*

A few days after Auntie's funeral, we kiss Papaw good-bye and we go back to our new home in Georgia.

Chapter Four

Our New Farm

We moved to Georgia in March of 1952. Mark had his first birthday on January 16 of this year. I had my ninth birthday on March 5. Mary will be eleven on June 19, Ruth will be fourteen on July 9, and Adam will be sixteen on October 8. Mama will be thirty-eight on July 15, and Daddy, who is ten years older, will be forty-eight on July 21.

I didn't get to see our new farm until the trip when the family was moving to stay. Daddy slowed the truck to turn off a paved road onto a dirt road. Mama pointed to the left and said, "Girls, there's your Aunt Karen's house."

I scoot up on the seat and hug the dashboard. I feel a sudden rush of excitement. "How much farther is it to our house?" I ask.

"It is one mile down this road," Daddy answers.

I turn around and see him smiling at me. For some reason I can't understand, I am irritated that Daddy answered. I had directed my question to Mama. I am angry with Daddy. I think Mama should tell him he wouldn't live with us in the old shack, so he can't live with us in this new place. I'll bet Aunt Karen feels the same way I do.

I feel better when Mama answers, "Our land starts here where you see the fence."

"I don't see a house, Mama. Where is our house?"

"You'll see. Half of the land is in front of the house. The other half is woods and the wooded fifty acres are behind the house," Mama explains.

We travel around the big square block of land and then we go up a driveway, which is about as long as a city block. At the end of the driveway is a big white house with four white columns on the front porch. I am speechless because it is such an improvement over the forlorn shack we left behind in Raccoon Valley in Tennessee.

Knowing Mama bought this house and hundred acres in a closed-bid auction, I am almost certain my Aunt Karen fixed the bid. Aunt Karen is Mama's youngest sister, and they wrote letters to each other every few days the last month or two we lived in the old shack. Mama had written to Aunt Karen of her wishes to live closer to her two sisters in middle Georgia. Aunt Karen wanted to help Mama move to Georgia, and this house is only one mile away.

The house is airy and cold. It has three propane gas heaters— one in Mama and Daddy's bedroom, one in the kitchen and the other in the living room. We do not heat the living room and front part of the house unless we have guest. The bathroom is in the middle of a big long hall—an afterthought built decades after the original construction of the house. Daddy still holds firm on his demand there will be *no* locks on the bathroom doors, as he did on Lay Avenue. The bathroom has two doors—one to the front hall and one to the back hall. I don't think the two-door bathroom is as strange as the bedroom we girls are assigned to sleep in. It has four doors—one to the back hall, one to Adam's bedroom, one to Mama and Daddy's bedroom, and one to the side yard. It is hard to find wall space to put bedroom furniture for three girls when there is a door on every wall. I'm not complaining; this house is still one hundred percent better than the house in Raccoon Valley where we rented.

I am in the third grade and frightened to enroll in a new school. I think I wouldn't be as scared if it were the beginning of a new year. As usual, Social Studies is my hardest subject. We cover only four of the chapters between March and the end of school. When it is time for the final exam, my teacher, Mrs. Jones, tells me I have to take the test, which will cover the entire book. I have been trying hard this past month to prepare for this final test, but I cannot learn the material in the whole book. On the night before the test, I cried until I could cry no more and I finally went to sleep.

Rebekah goes with me to my room the following morning. She faces Mrs. Jones with a withering stare. "Mrs. Jones," Rebekah says. "You should be ashamed of yourself, making my little sister take the test over the entire book when she was only in your class for four of the chapters."

"Wow," I thought. *"Rebekah's not afraid of anybody. She scared Mrs. Jones. I'm glad she did."*

Mrs. Jones blinked her eyes rapidly. "I don't intend to count off for the earlier chapters if she doesn't score high."

Rebekah is satisfied so she leaves to go to her class. After crying half the night, I am happy to hear what Mrs. Jones told Rebekah. I tried to study the whole book. When it is time for the test, Mrs. Jones hands them out and then wishes us good luck. I try my best on the test and I later learn I scored "ninety-six."

School is out and Mama makes us work from sunup to sundown on this new farm. But, every chance I can, I steal little moments to be alone. I believe Jesus helped me get away from the life in Raccoon Valley, and now I feel as if I am in a brave, new world. I want time to explore the boundaries of our new land. I look out and see rolling, sunlit countryside—not the ridges in Tennessee, which hemmed us in and crested the skylines on both sides, making it dark early in the evening.

When Mama goes in to start supper, I slip off for a quick walk in the woods. It rained earlier in the day and the overhanging branches are swaying and dripping raindrops on my head and shoulders. Still, it is a peaceful scene in these woods. Seeing a shadow on the path, I looked up to see buzzards circling overhead. They frightened me so I turned and went back home.

As one of our first tasks, we start digging out a spring for the cows to have a larger watering hole. The cows already have a watering hole on each side of the barn, but neither one is large enough. The front part of the farm is pasture and the back is wooded acres. Cows usually give birth to their new calves in the evening when they are in the back part in the woods. This makes finding them much harder.

If anyone doubts there is a God, he or she should live on a farm. I awaken each morning to find a beautiful green garden growing, new baby chicks chirping, little pigs squealing, and new baby calves trying, for the first time, to stand on wobbly legs. None of this could happen without God's touch.

Jersey is missing. Mama knows her calf is due any day. She asks Mary and me to go with her to search for the cow. It is late in the evening when we see her in the distance. She stands up for a while and then lies down for a while. She lies on her side and strains as if she is trying to have a bowel movement. Mama does not want us to see her suffer and she tries to send us home.

But, the cows are the only friends I have and I tell her, "No Mama, I don't want to go. I know Jersey is in trouble and we have to help her."

Finally, Mama realizes we are going to watch, and she says no more about us going home. Mama walks right up to Jersey and she is so tired and weak she doesn't get up and run away like she normally would if she weren't so tired. Mama talks soothing to her and rubs her hip. Then she pushed her hand inside the cow.

"What are you doing, Mama?" I ask with tears running down my face.

Mama's whole arm is up inside Jersey now and she is straining hard. "I'm trying to turn the calf around where its front feet and head can come first."

Jersey raises her head and her whole side moves up and then settles down again as the calf inside her turns. Mama breathes a sigh of relief; however, she then gets directly behind Jersey and pushes her other hand into Jersey too. She pulls with both hands and we soon see two little feet. Mama is breathing hard and I can tell she is tired. She says we should give Jersey a little rest. Every few minutes Jersey strains and Mama says she is having contractions like women do. She says Jersey will have the calf by herself now, since it is in the right position; however, she is so exhausted she thinks we should give her a little help. When Mama is rested, she waits until Jersey is pushing again, and then she pulls on the two little feet sticking out. The little calf slips right out. Jersey continues to lie there, so Mama drags the calf around to Jersey's head.

I knew Mama grew up on a dairy farm; therefore, I knew there must be a reason for her moving the calf. "Why did you do that, Mama?" I asked.

"Honey, sometimes cows reject their calves when they have a hard time birthing, especially if they can't get up to smell the calf right after its born. The cow needs to smell the calf and start licking it after it's born to begin bonding."

If Mama hadn't helped, the calf and maybe Jersey too, would have died because Mama said the calf was in the breech position. Now both the cow and calf are alive and happy. I am happy too, and I feel I have witnessed a miracle.

Each year Daddy hires someone to help butcher a pig and a steer to freeze for our own meat. If we want chicken for supper, Mama catches a fryer, hangs it by the feet with a rope on the clothesline or on a tree limb and cuts its head off with a knife. It flops around like crazy while the blood runs out on the ground. For Thanksgiving, she finds a hen, which has stopped laying. She can tell if the hen has stopped laying eggs by placing her fingers between the bones on the backend near their tail. If she judges wrong, she shows us the eggs inside the hen. The sight is unbelievable—so many eggs in varying stages of development. There are soft-shell eggs ready to be laid in a day or so, some are only yolks, some are smaller yolks joined, which gradually get smaller and smaller until they are pin-size. Mama uses these eggs for her dressing and giblet gravy. I wish she would make chicken and dressing more often.

Mama has a big garden. We work every day, trying to keep it hoed. A neighbor, who lives about a mile away, has two teenage daughters—one Rebekah's age and one my age. The neighbor comes to plow the garden spot for Mama each year, making it possible for Mama to have a large garden. During the summer, we prepare the vegetables for canning or freezing. The only vegetables we freeze are squash, peas, and lima beans. One summer we canned twenty-eight quarts of soup. Mama makes the best soup I have ever tasted. When Mama was young, she was Georgia's 4-H first place winner in the canning project, a title called Master 4-H'er.

For Christmas, while in the third grade, I receive twin paper dolls, Melinda and Belinda. I love them dearly. Mary loves to get paper dolls too. They are more fun than any doll I have ever received. With so many clothes, I can change them often and it is easy.

School has opened again. It is harder than last year. We have much more homework. I have little time I can call my own. It is a windy afternoon after school and only Mark and I are in the backyard. With ruffled feathers, wings low and head high, the old rooster struts toward Mark. I become rigid with fright. I think of the rooster's sharp spurs causing severe damage to Mark's two-year-old body.

Fear is knotted inside me as I scream, "Mama, Mama." It takes only seconds for me to realize Mama isn't coming in time to save Mark. The only hope for Mark is for me to stop the rooster. I spot the hoe leaning against the garden fence and I grab it. I swing at the rooster, who has by now knocked Mark to the ground and is on top of him. The rooster begins digging his spurs into Mark's chest. I swing at the rooster again and this time I hit the rooster in the head.

"Thank you, Lord, for that good aim." The rooster runs away. Mama has told us, if the rooster hurts any of us, his head is coming off. I decide not to tell her about the incident since I love the baby chickens. I know we will have no more baby chickens if the rooster's head comes off.

January 16 is an unfortunate date for Mark's birthday. Mama holds back some of his Christmas gifts for his birthday. She let me help with his cake, and sing "Happy Birthday" to him.

One of my responsibilities on the farm is to find the eggs our hens lay all around the farmyard. I love this job because it is like having Easter every day. Mama's words ring in my head, "Sarah, if you find a hen setting on eggs, run her off and get the eggs, because we need all you can find."

But if I find a hen on a nest, I don't disturb her. There is a saying, "She fights worse than a setting hen." You can't run a hen off her nest easily. She fights and pecks and it hurts. Besides, I like her to hatch the baby chicks.

Two or three days after the incident with the rooster, it happens again. No one is near this time to protect Mark from the rooster. His face and chest are scared for life. Some of the cuts are close to his eyes. When Mama learns this is the second attack on Mark, she not only kills the rooster, she almost kills me for not telling her about the first time. Mama gives me the second worst whipping of my life, the first being when I told the entire family I hated them and got up and walked out of the family meeting. Permanent scars remain on me too, but not from the rooster.

I leave the house and go into the woods. I cry for several hours, not from the pain of the whipping, but from the shame I feel for not telling Mama about the first time the rooster attacked Mark. I want to run away from home, but I don't have anywhere to go. I don't have anyone near I can talk to as I did the Michaels. I wish I was back in Knoxville living near them. I miss them. I wish I knew how to contact them. I would tell them the truth about Mama and Daddy now that we don't live next door anymore.

We buy several pigs, some sows, and one boar hog. When the baby pigs are born, they are precious. However, they don't stay clean long. They love to wallow in the mud created from the drain where our kitchen sink empties into the pigpen.

The beauty of our farm, the new life all around me, the calmness of the country, the green garden, the vast, rambling woods, and the sunlit pastures—all this helps my feelings and I rarely think about the time when Daddy and Adam bothered me. I feel safe sleeping in the room with both my sisters. Our bedroom opens to Adam's bedroom on one side and Mama and Daddy's bedroom on the other side.

It is time for school to start again. School is fun and I make good grades but I know little about the facts of life. Mama doesn't have time, or she hasn't taken time to tell us girls about the changes our body would undergo during puberty. One day my favorite girlfriend, Elizabeth, and I are swinging on the playground before school opens. I have heard other kids call one another "SOB." Well, I want to know what it means. I feel uncomfortable asking Mama what it means. Most likely, she would whip me. If I ask Elizabeth, I fear she will think I am stupid for not knowing. I decide the best way to find out is to call Elizabeth an SOB and watch her reaction. Wow! What a big mistake. She stopped the swing with one foot, hopped off the swing, and stormed into the schoolhouse. She didn't speak to me again for four days. I had a horrible time explaining my way out of that mistake.

My teacher, Ms. Black, calls home to tell Mama she needs to take me to get glasses. Ms. Black explains, "Mrs. Mahoney, Sarah needs to wear glasses. I have to sit her right under the chalkboard for her to work on her assignments. She cannot see from anywhere else. Are you aware of how poor her eyesight is?"

Mama has no embarrassment when it comes to telling others we are poor. She says to my teacher, "Right now we don't have the money to get her glasses."

I am embarrassed Mama told my teacher we couldn't afford to get glasses for me. For the rest of the school year, I have to sit right under the blackboard.

NOTE: I do not understand until many years later that, as a child, I never complained about anything. I internalized all my pain and disappointments; for example, I couldn't see. We often went to school without lunches or lunch money. We kids often had unattended medical and dental problems.

I did everything I could to make Mama and Daddy proud of

me. I was afraid for them to get upset with me. I didn't like to hear them yell or get angry. I never could understand why Daddy always asked Mama to whip me. I don't recall that being true of my brothers and sisters. I remember seeing him whip Mary sometimes.

In my efforts to please Mama, I continue washing clothes when

guests drive up, and she is forced to stop the washing machine. I turn the machine back on and try my best to run my own clothes through the wringer. (See Figure 4.1) I chose my favorite blue dress. When I try to send the dress through the wringer, it wraps around and around and gets hopelessly stuck.

Later, after our guests have gone, Mama says, "Honey, I will have to rip the dress to get it out."

Figure 4.1 Washing machine

My stomach is clenching tight and I feel a wave of apprehension I do not understand. I only know Mama cannot rip the dress. "Please, Mama, don't tear the dress."

Mama tries to untangle the dress from the wringer; however, it is caught up in the gears on the side. She yanks the dress and it tears away from the gear, allowing it to unwrap from the rollers. The gear part also spits out its chewed up bits of material.

My outstretched hands are shaking as Mama lays the torn pieces of cloth into them. "I guess you learned a lesson, Sarah. When you start a garment through the wringer, you have to hold the material away from the edges so it won't get caught in the gears. Just be glad it was an old dress. This dress was too little for you anyway."

I start crying as I tell her, "I loved the dress. It was my favorite dress."

NOTE: Since I have been writing this book, I remembered the reason the dress caused such an intense reaction in me. I was wearing that dress on the day Daddy took me to the studio to have my picture taken. Daddy's handwriting is on the back of the photograph. He took me to the studio when we were short on funds. He never took any of the other children to the studio. It upset me when I realized Daddy took me instead of Mama. I cried all afternoon.

Mary originally helped Mama at the barn but it didn't work out for her. She was afraid of the cows and they knew it. When Mama asked me to help, I was happy. I love the cows and helping Mama milk the cows became my permanent job. The neighbor boys used to come to the barn to watch me milk. I put the bucket between my legs and milk with two hands. At times, we have seven or more cows to milk. I always milk before going to school too. Mama tries to have time to get to the barn to help me, but if she doesn't, I milk all of them. We sell whole milk, buttermilk, and butter on a regular route every Wednesday and Saturday. We churn the milk by hand in a five-gallon crock and a wooden dasher.

When I am about nine years old, Mary tries to tell me about menstruation, but I don't want to hear about it. She gets angry with me and says, "Okay, when you want to know, I'm not going to tell you."

It made me sick to think about it, so I told her, "That's fine with me." When I did want to know, I had to get down on my knees and beg her to tell me. I had to say, "Please, pretty please, pretty, please with sugar on it."

Since it gets dark early during the winter, there is only an hour of daylight after school before time to go to milk the cows. Mark loves to drink the cows' milk straight from the bucket. One day he slips away from Mary and Rebekah and comes to the barn with his little drinking cup. We have a jersey cow named Old Red, who has sharp horns, and she is the meanest cow we have. Another cow named Spider is sweet. We chose that name for her because her face resembles a spider. As Mark reaches the barn, Old Red hooks Spider with her horns as she is coming around the edge of the barn. Spider knocks Mark down and almost steps on his chest. Realizing what she is about to do, she shifts her weight to her back legs and almost falls herself, saving Mark's life.

Summer comes and goes quickly. This was Adam's last summer at home. He will graduate at the end of the upcoming school year. I will be glad because he is always hurting me physically. He hits my arm in the muscle above my elbow and makes a big frog come up, and he twists the flesh below my elbow. He takes my arm and pins it behind my back and tells me he's not going to stop until I say, "I give." I won't give in until tears flood my eyes from the pain.

Not many changes happen during fifth grade. I change teachers for one subject and it makes me feel grownup. The seventh grade teacher comes to my classroom to teach math while my teacher goes to teach the seventh graders social studies. I become more active in 4-H Club work. I enter the muffin contest, the biscuit contest, the dress revue, leadership, gardening, canning, and citizenship every year at county level.

Mama never lets us go to 4-H camp at Rock Eagle because it costs money. However, if we are the county first place winner in our 4-H projects, we get to go free to Rock Eagle for District Project Achievement. Therefore, we work hard and we usually win first place and get to go to Rock Eagle for the district eliminations.

Mama's milk route is bigger now, and customers are asking for eggs. Because of cholera in Georgia, Daddy decides to sell all our hogs. We start buying eggs by the case from another producer. We run them through our chandler and grader, box them, and stamp them with our name. Eggs become a big 4-H project and demonstration for me now.

Summer has rolled around again and Adam is gone. He joined the army. I was usually the child Mama sent with Adam to help him with his assigned chores. Now that he is gone, I am lonely. I have more time for my 4-H projects and the cows.

The worst Christmas of my life occurs during my sixth grade in school. Daddy does not work during the fall and winter months; he quits his job to hunt during deer season. That means we have little Santa Claus.

NOTE: Later, while a teacher of middle grade children, I learned these middle years are often the hardest ages for most children, emotionally.

On this Christmas morning, I awaken at 3:00 AM and shake Mary. We slip quietly up to the living room, and see name tags attached to items spread about the room. It takes only a few seconds for me to find the tag bearing my name.

Mary asks, "What did you get, Sarah? I'll bet it is better than mine?"

In the corners of my eyes, tears began to glisten. "I don't think so. I didn't get anything except a pair of boots to pull over my shoes to wear to the barn. I heard Mama say I needed a pair of boots to wear to the barn, because the stalls are wet and full of cow manure. But I didn't want to get the boots for Christmas. What did you get, Mary?"

"Mama made me a skirt, but it's a mile too big."

"What am I supposed to tell my friends when they ask what I received for Christmas?"

"I don't know. I guess all you can tell them is the truth."

"And let them laugh at me. They already tease me about my hands smelling like the cows."

"Mama probably won't get my skirt taken up in time to wear on the first day back to school."

Sarah's voice is an expression of sadness and disappointment, "It's just not fair that Daddy is so lazy. Let's just go back to bed."

I also make the first "D" I have ever made in my life. I start hating myself because my life is not turning out the way I wanted. I should be blaming Mama and Daddy for their cruel methods of child rearing, which I believe is the cause of all my problems now and also for many years to come.

One morning later that winter, I am awakened by the sound of the wind blowing through the poorly framed windows and the howls of a coyote. I smell Mama's homemade biscuits baking in the oven.

I grab my old barn clothes and run to the kitchen to stand by the heater while I dress because it is bitter cold. After getting my clothes on, I slip on the red rubber boots Santa Claus brought over my school shoes and head for the barn. Mama folds the biscuits in a basket to keep them warm. She follows close behind me. Many times in the freezing weather the cows' udders will chap, break open, and bleed.

I lay the cow's tail between the bucket and my left leg to keep the nasty tail from slapping me in the face. By keeping my left leg on their leg, I can feel when they are going to kick and I am able to move. My legs never look like Mama's do. Mama's legs usually look like rotten strawberries.

I explain to her, "Mama, if you will hold the bucket between your legs and your left leg against their leg, you can feel if they begin to kick."

She retorted angrily, "I manage just as well with my head against their hip."

Obviously she doesn't, or her legs wouldn't continue to look like spoiled strawberries. In addition, she gets insects and trash in her hair from the cow's body.

Nevertheless, I am the child and she is the parent. To see her (or anyone) get angry makes me shake in my boots. From childhood through most of my life, I continue to be a people pleaser. I never again try to tell her how to milk the cows. I milk them myself. I want to be alone anyway, so I isolate myself in the barn. Many evenings I milk all the cows before Mama even knows I have gone to the barn. No matter how hard I scrub my hands when I finish milking in the mornings, the children at school still tease me about how my hands smell like the cows.

Seventh grade brings its embarrassing moments for it is this school year I start my menstrual period. The home economics teacher asks my friend, who lives one mile from school, to take me to her house and get me "fixed up." I have no belt to hold the pad and even if I did, I have no clue about how to use it.

When I arrive home, I am sarcastic with Mama. I tell her, "Thanks a lot."

She asks, "For what?"

I tell her, "For telling me all about my period so I wouldn't have to be embarrassed at school."

She says, "Oh, I'm sorry. I didn't tell you about your period?"

I say, "No. You told Rebekah, but you never told Mary or me anything."

Seventh grade is also the year my parents let me have a party on the evening of my thirteenth birthday. Most of my guests are girls; however, two boys come. One of the games is Spin-the-Bottle, and I ask one of the guys to walk down the road with me. This boy flirts with me at school, and I think his black wavy hair makes him the cutest boy in my class. During the walk, he holds me close and kisses me. I feel his penis as it begins to throb against my thigh. I will never forget the mounting sense of urgency as I feel the wetness in my panties. Mama had never taught us about sexual feelings, so I didn't know the reaction was normal for both of us.

Daddy is about the laziest man who ever lived. All he does is pretend to look for carpenter work. If he doesn't get to be supervisor of the job, he quits. No one, including Mama, is going to tell him what to do. When he is out of work, he lays around the house with his boxer shorts on and his penis lying out side them.

One day, when I come home from school, he calls me to his bedside. I get the straight chair and sit close to his head with the back of the chair toward his feet so I can't see his penis. He tells me how Mama will never give him sex and, if she does, she complains for a week about her back hurting.

He reaches for my hand and looks straight into my eyes as he tells me, "Sugar, it's not worth getting a little and then having to hear her complain about it."

I pull back my hand and look away. I know what he wants. He wants me to feel sorry for him. I don't know what to say. He should not be talking to me about this.

Taking a deep breath, I get up from the chair and say, "Daddy, I have a lot of homework. I have to go start on it now."

I go in the next room, which is my bedroom, and I begin working on my homework. I hear a click and I know Daddy is listening in on the telephone party line. This is a disgusting habit and he does it almost everyday. He has told the family at the supper table about a teenage girl he often hears talking to her boyfriend. I have been studying only about five minutes when I hear Daddy break into the phone conversation to say, "Why don't you let me give you a little bit?"

I feel my face grow red; I wish he were not my father. I hate to think of his blood flowing in my veins. I wish I could give myself new parents…and a new past…beginning with the day I was born. I deserve a better father than the lazy slob that is lying, almost nude and uncovered on the bed in the next room.

I wish Daddy would get a job. I believe he never thinks about anything but sex. I stay nervous wondering where he is in the house. He stealthily moves around to slip up behind me. In the mornings I am frequently standing at the closet door trying to decide what to wear to school. The closet is in the corner of the back hall next to the door, which opens to the bathroom. Before I know Daddy is behind me, he often runs one hand under my butt from behind. He pulls me to him with the other arm and I can't get away. He applies pressure with his fingers in the place he knows is sensitive. I try to get away and he simply tightens his grip on me usually over my tender breasts.

Mary tells me Daddy catches her at the door to this closet too. When he does, you are trapped because the closet is in the corner.

The bathroom wall is on one side and Daddy is blocking the other side. Sometimes Daddy stops by our bed at night and tries to feel of our breasts. I am beginning to hate him. Sometimes I feel like I hate Mama too because she knows what Daddy does to Mary and me, and still she does nothing about it. Mary told me she dreams about shooting him with Adam's gun.

The house and outbuildings on our farm are in much need of repair. Moreover, Daddy is a carpenter. While he is out of work, he could repair the screen door, the steps, or the door on the washhouse, which is hanging by one hinge.

Our cats and the flies can enter through the back screen door because it needs a carpenter's hand. The cats get on the table and eat out of our food. If Mama catches them, she throws the food away, but I wonder how many times they eat from our food and we don't catch them. When Daddy catches one, he kicks the cat about forty feet out into the backyard as if it were the cat's fault.

It is a wonder we don't all get sick because of the many flies, which come in the house and get on the food. The flies were not as bad after we sold the swine. I believe the hogs' mud hole was the breeding ground for the flies. But it would not take much effort for Daddy to drive to the hardware store and buy new screen wire to put on the back screen door. I would be happy to hold the screen wire while he tacked it to the doorframe. I help him with any carpenter work that he does do around the house. It would have been over in a day, and we would not have had all the trouble with the cats and the flies.

When someone smells cat "poop," Mama makes all of us look for it. One day Mary and I lay out our evening gowns on Adam's bed, hoping to get the wrinkles out of the net in the full skirts. Both of us are planning to enter the beauty pageant but we have not decided on the gown to wear. I decide on the one I am wearing in Figure 4.2. When we next go to look at them, we find a cat has done his job right in the middle of them. If someone left the closet door open, that is usually where we find the cat mess, but not this time.

Figure 4.2 Beauty pageant

Mama allows us to have a string from the light to our bed so we can pull the string from our bed to turn on the light before getting up. This easy access to the light is to encourage us to get up, go to the bathroom, and not wet the bed. For some reason this night, I cannot find the string to the light. I get up and wave my arms in search of the string. When I finally find it and turn on the light, there at my feet is a baby snake.

I scream, "Snake, snake."

It came under the door pictured in Figure 4.3, which opens into us girls' bedroom. My scream has wakened the entire household, but I don't care.

Since Rebekah has always taken care of Aunt Karen's three children during the summer months and after school, she is never around for

Figure 4.3 Side entrance to Georgia home

Daddy to see or bother. She graduates this year and leaves home to go to work for Southern Bell Telephone in a city nearby. She comes home on her off days because she is homesick, mostly for Aunt Karen's children. Her driving back home does not last for long because she soon realizes she must let go and begin anew with her own life. She is home little, except to sleep, during her last two years in high school. Aunt Karen had her ride the school bus to her house on school days to sit with her children until late evenings when she arrives home from work. They call Rebekah "Little Mama."

Eighth grade is a part of the high school, and I am excited about school starting this year. Mary is in the tenth grade. We have to ride the bus nine miles to the elementary school, and then transfer to another bus. Then we ride ten mile farther to the high school. If we could drive from home directly to the high school, the total distance is seven miles. Leaving seventh grade is exciting because I can get away from Ms. Louise. She knows my parents, and she and Daddy hate each other. She takes it out on me. She took it out on Mary before me. Well, guess what? She follows me. She is now my math and social studies teacher. Now I have had her three years. She is the teacher who swapped out with my homeroom teacher in fifth grade. I had her in seventh grade and now in eighth grade. I have never made a grade less than a "B" except under Ms. Louise. My first "D" was in seventh grade under her.

Mary and I have the best Christmas yet this year. Aunt Elizabeth, Mama's oldest sister from Atlanta, gave us the most gorgeous taffeta dresses. She gave Mark a cute little suit. Rebekah bought us each a wool skirt and sweater. She gave Mark toys. We never receive clothes except homemade, made mostly from twenty-five pound bag flour sacks saved until Mama had enough of the same pattern.

My favorite teacher is Mrs. Ledder, who teaches Home Economics. She encourages me to stop biting my fingernails, telling me it is the same as eating flies. Her explanation for making such a remark is, "Your hands touch where the flies have been and get the germs on them."

She wants me to start working on my Future Homemakers of America degrees, the first being Junior, then Chapter, and finally State. Being the "people pleaser" I am, I work hard on my degrees and complete all of them before leaving high school. I admire this woman and have a tremendous amount of respect for her. Everyone in the entire school looks up to her for knowing the proper etiquette to use in any situation. Her dress is always proper and immaculate. I decide I want to be like her.

NOTE: Mrs. Ledder makes such a great impression on me that I later major in Home Economics and receive my B.S. Degree from Georgia Southern College.

Since Rebekah is no longer in the house, the sexual harassment from Daddy begins to increase. He often hugs me from behind reaching over my shoulders to place his hands over my breasts. And he comes up behind me and rubs under my butt to see if he can feel a sanitary pad, thus learning if I am in my period. To my knowledge, he never bothered Rebekah except for one time when Mama wasn't at home. He mostly harasses me, and sometimes Mary.

When Adam comes home from Germany for a visit, Mary and I ask him to put a lock on the bathroom door that we can lock from the inside. He goes to the hardware store and buys the lock with his own money and installs it. The lock stays in place as long as Adam is home on leave. One day Mary and I come home from school and Mary sees the bathroom door lock has been broken.

She comes back into the bedroom where I am and asks, "Where is Mama?"

Her face is red and I can tell she is angry. "I don't know. What's wrong?"

"The lock is broken on the bathroom door, that's what." Mary turns around and stomps out of the bedroom and I follow her. She goes out the back door and I continue to follow. We find Mama at the wash house.

Mary is so angry her voice is shaking. "Mama, what happened to the latch on the bathroom door?"

Mama simply shrugs her shoulders.

Mary wants a response from Mama, so she continues to stare

silently at Mama with a dark, angry expression. I cannot understand where Mary gets her courage. I am afraid of Mama. I wouldn't dare stare at Mama like Mary is doing now.

Mama finally speaks and says, "Mary, you have to stop aggravating your Daddy so much."

Mary shouts at Mama, "It's not me who needs to stop, Mama, it's *him*. You don't know what it feels like to be taking a bath and he comes in and stands there looking and grinning. Mama, it's not right. You *know* it's *not right*."

Mama says, "Mary, men cannot help themselves. It is the way they are made. It's up to the girl to set the standard. It's your responsibility to hold the line. Your daddy is oversexed. His daddy (your granddaddy) and his brothers were all that way too. Your granddaddy was that way toward me when we were living with them in Alabama. Men will always go as far as you will let them. It is up to the girl to set the standard."

"Daddy is going to hell; he's going straight to hell. You should make him stop, Mama."

"Oh, no, he's not going to hell. His name is on the Lamb's Book of Life. Mary, you don't study your Bible enough. If you did, you would know that it isn't my place or your place to punish your Daddy. God punishes his own, right here on earth before they go to heaven. Your daddy's day will come, Mary. But for now, just try to get along with him and remember what I told you."

Mary starts shaking her head as she turns around and goes back into the house. I am sitting on my bed reading a chapter in my history book—a homework assignment—when Daddy comes home from work. Mary goes out the side door letting the screen door slam behind her. She meets Daddy in the side yard. I get off the bed and walk to the door so I can hear what Mary will say to Daddy.

Mary walks right up to him and asks him what happened to the lock on the bathroom door.

Wow, I can see the red rising up from Daddy's neck. I know he didn't expect Mary to have enough guts to confront him directly.

He glares at her and says, *"Nobody is going to keep me out of any room in my house."*

So, that is the end of it. Once again Daddy stands before the mirror and watches us through the reflection in the mirror. We have a choice—we can sit in the tub with our arms wrapped around our knees for an hour or more, trying to save our dignity because Daddy doesn't mind out-waiting us, or we can go ahead and bathe and let him watch.

It isn't fair that he should make us feel dirty. It isn't fair that he projects his nasty thoughts on to us. Sometimes he tells Mama we are whores. He sits at the table and says, "Any time there are three girls in a family, at least one of them will go bad." It isn't fair that Mama makes us live in the same house with him.

I wanted to be an achiever. I wanted a good life and I was willing to work hard for it. It isn't fair that we are not allowed to grow emotionally, intellectually, and achieve the reputation in our school and community that we could, if Mama would make him leave. Even animals protect their young if the adult male is a threat to them.

I have such terrible menstrual pain and Daddy knows when I am in my period. I experience chills, nausea, severe cramps, and diarrhea. It helps to curl up in bed with a hot pad on my stomach. Sometimes Mama fixes me a drink made of a little shot of Daddy's alcohol mixed with sugar water.

NOTE: Years later Mary and I learn why our menstrual periods have always been so painful. All the muscles, which normally hold the uterus in an upright position, have been torn away. My uterus and Mary's, have fallen backwards and is now upside down. My cramps are so hard because the blood is pushed from the top of my uterus instead of the bottom. As adults, both my sisters and I have numerous uterine suspensions, bladder suspensions, and early hysterectomies— Mary's at age twenty-three, mine at age thirty-two. Most of my siblings have back problems, knee replacements, and other joint problems. Some of us believe these physical health problems are due to the many one-hundred-pound feed sacks we lifted on the farm. Due to unbearable pain, I personally had to have surgery on both elbows, both shoulders, and both knees before I was forty.

Ninth grade comes quickly and this is my first year to play basketball. Mary is our school's top player. I feel grownup getting to stay after school with her to practice. Mary always gets to play the entire game unless she fouls out. I am lucky if I even get to play at all. I am carrying a full load—five classes. I have tons of homework, plus my degree work in FHA and my 4-H projects.

Mama lets us take the '49 Ford to school on Mondays, Wednesdays, and Thursdays so we will have a way to get home after basketball practice. It is nice not having to ride the bus on those long trips. Daddy has always been firm on his decision. We cannot play basketball, date, and go to school. He says three is too many things to keep up with at one time. He knows we have to go to school. He knows we will not give up basketball. He thinks he has a good reason to keep us from dating.

Daddy will quit a good job to go deer hunting in the fall. Last fall the man he went hunting with had a son who also went hunting with them. The boy was crazy about Mary. Mary began riding to church with his family on Sunday evenings. Daddy doesn't complain about him. It is different since the boy likes to hunt. Charles, a neighbor of his, came with him when he came to see Mary. They go to a different school from us.

Charles and I start going to the movies together on Friday evenings. We go to a drive-in theater because the regular theaters are too far away. We never see the entire movie because I have to be home by 11:30 PM.

Daddy allows him to visit on Sunday afternoon but we cannot leave home. We have no television so we often sit in the swing on the front porch. When 5:00 PM comes, I leave him to go milk the cows even if Mama is not yet ready to go to the barn. I have no choice but to leave him and he chooses to wait instead of leaving. At the barn I do my work as quickly as I can so as not to keep him

waiting longer than necessary.
(See my farm animals in Figure 4.4.)

District Winner in the 4-H Poultry Project (1957)
Competed in the State Level

Ashire bull calf sucking from the tit bucket. He was given to Sarah by a dairy farmer to use as a 4-H project.

Sarah loving her baby calves

Figure 4.4 Sarah's farm animals

The summer after ninth grade is a busy summer for me. I have saved money and paid my way to attend a week at FHA camp with my only girl friend Joyce. She is special to me. I can remember us hiding when we spent the night with each other so the other one could not see us in the nude. Later she told me she was ashamed of her large breasts and I told her I was ashamed of my small breasts. We could talk about *almost* anything, but I never told her about the way Daddy was abusing me. I was ashamed of that as if it were my fault. While I am there at camp, I talk to Joyce and pray to God about the decision I am about to make as to whether I should volunteer to do Vespers one evening. They had asked for volunteers. I am so frightened, but decide that I feel God calling me to do it. I choose Jeremiah 29: 11-14 as my scripture. After I read it to the young people, I explained to them that God has a plan and a purpose for us. All that we have to do is call upon him and he will answer. If we seek him, he will let us find him. I closed with my favorite Bible verse that I memorized many years before and asked those that knew it to say it along with me and that was Psalms 100. I am not surprised and am so thankful when more than half the crowd chimes in with me as we close with that Psalm of Thanksgiving. (See Figure 4.5)

Figure 4.5 Vespers at F.H.A. Camp

During that same summer, Aunt Agnes, Daddy's sister who owns a cabin on a lake in Alabama, invites us to come visit, stay at the cabin with them, and let Uncle Jack teach us how to water ski. Mama agrees to keep Mark and let Mary and me go with Daddy.

Mary says to me, "It will be okay; we don't have to worry because Aunt Agnes and Uncle Jack will be there."

"Yes, and Uncle Jack isn't like Daddy's brothers. We will have so much fun."

When we arrive, Aunt Agnes and her family are tired from the busy day at work and Aunt Agnes asks us to go on to the cabin telling Daddy they will come down the following morning.

Mary whispers, "Oh, no, we'll have to go to the cabin without them. I don't want to be there alone with Daddy."

"Just pray to Jesus that he will be too tired to wake up and will stay in his own bed."

Daddy tells Mary and me to sleep in the bed on the porch and he will sleep in the bed in the big open area inside. I remind Mary to pray. During the night, Daddy *does* get into the bed on Mary's side and puts his hand down the front of her pajamas into her panties. It awakens her. She is trapped by Daddy on the front side and me on the back side. Mary stands up and gets out of the bed over the footboard. She crawls across the floor, and goes out the back door to the outhouse. I awaken and realize Mary is gone. Just as I awake, I see Daddy's shadow go across the foot of the bed.

Daddy goes back to his bed. I wait and wait for Mary to come back. I am too afraid of the dark to go outside to look for her. Later, I learn she is too afraid of Daddy to come back in to check on me. She fears Daddy may be bothering me too. I begin praying....

Jesus, you know Mary is outside alone and afraid. You must take care of her. Wrap your arms around her and protect her from all harm. You know I am in here alone with Daddy. Please make him stay in his bed now until morning when Aunt Agnes arrives.

I may have gone in and out of twilight sleep, but never sound asleep. Soon the sun is breaking the horizon and I get dressed, go outside, and find my dear sister, Mary. While I am outside, Aunt Agnes, Uncle Jack, and their two boys come. Mary and I go inside and tell Aunt Agnes we have been to the outdoor toilet. Aunt Agnes starts cooking bacon, eggs, grits, and toast. Mary goes through the main room where Uncle Jack and Daddy have settled down, and I follow her to the screened in porch, where she sits on the side of the bed. Mary seems to be exhausted and she starts crying. I just hug her, but neither of us says a word. We are afraid someone might hear us. After a while, Mary seems to feel better and we go to the kitchen to help Aunt Agnes.

Today I learn to water ski, but Daddy has spoiled the whole weekend. Daddy doesn't mention what he did on the way home and neither does Mary.

NOTE: It has only been in the last ten years that Mary and I have talked about that weekend. I never knew she felt guilty for not coming back into the cabin to make sure Daddy wasn't molesting me. And I felt guilty for being too afraid of the dark to go and check on her. We both carried guilt over that night for many years.

Soon after our trip to Alabama, Daddy gets into trouble and this time the secret comes to light. The neighbor man who once plowed our garden plot each spring for Mama has a daughter who often visits my sister. Daddy starts fondling the girl when she is visiting. He offers to teach her to drive because her father has a severe heart condition and his wife cannot drive. Daddy says the daughter needs to know how to drive in case he has a heart attack. While teaching the fourteen-year-old girl to drive, he is frequently alone with her. The girl tells friends at school about Daddy molesting her when they are alone. The school principal sends a letter home asking my parents to come to school for a conference. Mama says if people continue to talk about it, she will divorce Daddy.

It is strange to me Mama has gotten angry about this neighbor girl. She knows Daddy comes into the bathroom to watch when we bathe. She knows he continually stops by our bed at night to try to feel of us. She knows he tries to feel of our breasts and runs his hand under out butts. We've told her all this and she does nothing. Later, she tells us children we must obey and respect their elders.

Mary is a senior this upcoming school year and I am a sophomore. When Mary was in the tenth grade, she entered the Farm Business Project in 4-H. She won second in the state in the girls' division. The state traveled out west for ten days. My goal is to work on the Farm Business Project this year because I want to win first in the state competition.

In this project 4-H'ers visit co-ops and then give speeches and demonstrations to explain what the co-ops are and how they help farmers. The 4-H'er earns fifteen points for giving a talk and fifty points for a demonstration.

During the school year, my home demonstration agent carries me to visit a co-op and then helps me write the speech and plan my demonstration. Going to visit schools, churches, and local clubs to present the information is a wonderful learning experience for me.

Daddy and Mary are constantly fighting now. Mary is dating someone Mama likes, Daddy hates him. Daddy slips outside when Mary and Henry are in the living room and watches them through the window. One time a boy came to see Mary and Daddy shot at him. I worry about not having Mary here after this year. I will be lonely. Mary is angry with Daddy. About a month ago, Daddy had told Mary to make a choice…she could tell Henry to not come again or he would tell him. She and Henry made plans to run away and get married. Mama found Mary's packed suitcase and called the sheriff. The sheriff came and talked to Daddy. He told Daddy if he wanted Mary to finish high school, he had to agree to let her and Henry see each other for the remainder of her senior year. Daddy agreed to let them see each other.

I work hard on my speeches and demonstrations. Finally, spring arrives with all its beauty. This is the time to send in the signature cards and the summary of points to the District 4-H office for final judging. State winner and all district winners will travel by chartered buses to Urbana, Illinois, for three days where all states join for a meeting about co-ops in their respective states. The Georgia winners' reward for their efforts is to go sightseeing in Chicago, the Great Lakes, Canada, and Niagara Falls.

I pray, *"Oh, God, you know how hard I worked on this project and how much I want to win this trip, but I think Mama can't get along without me. She needs me to help with the cows. What shall I do?"*

Inside I believe I hear an answer, *"You worked hard on this project and, if you win, you deserve to go. Traveling is a good way to learn and Mama can manage without you."*

The time finally comes. The telephone rings. My heart is beating so fast it feels like cymbals beating against my chest. Looking up toward the ceiling, then closing my eyes, I say one last prayer. *"Remember Lord, I want what is best for Mama, as well as for me."*

The call is from my home demonstration agent. There is a trace of laughter in her voice when she asks, "Are you ready to hear the good news?"

I wonder exactly what 'good news' means. I try not to sound too excited when I answer, "Yes ma'am."

"Really? Is it true?" I cry as joy fills my heart and I say, "Now I am a Master 4-H'er like my Mama."

I go straight to the barn and begin my usual conversations with the cows. "I love you so much. How will I ever be able to cope if I don't see you for ten days? Mama won't talk to you the same as I do. When your tits are sore, she won't be gentle with them either. You will miss me too."

We have two months left of school. These months pass slowly. Mary spends all her spare time on her wedding. Mama promised her if she would finish high school, she would let her have a small church wedding. Mary is making her wedding dress and all her brides' maid dresses. Mary graduates as salutatorian of her class on Tuesday night and marries Henry the following Sunday.

Mary is not married long before Daddy starts causing problems in her marriage. He stops by her house on the way home from work. He tells Henry, her husband, "Let's go sit down in the living room and watch the news." (We didn't have a television at home until after I was gone.) After Henry sits down, Daddy gets up, goes into the kitchen while Mary is cooking. He puts his arm across her shoulder and lets it fall down over her breast. When she slaps his hand he pinches her butt, just as he did when she was a child.

When I visit Mary she tells me about it. I can tell Mary is feeling a great deal of stress about Daddy stopping by her house on his way home from work.

> *We three girls take Mama off on a dirt road to discuss the problem Daddy is causing for Mary. Mary has to tell him he cannot stop by her house on the way home from work. We girls had decided it was time to let Mama know about some of the things Daddy was doing to me too. I am still living at home and in the eleventh grade when we had this talk.*
>
> *Before Mama lets us say anything, she says, "I probably know more than you think I do."*
>
> *If she did, why didn't she leave him instead of letting him mess up our lives? She threatened to leave Daddy for messing with a neighbor girl but not for messing with us. I did not understand Mama's attitude then and I never will. Not until I went to a hospital in 2003 did I know how much my parents messed up my life.*

The important day for me finally arrives and my bags are

packed. I meet other winners in Atlanta. Aunt Karen drives me to the hotel for Mama. I am scared because I have never stayed in a hotel alone in my life, much less in a large city like Atlanta. The dress I am wearing in Figure 4.6 is the one I made and designed myself for the last senior 4-H dress revue. I won first in the county.

Figure 4.6 Leaving Atlanta on 4-H trip

The first night is fun

because I meet others my age. Waiters serve us a meal in a huge dining room. I feel like a queen. The second night is not as glorious. There are drunken women on the street screaming and causing a ruckus. One of the boys and I start to go to the movies until we learn the admission fee is $3.00.

He tells me, "I cannot afford it. Maybe you can, but I can't."

I don't know how much he has to spend; however, I have only ten dollars for the entire ten days.

I tell him, "I can't afford it either."

We decide to go back to the hotel to get a coke. A coke normally costs twenty-five cents. At the hotel, we sit down and order a coke. A waiter serves it to us in a bottle...no glass, ice, or napkin. When we receive the ticket, the cost is a little over a dollar each.

The third day we arrive in Urbana, Illinois, where all the states are gathered. This is marvelous. We Georgia girls go crazy in love with the boys from Ohio. They all wear the same kind of hat, singing and marching together everywhere they go.

In Chicago, everyone has to stay with the chaperones and go to a movie together. The chaperones scare us about the Blacks before we reach Chicago. They were warning the southern country boys about calling the Blacks names, but it still scared me.

The next day we leave and have lunch on Lake Michigan at the Hayes Hotel. It is a beautiful lake. Crossing the border into Canada gets the adrenaline going for many of us. Someone starts a rumor that the customs inspector will go through our luggage and look at everything. We girls worry about them seeing our sanitary pads and tampons. Our worries are useless; they don't open one piece of luggage. We spend the night at Niagara Falls, New York.

It is Saturday morning and the excitement of the trip is wearing off; I am homesick for the cows. Our chaperone tells us to sleep late, but I can't. Daddy doesn't allow anyone to sleep late at home and I can't this morning either. My itinerary lists a special tour for this afternoon. It carries us to both sides of the falls—Canadian and American. The stories we hear of the suicides are unbelievable.

The long drive home tires us out; most of us sleep on the bus. We spend Sunday night in Cincinnati, Ohio. By Monday, 6:00 PM, we arrive back in Atlanta, Georgia. It was a wonderful experience for me—one I will never forget for as long as I live. We travel during the month of August before I begin my junior year of high school.

School, home, nothing in life is the same since Mary left. She lives about forty miles away and I never see her. I am still dating Charles—the same person I have dated all through high school. Going to different high schools has advantages. We don't have to worry about walking each other to class and getting jealous when we see each other talking to someone else. Daddy has us in a "Catch 22" with his rule about we cannot date, play basketball, and go to school. We don't date. He is more lenient on that rule since the sheriff told him to let Mary see Henry if he wanted her to finish high school.

Only one good thing happens this year. I complete all the work for my Future Homemakers of America State Degree. Only three of us finish this year and the other two are high school seniors. We are honored at a FHA banquet where we are awarded our pins and certificates. The picture in Figure 4.7 was taken outside the banquet hall.

This year I break the frames of my glasses playing basketball. Mama's nerves are always on edge and, when I tell her about the glasses, she flares

Figure 4.7 Just received FHA State Certificate

back at me, "I told you if you broke another pair you had to stop playing basketball." I don't stop playing basketball, but I never play with my glasses on, and I can't see without them.

One of Daddy's brothers dies. Daddy, Mama, Mark and I go to Alabama to the funeral; however, after the funeral, Mama stays in Alabama to help my aunt to settle her affairs and to catch up with the laundry business she owns. Mama wants the rest of us to go home to take care of the farm.

The first night we are home, Daddy gets into bed with me. I think, *"Oh dear God. Mama isn't here to stop him."* He moves over close to me and puts his hand under my pajama top. I feel a pressure in my head. *"I can't take this. I can't take this."* I feel as if I am going backwards through the air...as if a vacuum cleaner was sucking me up in slow motion.

Susie is in Sarah's bed and she is thinking it has been a long time since she has had control of the body. The body has grown since she was out the last time and she feels a lurching excitement within. Her vaginal juices are flowing even before he touches her. Still, her feelings are passive; he is her father; how can she resist him?

Daddy's touch is light and teasing as he gently pushes her legs apart. He is surprisingly restrained, pausing to kiss her, whispering his love for her. His fingers part her soft curling hair and then he begins to stroke her clitoris. It sends jolts of pleasure through her and she moans softly.

Jim has wanted for a long time to have this opportunity. He knows there may never be another time when he is alone with her without his wife in the house. He snuggles her against him and presses his throbbing hardness against her. Susie groans, and turns her body away realizing how fired up her dad is. Knowing that this will be his only opportunity, he angrily pulls her back over so that she will be on her back. He places one leg over both of hers so that she can't move. He sucks on her breasts and then places her hand around his erect penis. He parts her legs and uses his hand to play with her clitoris again and then gently pushes his finger as far as it will go into her vagina. Now he slides his entire body upon hers. She tries to push him off, but there's no use. He is too strong. He kisses her ear and tells her it will not hurt if she will just be calm. She remembers no more. "Please don't ever tell anyone about this. You know your mom won't give me any."

Susie is shaking uncontrollably, and he tries to put his arms around her, but she turns over on her stomach, tightens her buttock muscles, and lays her arms by her side so he cannot get to her. He tries to turn her over, but she is rigid. He stays there for a few more minutes, then gets up and leaves.

The following day, Daddy asks me, "Sarah, why won't you give in to me completely?"

I feel like Daddy is ruining my whole life. I am sick at my stomach because he would even ask me such a question. I tell him, "Because it is wrong and beside, I don't know what you're talking about. Why would you ask me such a question?"

Slowly and seductively, his gaze slides over my body. "Sugar, nobody will know unless you tell them."

My body feels numb. I cannot believe we are having this conversation. I answer, "Daddy, I will know and besides I have never done it."

He says, "I don't believe you. I know you've let Charles have your cherry."

I feel my soul shriveling a little from being a participant in this conversation. Daddy wants to bring everyone down to his level. Sometimes I think I hate him. I tell him, "No, I have not. I told you I have never done it. You shouldn't be talking to me like this. Let's stop talking about it."

The next night, when I go to bed, I find blood on the sheets. I am terrified because I can't remember what happened the night before. I go to the bathroom and close the door. I put the lid to the toilet down and sit on it. I begin crying uncontrollably, rocking back and forth. I am terrified that Daddy might have raped me and I cannot remember. Daddy comes to the bathroom door; he opens the door, comes in, and asks me what's wrong.

I get up and he tries to put his arms around me. I begin beating him with my fists. I manage to get around him and go out of the bathroom. I go to the barn because it is time to milk the cows.

Surprisingly, Daddy does not bother me again while Mama is gone. Thankfully, she is gone only three days. Daddy causes me to feel trashy and filthy.

Death may not be long for me because I will commit suicide if I do not soon leave my parents' home. I feel I cannot even tell Charles about Daddy, what he is doing, what he has accused the two of us of doing, and my suicidal thoughts.

Part III
Kristen Appears

"I will trust you always,
tho' I may seem to be lost and in the shadow of death,
I will not fear for you are ever with me and will not leave me.
I will not face the perils alone. Amen
- Thoughts and Solitude, by Thomas Merton, cc. 1968

You Love Your Daddy, Don't You?

Chapter Five

Life Away From Home

When I finish eleventh grade, I will have fifteen credits. Students need have only sixteen credits to enter college. Adam is a freshman at Middle Georgia College in Cochran, twenty-eight miles from our home. When he had completed his term in the army, he worked as a plumber for a while and then decided he didn't want to spend his life as a plumber. When he entered college, they gave him the job as dorm leader, because he was older than the other freshman students. He was dorm leader for Ebenezer Hall, the smallest boys' dorm on campus.

The mother of a girlfriend in my class, Mrs. Smith, works at the county board of education office as a visiting teacher. When she is at my school one day, I ask her how I can enroll in college after my eleventh grade of high school. She offers to check with Middle Georgia College and let me know.

Upon calling the college, Ms. Hardy answers the telephone. They discuss my situation and my wishes. Mrs. Smith tells her that the student is Sarah Mahoney.

Ms. Hardy asks, "Is she related to Adam Mahoney?"

"Yes, Sarah is Adam Mahoney's sister."

Ms. Hardy obviously gave her good news because the next day Mrs. Smith stops by the school and I am called to the office. She tells me I can enroll in college in the fall if I can get my senior English credit this summer. The only provision is I pass entrance exams, and my transcript is at least a GPA of 3.0. Mrs. Smith agrees to monitor my English through correspondence from the University of Georgia.

My head starts spinning, "Oh, how wonderful! Neither of those two requirements should be a problem. I always make good grades, and passing entrance tests should not be too difficult either. Then I remember I haven't said a word to Mama about going to college early."

When I finish my eleventh grade, my report card grades are History-92, English-97, Typing-92, Physics-87 and Bookkeeping-92. I have no problem with the GPA of 3.0 because most of my other ten subjects have averages in the high nineties.

On completing my high school English with Mrs. Smith, and I have sixteen credits, I ask Mr. Fulbright, my principal, if he will give me a high school diploma since I have finished all the course work. He said, "No, I can't since you are in the age group that was told in the ninth grade you had to complete eighteen credits to graduate."

I reply, "I can respect your opinion, but I don't agree with you since I will enter college in a few days." Then I leave him, waving good-bye.

As time grows nearer to my leaving for college, I can see a change in Mama for the better. She is glad I will be gone. She isn't stupid, merely in denial. She knows more than she pretends to know. She has been turning her head, hoping what she sees is not what she sees. She remembers the trip we girls took her on several months ago. When I leave, all the girls will be gone, and she won't have to worry about having girls at home. Mark will be going into the fourth grade this fall.

Where did my childhood go? When I look back, I cannot say I had one. My abuse started the first time I sat on Daddy's lap at age four, and continued until I left home early to escape it. Am I prepared for the future? Not in the least. I have many fears. I am the youngest student in my college, and I am afraid of my own shadow. With God's help, I will make it, but I fear it will be rough.

I begin my first year of college in the fall quarter of 1960. There are five boys' dormitories and only one girls' dorm. Charles, my high school boyfriend, wonders why I won't go steady anymore. I tell him I want to be sure he is the right person for me. He tells me if he can't have me all to himself, he doesn't want me at all, so we say good-bye to each other.

Only one girl in the dorm has a car. Luckily, she is my roommate. Pat invites me to go home with her for the weekend, and I see how she treats her mother. She tells her mother her plans, instead of the other way around. All the students want Pat as their best friend.

Everyone smokes, so I try it too. I cannot inhale without choking, so I quit inhaling, temporarily. I hold the smoke in my mouth for a few seconds, and then blow it out, hoping no one notices I haven't inhaled.

Several girls call me on it at the same time saying, "Sarah, you aren't really smoking."

I demonstrate I *can* smoke, and have been doing a good job of inhaling since.

The college looks like a ghost town on Friday nights and Saturdays. Students begin coming back on Sunday mornings. We have a local hangout where the students meet on Sunday afternoons and tell jokes to one another. One guy can tell jokes so fast he doesn't give us time to laugh before he starts another.

Mama expects me to come home on weekends to help wash jars, churn milk, mold butter, and drive the truck for her to peddle the produce on Saturdays. I dread the weekends.

I try out for the girls' college basketball team and I make it, because I played high school basketball and because so few other girls try out. We have a game every Friday evening. Unlike high school, where there are many girls to select from for the team, there are only eight of us. In the sixties, six female players are on the floor at one time—three guards on one end and three forwards on the other. Also, girls do not run the full court as the boys do. I start out playing some games and play nearly all four quarters.

The college assigns me to the Dean of Students for my work program. His office is located right off the student center. I have no time to socialize. Dean Taylor smokes cigars and, with his small office and no windows, some days I think I will choke to death. However, I soon adjust to the smell of his cigars, and I grow to love Dean Taylor with all my heart.

One day I remark to him, "Dean Taylor, I need to work enough hours to pay the balance of my tuition after the first $100 each quarter. I have only $300 for this whole first year."

He pats me on the shoulder as he replies, "I don't know if I have enough work for that many hours, but we will work something out." And, bless his dear soul, he did too.

Mama gives me an allowance of $1 a week. Cigarettes are twenty cents a pack and I spend my dollar on five packs of cigarettes a week. I not only start smoking, I begin drinking alcohol too. We have a little town close by that has dances with a live band. I begin having what friends in my dorm tell me are blackouts. I cannot remember the next day what happened the night before. One friend tells me I am drinking too much. I only know I want to chill out and forget the past—all of it—Daddy, Mama, Adam, Charles, and my suicidal thoughts. It seems alcohol does that for me. When I drink, I forget the past, and I let the other side of me come out—the side that isn't inhibited by all the rigid rules that inhibit me.

Frank, the student I have been watching since the beginning of the year, calls me aside one day. His dignity and composure impresses me like no other male on campus does. My mind takes over for a second, "*Maybe he is going to ask you for a date finally.*"

When I reach the bench in the park where he is sitting, his words devastate me, "Sarah, why do you smoke and drink? It causes the guys to think they can get anything they want from you."

The realization that he might care some for me had I not turned out to be so bad overwhelm my brain. It takes several minutes before I can speak.

When I do answer Frank it is not the truth, "I don't know except all the other girls do. I never had the opportunity to smoke and drink at home."

I don't remember him ever speaking to me again. I cared

106

sincerely for him and our conversation caused me to want to die.

It is Tuesday and I am going out with my friends this evening. I have to stay sober so I can sign myself back into the dorm at the end of the evening. Susie and I begin to battle with each other. Susie cries, "You know I don't want any responsibility. My only care is to have fun."

Sarah responds, "I know, and that's why I'm stressing to you that you have to get me back into the dorm tonight and safely too. I can't afford to get kicked out of college for drinking or being late to sign in this evening."

My friends and I leave campus after classes end. My mind keeps returning to Frank's question, "Why do you smoke and drink?" My thought is, *"You would too, if you had been abused like me."*

We are going to the dance in Hawkinsville. I have my mind made up before I get there that I intend to get drunk. Frank's remarks destroy me and I want to forget him. I don't have money for my drinks so I dance with whoever will buy me a drink.

10:00 PM: "Hey Baby, can I have this dance?"

By this time, Susie is ready for action and this guy looks and sounds good to her. She mumbles, "By all means."

"What's your name?"

"I'm Susie, and your name?"

"Fred. Where have you been all my life?"

"I am one of the more enlightened students at Middle Georgia College."

"How are you going to get in the dorm as drunk as you are?"

"I don't know. I'll figure it out later." Susie looks at her watch and growls, "It's almost two hours before time to go, but I guess I *should* stop drinking now."

"Well, let's go get some fresh air and that will help sober you. We could ride around for a while."

I think about the window rolled down and the cool breeze blowing on my face. Fred is right; the air should sober me before I have to check back into my dorm. I tell Fred, "Let me go tell the people I came with."

Fred grins at me and says, "Now you're being smart; meet me outside."

When I get outside, two other guys are standing with Fred beside a car. I walk up to them and they force me into the back seat of the car and the two guys get in on either side of me. I fight to get out; however, it is useless. Fred is alone in the front seat, and he drives a short distance before turning off the main highway onto a dirt road. We are surrounded by trees when he stops the car.

One of the guys sticks his face in mine and growls, "You can scream all you want. No one will hear because we are miles from civilization."

He gets out of the car and pulls me out by my arm. In the half-light, the moon is casting grotesque shadows through the treetops.

I see the weatherworn cabin Fred is now unlocking, and I fear if they take me inside, I may not come out alive. I dig my feet into the dirt and push backwards.

"Bring her on, Kent," Fred calls over his shoulder.

"This pussycat is putting up a fight."

The fight goes out of Susie when the third guy walks up to her and slaps her across the face. She goes limp and falls to the ground. Jason weighs about 230 pounds and he easily picks Susie up and carries her into the cabin.

"It could have been fun, but you've spoiled it," Susie tells them.

"No we haven't," Fred says. "Just wait and see."

They strip Susie of all her clothes. Then Kent and Fred hold her lying flat on the bed, as Jason ties her arms to the headboard of the bed. Fred has first claim to Susie, since he brought her out of the dance hall. He tells Kent and Jason he will take his time; they can go somewhere or they can stay and watch, but, if they stay, they are not to interrupt him as they will have their turn later.

Fred positions his upper body over her, with his knees straddling her. The shapely beauty of her naked body taunts him. He wants to take time to explore, to arouse, and to give her pleasure; however, he knows Kent and Fred won't wait long for their turn. His hands roam intimately over her breasts. It is flesh against flesh, man against woman.

"Shit, man, hurry up," Jason bellows.

"Man, I told you to go somewhere else if you couldn't keep your mouth shut. I found her. I have first turn. Shut up or go away."

"Oh, God, oh, God, oh God," says Susie. "Please let me go, Fred."

"Just shut your mouth."

Fred's knee parts Susie's thighs and he rises to get between her legs. With no preliminaries, he gives a hard thrust that drives him deep into her.

"Oh, God," Susie moans. "Just please don't hurt me and let's get it over with." A vaguely sensuous light passes between them.

His ferociousness climbs with each thrust until he can last no longer. Afterwards, Fred drops his weigh over Susie. When he feels her trembling, he kisses her on the cheek, and rolls off her.

Susie grabs his arm and he looks into her eyes. Fear, stark, and vivid, glitters in her eyes. "Fred, don't go away. Please don't leave me with those guys. Please don't let them rape me."

"I'm sorry, Sarah; we made a deal before we brought you here, and I can't back out now." Fred then gets off the bed and walks out of the cabin, without looking back.

Susie's gaze is now on Kent, who has taken off his shoes, pants, and is now taking off his boxer shorts. He is gazing at her intently.

"Please," Susie begs. "Untie my arms for a while. They are hurting from being in this upright position so long. And the ropes are cutting into my wrists."

Kent comes to the bed and gets over me. He hits Susie on the side of her face. "Shut up, Bitch. We didn't come here for your comfort."

Kent sucks on her breast and then he grabs her by the knees, forces them up, and apart. Then he rapes her.

Jason is the largest of the three men, his penis is the largest, and he is the most violent of the three. When she doesn't do exactly what he says, he slaps her in the face and asks, "Does that feel better?"

When he is finished, the three of them return to the inside of the cabin, make coffee and rest for a while, talking to one another. I cry and plead with them "Please untie my arms." When neither of them listens to me, in my frantic state of mind, I shout out in a piercing voice, "You are all terrible men, just wait until I report you to the police."

Jason responds, "Oh yeah, what do you think we should do boys? She can't if we leave her tied up.

She cries and pleads, "Please let me go. I will be kicked out of college; I have to get back to the dorm. I promise I won't call the police if you will just let me go."

Fred says, "It's after midnight now, so time is not a factor anymore."

"Well boys, do you think we should leave her tied up?"

Kent says, "No, I think we should all get another turn with her to teach her a lesson and make her promise not to call the cops."

"Sounds good to me," says Jason. "I'll go first."

Fred and Kent left and went outside. Kent asks Fred if he can go ahead and untie her hands. Fred agrees to let him.

Soon Kent comes in and tells me he is going to untie my arms. Then he flips me over on my stomach and up on my knees. He rapes me from behind, showing no mercy. When he pulls out, I curl up in a ball. He dresses and goes outside with the others.

Fred comes in for his turn, and surprisingly sits down in the curl of my thighs and chest. He puts his arm over my back and I hear him sobbing. Do I see tears coming from his eyes? He whispers in my ear, making sure his macho friends cannot hear him, "Can you ever forgive me? This is all entirely my fault. I am truly sorry about the whole situation. I know now I have some new friends to make as I am not going to let this happen to another young girl like you. If you can forgive me, I can promise if you ever see me at that dance again, I will not be hanging around with Kent and Jason. If you give me the opportunity, I will prove it to you. We are leaving now."

"No, no, you can't leave me here alone," I cry.

"Just follow the dirt road back out the same way we came in. When you get to the highway, turn right. The campus is four miles down the highway." Fred turns around and leaves.

I reach down to the foot of the bed and pull the cover over me. I have no light, so I curl up like a baby in its mother's womb, trying to stay warm until daybreak, sobbing and thinking about what I will do now. I believe I will be kicked out of college for staying out all night. "What will I do? Where will I live? I'm not going back home and that's final."

Susie begins talking to me in my head. "Oh, Sarah, you've done it now. Who is going to help Dean Taylor? He is going to be so disappointed in you."

Sarah thinks, *"I wonder if I can report this to the police and they can find these men."* So many thoughts and questions pour through my mind, and I have no answers.

Susie is the sexual alter of Sarah's system; however, Susie's idea of sex is to enjoy it. She has never been violently raped. She can no longer deal with this scene. Her eye lids grow heavy against her will. She is tired, so tired. She feels herself going away, much the same as if she were simply going to sleep, only this time she is floating away in the air, leaving her body behind.

Somebody new is in the body. She *had* to come. It was obvious to her Susie was desperate. How could Sarah let Susie get her in so much trouble? Kristen felt she had to come and try to watch over them, or Susie would eventually get them killed. Sarah's third alter had just been born.

Tears begin to flow down Kristen's face; however, she knows her whole

Figure 5.1 Kristen appears

reason for existence is to save Sarah, so she decides to access her situation. First, she is glad to be free from her rapists.

NOTE: Kristen, my third and final alter, appears during my first year of college, when I am seventeen years old. From this night, until I enter WIIT hospital, when I am fifty-nine years old, Kristen comes to rescue me from pain or dangerous situations.

Daybreak finally comes. Kristen knows it is now time for action. She rises and finds blood between her legs and on the sheets. Quickly, she cleans herself and puts on her clothes. Looking in the mirror, she finds marks on her face where Kent and Jason slapped her. She runs her fingers through her hair and then leaves. She begins walking and singing a gospel song, "Count your blessings, count them one by one. Count your blessings, see what God has done."

I have walked for about two miles when a man stops and asks if I want a ride. Kristen gets in and says, "Thanks, I'm a day student at the college."

He asks, "Do you walk everyday?"

"No sir, my car is in the shop."

We are soon at the college. Kristen slips into the dorm and up to Sarah's room, without being seen. Thank God, for that blessing. She breathes a sigh, and gladly turns the body back over to Sarah.

My roommate says, "Where have you been? What happened to you? You look terrible."

"Pat, you won't believe it. I got raped and beaten by three men last night. They left me alone about 3:00 AM in a dark cabin four miles from here. Did you sign me in last night?"

"Yes, I was waiting up for you to tell you about my wonderful date and you didn't come. It was ten minutes before midnight and you still weren't here. I didn't know what happened, but I wasn't going to take any chances. I signed by your name, believing, if you came in, you would know I signed in for you.

"Thank you, Pat. You kept me from getting expelled."

I begin crying, as I gather clean clothes, preparing to take a shower. Then I remember Dean Taylor. "Oh, Pat, please go by Dean Taylor's office and tell him I'm sick and won't be in to work today."

After my shower, I go to bed and miss all my classes for the day. I attend classes the following two days, and then it is time once again to go home for the weekend. *How* do I pretend to be normal? *How* do I go on after what happened to me? I *force* my body to move, but I feel as if my mind, spirit, and soul are not in my body. My loss is beyond tears and I suffer in lonely silence.

Causing me to feel worse, Mama finds my cigarettes in my purse and she gives me holy hell. "If that's what you learn at college, I wish you had never gone. I'd rather you scrub floors for a living than start smoking."

Mama tells Daddy about my smoking. He had stopped smoking eight years ago. The doctors had told him if he didn't quit, he would die of emphysema and bronchitis. Now he starts bumming my cigarettes and begins smoking again. I blame myself for Daddy starting back smoking again. Mama blames me too.

Words to my book before I started editing it, June, 2007:
I was a virgin when I left home...or I think I was. The sad part is I don't remember when I had intercourse for the first time, because I can't recall much of what happens when Susie has control of my life. I can't say for sure it didn't happen the night Mama was in Alabama, when I was in the eleventh grade.
While a patient at WIIT, I asked, "Why can't I remember who took my virginity?
The counselor responded, "You will remember when the time is right."

NOTE: While editing my book, I feel no threats anymore and now I know that I did lose my virginity that night with dad. It is so good to have finally remembered even though that in itself is traumatic.

Except for the rape trauma, I loved my first year at college and summer comes all too soon. I go to Atlanta to live with Aunt Elizabeth. The city bus comes right by her house and I find work at a local restaurant. At work, I meet all kinds of men. I sometimes become Susie on the job. As Susie, I do everything I can to make tips; I even meet men after work. I serve one man who is a baseball player from Syracuse, New York. I agree to go to his motel room across the street. I am afraid, but, knowing I am having my period, I think he will not want sex. I am right; he doesn't want sex when he learns that fact.

Another man proves not to be a one-night stand. We get together often. He is married and twice my age. He is a white-collar worker from here in the city, and it appears he is wealthy. He is a little overweight, but I still enjoy having sex with him. If he knew how much I needed the money, he probably would give me several hundred dollars; however, I have too much pride to ask. He is another server's regular customer in the restaurant. Therefore, the only time I get to wait on him is on her day off.

Fall quarter begins soon. I don't have enough money saved to pay tuition. About a year ago, a dairy farmer near my home gave me a day-old bull calf to raise for a 4-H project. Selling the calf will help. Also, I can cash the bond given to me at birth by my Aunt Sarah. She was proud I was her namesake. With money from those two sources and the little money I made this summer, I hope I can make it.

When fall quarter begins, I meet with my counselor to find out if I can overload my courses. I learn I can graduate in two more quarters. I take the money I have, divide it and use half on each quarter. Dean Taylor allows me to work enough hours to pay the rest. The closer I get to finishing, the more frightened I become about my education. I have no diploma saying I graduated from high school and only two years of college. An Associate Degree is not impressive when looking for a job.

I tell Dean Taylor, "I plan to drop out of college after winter quarter. Mama and Daddy impressed on me never to borrow money."

He tells me, "We will look and see if we can find you a scholarship."

I began my first year of college majoring in Business Education, aiming to get a one-year education degree and then marry Charles. I took shorthand, typing, and accounting all the first quarter. I never had shorthand in high school, only one year of typing, and no accounting experience except for the one year of bookkeeping. I passed the shorthand with a "B" because the 100's on my forms tests pulled my dictation tests up to eighties. There was no way I wanted to continue studying this curriculum area after I broke up with Charles. I changed my major to what I had always wanted—Home Economics. Now I could be like Mrs. Ledder.

The first scholarship Dean Taylor helps me apply for is the Georgia State Teachers' Scholarship. Dean Taylor says, "Don't get your hopes up because this scholarship is normally given to high school seniors."

He reads me the statistics on how few are given to students already in college. It does not sound too promising. He convinces me Student Defense Loans are always available. In these loans, the student pays back half the money and works for half of it over a five-year period.

The closer it comes to the end of the winter quarter, the more depressed I become. Daddy has always made it clear, once we leave home; we are not welcomed back. If I quit college, what will I do? I will not go back home, but I am scared to live alone and have no idea what type of job to seek. I start drinking every opportunity I have and drinking leads to sex.

Dean Taylor calls me into his office the following week.

He says, "Guess what?"

I reply, "I don't know." The scholarship doesn't enter my mind, because I don't think there has been enough time for an answer to come back yet.

"They have accepted you for the scholarship. They are giving you $2,000.00 to finish your last two years."

I hug his neck and almost don't let go. I feel happier than I have ever felt in my entire life. A check for $2,000.00 sounds like a million dollars to me. I won't even have to work those last two years. I am sad, though, leaving my small college in the middle of the year. I cry while I pray to God for thanks and gratitude that night.

Entering Georgia Southern College during the middle of a school year is scary. This college has about twenty times the number of students as my small junior college. I haven't learned any social skills since I spent all my spare time either working on campus or at home on the weekend.

Most of the courses remaining are in my major, Home Economics. No boys in those courses. My favorite course is Child Development. We go to the pilot school located on campus—first simply to watch the children and then to choose one child to observe. We must complete several written assignments on the chosen child.

Summer comes quickly and I decide to attend the first session of summer school before returning to my Aunt Elizabeth's in Atlanta to work at the restaurant. Being a server is so hard for such little earnings. It is during this summer I meet the man of my dream. I believe or hope he will ask me to marry him someday. He works at the same company as Mary's husband and they know each other personally. Neither Susie nor Faith appears while Bill and I are together. Alcohol and sex are no longer a threat for me. It appears this could develop into a long term relationship. Bill comes from a big tobacco farm in Vidalia, Georgia. His family was not poor like mine, but he worked hard on his Daddy's farm. There were two other boys and one sister in his family.

The summer is over before I want it to be. He asks, "Can I drive you back to Georgia Southern College a day early? If you will allow it, we will get a room at a local motel and stay before you sign back in and then I will go on to Vidalia to see my parents before coming back to Atlanta."

"That will be a blessing for me. Then I won't have to call around to other students trying to bum a ride back down there."

As we travel the five hours south, I discuss my college plans, and how I will be able to finish the four years early since I completed the first two years at Middle Georgia College a quarter early. He tells me about his parent's tobacco farm and I tell him how much I have always wanted to see tobacco growing and hanging in a barn. He promises to take me someday and I can meet his parents at the same time. When you enjoy the company you are with, time passes so quickly. We are in Statesboro, so we get checked into a motel and go to find something to eat.

When we return to our room, I tell him, "My turn first, for the shower."

"You better hurry or I'll be in there with you." I did hurry because I wanted to surprise him with the new negligee that I purchased just for the occasion.

"Oh, Sarah, you are beautiful. Come let me hold you." He does hold me as he kisses my tender breasts and then whispers in my ear, "You won't have this on long." Then I send him away for his shower. I lay in sweet anticipation of our next hours together. They are total ecstasy for me.

He sits at my feet; first removing the bottom of the negligee, then begins massaging both feet, moving gently up my legs until he reaches my clitoris. He teases me by stimulating it for a few seconds and then removes my top. He caresses my breasts with his large strong hands and then sucks on each of them, first one and then the other.

"Oh Bill, my body is throbbing and yearning for yours. Please, give it to me. I want to feel your body against mine."

I spread my legs in invitation for him to enter. His eyes glow as his whole body becomes aflame. The passion climbs with each thrust of his penis until the crucial time when the sky is lit by a thousand blazing stars. Bill knows just how to make me happy.

Upon awaking the next morning, I take the lead, and position myself on the top. We have beautiful sex one more time before we separate. He has asked me to not see any other men, so we exchange class rings as he leaves at the door of my dormitory.

I miss him so much. He drives down to spend a weekend with me during the month of November. I sign out of the dorm as if I am going home. We stay in a motel again. I am nervous for fear my parents will call the college asking for me and I will get caught. It turns out great too, but not as exciting as the first we spent together.

Christmas holidays arrive and I have about four weeks out of school. When Bill is not working, we are usually together. He takes me to his parents' home to meet them. I am nervous, yet excited. After Christmas is over and winter quarter begins, weeks go by without a word from Bill. I am sick with worry so I catch a ride home for the weekend and call him.

He comes to Mama's house and I ask, "Bill, what's wrong? Why haven't you called me?"

He says, "I'm ready to get married now, and I don't feel right about marrying you. If I marry you, you might not finish college. You are too close to finishing for me to mess it up." He continues, "I would never forgive myself if you quit and didn't finish. We need to call it quits."

Reluctantly, I take off his ring and give it to him. I ask about my ring, and he tells me it disappeared off his mantel when the housekeeper was there. Bill leaves, and I throw myself across one of Mama's bed, crying. I cannot believe he isn't willing to wait for one year.

Later, Daddy says Bill pawned my class ring. I bought my ring from my junior college, because I didn't get one from high school since I skipped my senior year. The cost of that ring was a tremendous amount of money for me at that time and I am extremely upset with him. I learned an important lesson though. I never gave my class ring from senior college to any boyfriend.

On Sunday I catch a ride back to Statesboro with a young

preacher and a friend of his. I am alone in the back seat and I am unaware that Joseph, the young preacher, is watching me in the rearview mirror. I cry much of the way back to Statesboro.

When we reach the campus, Joseph drops the friend off and then he turns around and asks, "Sarah, do you want to ride some place where we can talk? I'm a good listener."

I am unable to give a verbal answer; but my head goes up and down. Joseph drives to a secluded spot that overlooks a lake. When he gets out of the car, I follow. He opens the trunk of his car and takes out a blanket. He throws the blanket on the bank of the lake and I tell him I didn't hear from Bill for four weeks. Then I told him about the past weekend. I am sitting with my knees propped up, my elbows on my knees, and my chin propped in the palms of my hands.

Since he is a preacher, I assume it is safe to talk to him, and I turn and look into his kind, compassionate eyes. "Joseph, I gave everything I had to him. I loved him with my body and my soul. I held nothing back. Tell me what I did wrong. What's wrong with me, Joseph? I end up losing everyone."

Joseph reached over to put his arm around my shoulder and I laid my head against his chest. "Sarah, I can't tell you why Bill did what he did, but there is nothing wrong with you."

I continue to cry and Joseph cradles me as if I were a child. He leans down to kiss me on top of my head. This act of kindness means so much to me. I want to tell him, "Thank you." Then I fear he will think I am ridiculous. It is cold and I am shivering; Joseph pulls the blanket around us and his strong arms hold me tight, causing me to feel safe. Joseph is about five feet, ten inches tall. I'm guessing he weighs about 190 pounds. I don't know if he works out in a gym; however, I'm sure he could hold his own in a fight.

I am glad that we are comfortable with each other without talking. I look out over the lake and see a deer on the bank on the other side. I point out the deer to Joseph and he nods. We watch as bass strike in the lake.

There is an inherent strength in Joseph's face. His compelling dark eyes, his tanned features, and the confidence apparent on his face draw me. His dark brown hair shines with blond highlights. Tendrils of hair fall down and curl on his forehead. He leans back and props on his arms, watching me.

I turnover on my side towards him and say, "Joseph, you are beautiful."

He laughs at me, as he leans backwards, pulling me down beside him. Gently, he takes me in his arms and makes love to me. Joseph and I continue to see each other until the end of the quarter.

Between winter and spring quarter Rebekah sells me a Rambler wagon for only $400. It is worth much more; but she knows how badly I need a car. I will live in the Home Management House this quarter. Living in the Home Management House will earn me ten hours college credit. I can't leave the house overnight. I take an extra ten hours credit to finish college by Christmas. Our college offers two of the courses I need during the first session of summer school. The other required course, bacteriology, is taught at a college near my parents' home. It is only a three-week course. I hope I can tolerate being back at home for three weeks. I will be at the college except to sleep. My Student Teaching is scheduled for the fall quarter. By the middle of December, I will have my B.S. Degree in Home Economics.

During the first session of summer school, I have a blind date with an Air Force man stationed at the Radar Missile Base about three miles from the college. When he comes to pick me up he is wearing white shorts and a blue polo shirt. His name is Noah and he is an attractive young man with brown wavy hair and the most gorgeous blue eyes. As we head for his car, I almost flip out. He drives a '57 Chevrolet. I learn on the second date he is Catholic and from Ohio. I think about the boys from my 4-H trip in tenth grade who were from Ohio. That excites me even more. By the third date, my alter Susie has us taking showers together in his apartment and having sex with each other.

I burn myself at the beach the next weekend. When I am with

Noah the following Sunday evening, I tell him about my burned back. He wants to see it; then he uses a hangnail from his thumb and cuts my blistered back. Before the evening ends, he uses the same hangnail to ruin my last pair of hose. I have no money to buy another pair.

"Suzanne," I later complain to my roommate. "Look at my back."

"I see," Suzanne says. "It's blistered. What caused this cut in your back? It's going to get infected if you don't put something on it."

"Noah cut my back with a broken fingernail. Then he tore up my hose with the same hangnail."

Suzanne's brows draw together and she begins shaking her head back and forth. "Sarah, you are crazy if you go out with this guy again."

But, I continue going out with Noah. I do ask him "Why did you do such a thing?"

He said, "I wanted to see how much you could take."

I never mention it to him again. His money is as short as mine. One evening we go to the drive-in theater. He cleans out the glove compartment of his '57 Chevrolet looking for change. We are short three cents, but the admissions clerk admits us anyway.

I have never been happy with my parents' Primitive Baptist religion, so I visit all denominations while in college except Catholic. Since Noah is in the Air Force, he is inactive in the Catholic Church. Noah and I begin attending together.

I say to him, "This is it. I like the reverence and total quietness of this church. I can feel the Holy Spirit." I begin instructional classes to become Catholic.

The first session of summer school is over in five weeks, and it is time for me to go back to Mama's house to register for my last official class, bacteriology. Noah follows me to see where I live and to meet my parents. He is not afraid of meeting Daddy like all the other boys have been who dated us girls because he does not know of Daddy's history.

When he tells Daddy he is Catholic, Daddy says, "I dated a Catholic girl once, and I learned that all Catholics are Communists."

I watch for the reaction on Noah's face. He looks my father squarely in the eye and says, "I don't know who told you that, but your information is wrong."

Then Daddy says, "Well, as long as you never mention the word 'Catholic,' we may get along all right."

Noah has already asked me to marry him, but Mama and Daddy know nothing about it. We've only known each other for three weeks. Our tentative plans are to get married during the Christmas holidays after I graduate. Noah sleeps in Adam's old bedroom before going back to Statesboro the following day. I get little sleep that night, because Mama and Daddy have never allowed male friends to spend the night. My thoughts are, *"After he sees how poor we are, he will consider my family 'poor white trash,' and I will never hear from him again."*

Surprise! Noah calls each evening unless he is working the swing shift. The next three weeks pass so slowly. I am driving to a college forty-five miles away to take my last course. The time comes for my menstrual period. I am a week late and then two. I begin to wonder if I could be pregnant. I call Mary and ask her to help me get a pregnancy test. I tell her I might as well kill myself, because Mama will kill me if I am pregnant. Mary has a sister-in-law who is a nurse and will perform the test free. Pregnancy tests at this time require a blood test and several days to get the results.

Mary tells Mama about my fear of being pregnant. She would not normally have told Mama my secret, but she feared for my life—what I might do with my low self-esteem if I were pregnant. If I committed suicide and she had not told Mama, she would have never forgiven herself.

It is the last day of my bacteriology course except for the final when Mama learns I might be pregnant. She comes to me and says, "It doesn't matter if you are pregnant or not, marry him, the sooner the better. It is wrong to have sex before marriage. You need to go ahead and marry him."

I wanted to meet his parents in Ohio before I married him, but I guess there is no way now. I feel numb as I call him and tell him what Mama said.

He says, "That's fine with me. I'll talk to Father Chris to see when he will be available to marry us."

Mama starts planning a home wedding in the living room of our house. I call Noah back and he lets the priest know my family is also planning a home wedding.

Father Chris says to Noah, "Let me think about this. I'll get back in touch with you tomorrow."

I started my period; however, that makes no difference to Mama. She is determined to go through with the wedding. I am confused at this point, because I have no input in this most important decision about my life. I have not known Noah but five weeks.

Mama calls our Primitive Baptist preacher and asks him to come over. When he arrives, she tells him the man I am marrying is a Catholic. When everyone leaves the room except the preacher and me, he explains the commitments of marriage. He doesn't say anything rude or contradictory about the Catholic religion; however, without warning, he says, "I had rather my daughter die than marry a Catholic."

Total shock comes over me when I hear him say this. I cannot speak. This man is not going to marry Noah and me. The sound of the telephone ringing breaks the silence. Mama calls me to the phone. I am so relieved.

The call is from Noah and he says, "Sarah, there can't be but one wedding."

I say, "What?"

Noah repeats, "Father Chris says there can only be one wedding." He says, "If I start out letting you have your way by getting married there in your home to satisfy your parents, then we drive straight back here to Statesboro and get married again, he says I will have gotten off to a bad start first thing."

I am happy to hear from Noah. I say simply, "All right."

Noah continues, "I'm going to leave here now and we will talk about it when I get there."

I'm afraid he will hang up before I can talk. I say, "That sounds great to me, because this Primitive Baptist preacher is sure not going to marry us."

What else can I say? Without knowing if my parents will allow me to leave with Noah, I return to the living room where the preacher and Mama are sitting and tell her, "Noah is on his way to get me and he says we are not having but one wedding." I excuse myself and go to pack my clothes, not knowing what the next few hours will hold. Mama slips into my suitcase a beautiful gown, which she bought for my wedding night. I love her for doing this. The gown is not expensive, but it means much to me, knowing it came from Mama.

My nerves are in jitters while I bathe, fix my hair and face, and prepare to leave my parents' home for the last time as their unmarried child. Noah will be here in two hours.

When Noah arrives, it seems he and Daddy talk forever. Only my parents, Mark, Noah, and I are here. The preacher understood he would not be performing the wedding, and he left. Again, Daddy says to Noah, "If you won't ever mention the word 'Catholic,' we will get along fine."

Noah takes my bag to his car and throws it in the trunk, while I say good-bye to my parents and to Mark. Noah opens the door of his '57 Chevrolet for me, I get in and he closes it. When Noah backs out and then pulls down the driveway, I turn my head to look back toward my parents, who are still standing and waving. In my mind I am thinking, *"This is it, Daddy and Mama. You no longer control me. No matter what happens to me in the future, I will never come back or ask for your help again."*

I feel we are going away, forever, out of their lives. I never live close to my parents again or allow them to know much of what is going on in my life. Many times Daddy told us as kids, "The day you leave home, it is your 'little red wagon.' Don't come back to me wanting help."

It is one thing to leave a happy home to go into a marriage with the knowledge that, if it doesn't work, you have loving parents who will give you emotional support and let you come back home until you get back on your feet. Yet it is terrifying to know you cannot go home again, no matter how desperate your life becomes. I now know I do not have my parents support, and I know I will not be welcomed back home, and to me that is a terrifying thought. A desperate person will do things a normal person won't.

Chapter 6

My First Marriage

The trip to Statesboro is long and silent. I go in and out of dissociative states and I feel fragmented—as if my hold on reality is uncertain. My life has become one bitter battle after another and I now feel I am losing the war. My sense of loss is beyond tears.

How did this happen? This is only the second month I have known Noah and now Mama is forcing me to marry him. Oh, if she only knew about my past and all the other sexual encounters I have had with other men. She would have had me married many times before now. Now I am leaving her house never to return and worse…I am marrying a total stranger. Having never met his parents, or knowing where he lives, except somewhere in Ohio, makes it even more frightful. How can I let Mama rule my life after I loved Bill so much? I'm not sure if this is love. I cannot forget some of the verbal abusive remarks Noah frequently says to me. And I remember the look of enjoyment I saw on his face when he ran his fingernail down my sunburned back.

Time looses its objective meaning when I'm not present all the time, and sooner than I had expected, we arrive in Statesboro. Noah goes to ask Father Chris if he can marry us tonight. He tells Noah, "I don't see why not. I will tell the missionaries to grab their hats and come on over to the church, because they have a wedding to attend."

Soon the missionaries have the entire wedding organized. We have a maid of honor, best man, brides' maids, ring bearer, and flower girl. The wedding party throws rice at us as we leave the church. I have not completed all the classes to become Catholic yet; therefore, I have not been confirmed and cannot go to confession or receive other sacraments before marriage, but Noah

126

does. We are also required to sign a book stating we intend to bring our children up in the Catholic faith.

After the wedding we get a room at the Stiles Motel even though we can go to his apartment. Noah says, "It's our honeymoon."

When we awake, we go to his apartment, pack his clothes, and begin the long drive to Ohio so I can meet his parents. He starts out driving while the roads are straight and present no driving problem. When we reach the North Carolina Mountains with the curvy "S" turns that the motorcyclists call switchbacks, he asks me to drive. I almost loose control. He jerks at the wheel to pull the car back on the road and this upsets me.

He grounds the words out between his teeth. "Pull over. I thought you could drive, but I see you can't."

I am too angry to speak because, if I do, I will cry. I pull over and return to the passenger seat. When we stop for a restroom break, I feel as if I am with a stranger. I wonder whether the car will be there when I come out. I worry about the possibility that Noah might leave me. I have no cash in my wallet. If he should leave me, I don't know what would happen to me.

When we reach his parents' home, I am impressed; however, they have a hard time understanding my southern accent, and I can hardly understand their northern accent. His mother is especially polite to me. I can tell she wants me to be happy and to feel welcome in her home. We stay only one night because Noah is in a hurry to reach the farm where his family lived when he was a young boy. His family still owns this farm and it is about one and one-half hours away. The location is at the top of a road named Winding Hill.

We spend our honeymoon week here at this farm on Winding Hill. Figure 6.1 shows the house in the distance; the barn is the larger building. While we are going up Winding Hill, Noah shows me where his old high school girlfriend lived. He tells me how much he loved her and he says he always will. I did not tell him about Bill and how much I loved him. That was the past and I did

Figure 6.1 Noah's childhood home

not see any need to hurt him.

He says, "I tried my best to get in her pants but I couldn't. By our third date, you let me in yours." (I also did not tell him I dated Charles all through my high school days and never had sex with him either.)

No one can see us, but we can see for miles because we are far from civilization.

Two days later, I can't describe my feelings. A tired sadness has settled over me. I walk around outside with a cup of coffee, dressed in my nightgown, and cry. Put down, put down, and more put downs. Why did I ever let Mama force me to marry this man? It gets worse. While on our honeymoon, he forces me to wash, starch, and iron all his long sleeve dress shirts. I do not understand why he could not have shown me more love. Maybe he just never learned how to love.

My student teaching fall quarter is scheduled in Vidalia. I am too afraid to live there alone. I have never even made an important decision on my own. How could I have ever thought I could live there alone? Mama never taught us or gave us the freedom to make our own decisions. Fear of the unknown was one reason why I allowed Mama to force me to marry Noah. I was terrified of the thought of living in an apartment in Vidalia all by myself. However, the college reassigns my student teaching to Statesboro High School when they learn about my marriage.

When Noah and I return to Statesboro following our honeymoon, I feel numb and disoriented. The supervising teacher for my student teaching has a trailer for rent. We decide to rent her trailer. I am not making money and Noah makes little, since he is only an Airman Second Class. Before I finish my student teaching, I become pregnant. I have already started applying for jobs, because the Georgia State Teachers' Scholarship requires you to teach in Georgia for three years as repayment for your scholarship.

I am having no luck in finding a teaching position, with my major in Home Economics. I decide to write to the scholarship program and tell them about the problem I am having. I ask to wait until the fall of the new school year, which will be school year 1964-1965.

The response from officials managing the Teachers' Scholarship Program stated, "You accepted this scholarship with the responsibility that you will teach in Georgia for three years. We advise you to start looking for a teaching position immediately."

When I learn Noah has to leave in January for a temporary duty (TDY) in South Carolina, I feel panicky. I have no job and no money of my own. I apply for a job near my parents' home, since I have exhausted all chances of finding a job near Statesboro. The principal of a small school nearby accepts me as a third grade teacher to finish the year for a woman whom the principal wants to move into the library for the rest of the year. I start out driving forty miles to the new job from Mama and Daddy's house.

I am again living in my parents' home and I do not remember making the decision to move back home. I am panicked because I sometimes hear voices in my head and I lose blocks of time. It is a secret I guard with my life. All I want is to be normal. To believe I moved back in with Mama and Daddy is beyond me; I have to get away from here before Daddy makes a move on me. In a few days, I find an older woman who agrees to rent me a bedroom and kitchen privileges. She is sweet to me. Right away I feel the panic easing. Mama didn't seem too surprised when I moved out again. My landlady is teaching me how to crochet using a baby afghan kit I ordered from Sears. She teaches me the design she calls "Down in the Valley and Up on the Hill." It is pink, blue, and white. I think it will be gorgeous for my first baby. We work on my afghan every evening while we visit.

Our baby will not be due until late July, so I feel sure I can complete the school year. On January 29, I start hemorrhaging at school. Mama and Mary come to take me to a local Air Force base hospital. After my admission, I call Noah and tell him where I am.

In a shaky voice, he says, "Hold on. I will be there as quick as I can."

I tell him, "Don't drive too fast, but get here as quickly as you can because I am hurting."

I know women have miscarriages, but I never dreamed it would happen to me. Before Noah arrives, the contractions become unbearable. After three hours, he arrives. As he holds my hand, he cries. It is as if the pain leaves through my hands and enters through his hands to his body. The doctor comes in and tells us he is sure the fetus is dead, but will wait until morning to perform the D & C, the scraping of the walls of the uterus.

That night is like a long nightmare. Noah and I talk as he tries to comfort me. The nurse keeps both of my arms taped down and they ache badly. Glucose is running in one and a blood transfusion in the other. While Noah is getting a nap, I watch the glucose bag with great intensity praying for it to empty so I can ring for the nurse and ask her to take the needle out of my arm. As soon as one bag empties, they bring another. I break down and cry from the pain and frustration.

At 8:00 AM the interns come for me. The bottle of glucose hits the top of a doorway and tumbles down, nearly hitting me in the head, but I catch it. The attendants are so upset I feel sympathy for them. Knowing I am on the way to have my baby scraped away, it wouldn't have mattered if it had hit me in the head.

When the anesthesia is started, I fight it. In my mind, I am determined to stay awake as long as I can. I know the doctor is going to scrap the walls of my uterus and any hope of a baby will be gone.

The next thing I remember is looking up and seeing Noah and

Mama. In a choking voice, I cry, "When are they going to do it?"

Mama tells me, "They are done and you are waking up."

My body feels so empty. The life I was carrying is gone now for sure. Noah says, "The doctor reported it was a blob of living matter and could never have matured normally."

Our lives must go on. Noah has to get back to South Carolina, and I have a duty to those third graders. Noah's TDYs last only two months. Instead of staying in Statesboro alone, he volunteers for another TDY for April and May. We will arrive back in Statesboro about the same time.

When Noah's TDYs are over, we look at apartments, but the available ones are terrible. The neighbors are loud, the apartments are trashy, and they are in undesirable sections of town. We look at mobile homes to buy. They are gorgeous. We even find a mobile home park where only couples from Noah's military site live at one end. I am now getting a paycheck, so it is not as hard financially as it was before. We settle into this park with our new mobile home and other military couples. I find a teaching position in a county outside the one we live in teaching fourth grade.

Before Mama's fiftieth birthday in July of 1964, my parents sell the farm in Georgia, and purchase a home on the lake in Alabama where many of Daddy's family have a second home. Those homes are similar to the one Mary and I visited with Daddy's sister and her husband the summer we learned how to water ski.

It has always been Mama's dream to become a nurse. She thought she didn't have a chance to fulfill her dream after she had more than two babies. She couldn't leave us all at home to get training. The city was too far away and she didn't have transportation. The hospital wouldn't hire a woman, even for a nurse's aide position, after the age of fifty. She gets a job at Russell Hospital.

The house has a big dock where Daddy can sit and fish. He buys a nice fiberglass boat. Sometimes he takes the boat out on the lake to fish. He also buys water skis. Daddy enjoys pulling Mark.

He allows Mark to use the boat with his friends. We four siblings go to visit my parents, but not often because it is far from where we live in Georgia. How wonderful for Mark. All through his high school, he lives on the lake with a boat and water skis—no farm work, no garden, and no animals to feed or care for—simply pure pleasure.

Late in the summer of 1964, after my first miscarriage in January, I become pregnant again. I go to the doctor regularly, but I try not to think about being pregnant for fear I will miscarry again. Roughly, three and one half months after conception that is exactly what happens. My doctor advises me to have a uterine suspension if I intend to try to get pregnant again. Well, I intend to get pregnant again, but I do not feel like having surgery now. Neither do I want to take time off from teaching at present. The doctor tells me my uterus is inverted and tilted, and this could be a contributing cause of the embryo not developing properly. Noah is on a temporary assignment in another state. He comes home to me as soon as I call to let him know of this second miscarriage. All I ever wanted from life was to be normal, have babies, and be a good mother to those babies.

I keep my job and lose only a few days. I love these children in my fourth grade class. Since I am not being successful in having my own children, I refer to my students as "my children." Even though Noah and I are practicing Catholics, the emotional and physical strain on my body of continually having one miscarriage after another is too much for me. I begin taking birth control pills. My principal offers me a contract for the next school year, 1965-1966. That year becomes the best school year so far in my career. During my first year at this school, I learn much about being too easy on students. I become stricter the second year. Oh, how I love my job. My health is better now, and we are managing better financially than we ever have.

In February of 1966, Noah decides to reenlist. He gets about $900 reenlistment bonus. He plans to make the Air Force a career. Financially, Noah and I are doing well and we decide to try again to have a baby.

When I make my first visit to the doctor in September, he confirms that I am pregnant and says, "With your history, you should quit teaching and stay off your feet as much as possible."

The attachment to my students, the faculty, and the principal make it hard for me to quit my job; however, I know I must. I give my principal two weeks to find another teacher.

I keep myself busy with odd chores and visiting the military wives to keep my mind occupied and off the thought of having a baby. I am afraid to get my hopes up too much. However, I am home only two weeks when I begin hemorrhaging again. After we enter the base at Fort Stewart hospital, the military police stop him for speeding. After they learn he is on the way to the hospital, he is escorted the rest of the way. Of all the rooms in the hospital, I am put in a room on the maternity ward. Seeing the young woman in the room with me love and nurse her baby causes more pain than I can bear. What have I done to deserve this? I realize I am on the edge of "cracking up."

When anything bad happened to us as children, Mama always told us it was our punishment. She said, "It's because you have been bad. God knows everything you do. You cannot hide anything from God."

That was the belief of the Primitive Baptist Church. That was why Daddy didn't want us going to the Missionary Baptist Church. He was afraid we would learn something different from Primitive Baptist doctrine. Our current pastor just had a "calling" from God and started preaching. He didn't have college or seminary training. Not long before his calling, one of his daughters had gotten pregnant out of wedlock. And yet this same preacher told me he had rather his daughter die than marry a Catholic. The Primitive Baptist doctrine, taught to me by preachers and my parents caused me much heartache and shame until the age of fifty-nine when I entered the Women's Institute for Incorporation Therapy at Hollywood, Florida.

Mama had drilled deep into my subconscious the belief in the "vengeful almighty God" who punishes each of us for our sins. At this point, I believe God is punishing me for my past sins by causing my miscarriages.

I cry out to God, "Please dear God, punish me but not my babies; they are innocent."

I can't understand the cause of the miscarriages and the doctors can't tell me. My doctor gives me the label, "habitual abortor." The Catholic faith teaches that once a child is conceived, it has a soul. During all these pregnancies and miscarriages, I always said a baptism over the commode when I hemorrhaged just in case one of the larger clumps of blood was the fetus. In each of the miscarriages, I lost so much blood that I was given two pints of blood.

From this miscarriage, I not only lose my baby but my job as well. I have to find a job, but I barely have the energy to get out of bed in the morning. I feel a wretchedness of mind I have never known before. I drag myself out to look for work and I cannot find another job teaching.

The local newspaper hires me to set type for the "Women's Gossip Column." I feel useless and unhappy sitting behind a machine, so I start looking for a teaching job again. Children are my first love. I am beginning to see a tiny ray of sunlight again, and I cannot wait to get back in the classroom.

Funds finally become available for some remedial work in the areas of reading and mathematics for one of the smaller schools in the county where we live. The school board hires me to begin the program in January of 1967.

Before Christmas of 1966, Noah receives orders to report to Kessler Air Force Base at Gulf Port, Mississippi, to attend a Radar Technician School for five months beginning in January. He says nothing about me going with him.

I have worked on my new job one month when Noah calls and says, "I don't want to stay here alone for five months. Let's get an apartment and you can come down here."

Normally, I would have been excited about going to the coast and being with him, but, if he wanted me with him, he should have let me go with him originally? Why did he let me take a new job on January 1?

"I can't; I just took this job a month ago."

"I didn't know classes were going to be just six hours a day and I would get so lonely. Please come."

It isn't easy to find a teaching position in a university town. I am embarrassed to resign my new job so soon after taking it, but, since he begged; I resign and go to Noah.

By the time I work out a two week notice for my job and get moved to Gulf Port, Noah has three of the five months remaining. Gulf Port is an eye-opener for this little country girl. The places and events I see are a shock to me. Wow, I have more fun and excitement in these three months than in all the previous time of my marriage. We go to a little bar called Sam's Beach Lounge every night, and we shoot billiards, play pinball machines, and drink beer by the pitcher. We buy a boat and go out into the gulf every weekend. I don't want to leave when Noah's classes end and it is time to leave.

Only one problem marred the time we were there and it follows us home. When Noah and I have been with other military personnel, Noah waits until we are home, and then he accuses me of flirting with the men. I try to explain I am not flirting; I am only being friendly. I tell him Mama taught us to be friendly with people. Later, however, I learn some of the men obviously did take my friendliness as flirting, because I did receive some telephone calls from them when Noah was gone on TDY.

I become pregnant for the fourth time in the spring of 1967. Noah is scheduled to leave for a six-month tour to Viet Nam in the middle of July. When he leaves, I will be two and one-half months pregnant. I don't want Noah to leave me, but it is not my call.

My doctor, knowing I am an habitual abortor, decides to prescribe some powerful hormones he thinks will help me carry this fetus. In the event intercourse may be a contributing cause, the doctor asks us to avoid sexual intercourse. This is the first time I have been on hormones; I am taking them by mouth and by injection. I like this doctor. He has thoroughly studied my history, and I have faith he will do everything he can to help me carry this baby. I allow myself to get my hopes up once again.

After Noah leaves for Viet Nam, it is exciting to get his letter about our baby. He writes about how big I will be, and how great it will be for both of us. The baby is due January 31, and Noah is due to arrive back home the middle to late January.

Noah has been gone two weeks. I wipe after urinating and I see a speck of blood.

"Please, dear God, no."

All the other miscarriages began this way. I feel terrified and I pray I will not wreck the car as I drive to my doctor's office. I tell the receptionist I saw a spot of blood and I have to see the doctor. In no time I feel his hand on my shoulder. I look up and see kindness and concern in his eyes.

"Sarah, come with me. Let's see what's happening."

I start crying as I follow him to the examining room. I feel special because he came himself to get me and take me to the room. After a brief examination, he asked the nurse to call an ambulance to transport me to the hospital and to call in orders for a pregnancy test to be done.

The first pregnancy test comes back positive. This gives me hope. The following morning the doctor orders another pregnancy test. This time it comes back negative.

With a pained expression on his face, my doctor asks, "Sarah, do you understand what the negative reading means?"

The massive doses of hormones are preventing me from hemorrhaging; therefore, I know I have not lost the fetus. I had assumed the tests would continue to come back positive. So I answer his question, "No, I don't understand what it means."

He answered, "It means the fetus is dead."

"No...no...no, no. Please don't say that." I am looking at him and I see his mouth moving but I can't hear what he is saying. He puts his hand on my shoulder and I recoil from his touch. My eyes aren't focusing. I am so tired. I close my eyes and it feels as if I am floating.

When I open my eyes Rebekah and Mary, my sisters, are in my room. I guess a nurse from the station got Rebekah's phone number from my chart and called her. I am so glad they have come.

Rebekah comes to my side, "Well, little girl, we thought you would never wake up. I told your doctor I wanted him to run another pregnancy test."

I start crying, "You two shouldn't have come. You have your children to take care of and meals to cook for your husbands."

"Nobody is more important than you are right now, sweetheart," Rebekah says. "I'm going to the nurses' station to let them know you are awake."

When Rebekah is gone, Mary comes to my bedside to hug me. "Sarah, I love you so much. I'm so sorry."

I ask Mary, "What about your children?"

"We put all five of them in day care."

At Rebekah's request, another pregnancy test is run; however, it too comes back negative. I cry out to Rebekah and Mary, "I can't bear the thoughts of another D & C. I had rather risk getting gangrene than let them scrape away another baby." I liked it when it seemed as if I were floating in the air. I wished I had not awakened to this agonizing sense of loss.

"Darling," Rebekah says, "please go home with me and let my doctor give you his opinion before your D & C."

"I'm too tired to ride that far, and besides, I trust my doctor's opinion. I just don't want to have the D & C."

"You have no choice about the D & C. If you don't let them operate, then we would eventually lose you and the baby."

"I know it must hurt like hell to have one miscarriage after another, but Rebekah is right," Mary said, holding my hand. "You have to have the surgery, sweetheart."

"I know you are right. I just can't understand why it keeps happening."

The Red Cross reports the news to Noah. Rebekah and Mary must leave the same day because of their children in the day care program. My spirits sink even lower.

I receive a letter from Noah telling me his country needs him and I will have to weather the storm alone. He writes, "I told my boss, 'This is my country and my job. I am needed here and I feel obligated to stay.'"

The doctor had sent the results from my surgery to a lab in Savannah. Since the hormones I had been taking had not allowed me to hemorrhage, the doctor knew the placenta and fetal parts were all present when the D & C was performed. When the report returns, it states, "The placenta looks normal; however, no fetal parts are present."

I stare at the doctor, speechless, feeling like an abnormal freak. Why is it I cannot grow a normal baby? I wonder why no one can give me answers.

"Please, dear God, help me. Help me to understand."

I am dismissed from the hospital and I go home alone. I am faced with the harsh realities of loneliness. I am reminded of Noah's words, "You will have to be brave and weather the storm alone." I'm not sure how brave I can be but I guess I'll find out, because I sure am alone. I must find a job quickly or I will go insane. It is time for a new school year to begin.

NOTE: As I look back on my life today, I realize I was suicidal during that time because I didn't know where to turn for help. I needed medication for depression, but I didn't know how to ask for help. I wasn't in therapy to help me cope with my childhood trauma, Noah's verbal put-downs, or the miscarriages.

Searching the newspaper, I notice an opening in an adjoining county for a Home Economics Teacher. Out of hopelessness and frustration, I think, *"Lord, this would be great. If you are not going to let me have babies, then at least answer this prayer. Please allow me to find a job as a Home Economics teacher."*

Obtaining this position would be the answer to my dream and my opportunity to teach in my field. It would be my chance to be like Mrs. Ledder, my high school Home Economics teacher. Everybody in the school will look at me as an example of correct etiquette and rules.

"But wait," I think. *"I don't have the job yet."* I dress my best and drive forty miles one-way to the high school. My interview goes well, and the principal promises to call tomorrow. He says he has one more person to interview before he makes a final decision. He asks whether I can begin Monday if offered the position.

I'm sure he can hear the excitement in my voice as I answer, "Yes, of course. There is nothing that would prevent me from starting work Monday morning."

The next day the principal calls to officially offer me the job. After hanging up the phone, I jump for joy. I will finally be teaching in the field I love most. I go to the first military wife and say, "Guess what? I begin a new teaching job Monday. Guess what course I'll be teaching?"

Beverly asks, "What?"

"Home Economics."

"That's nice."

She doesn't seem too excited for me. I go to three more of my best friends to share my good news. They all have children except me. We meet at one another's houses sometimes when our husbands are TDY and play Yahtzee. They rarely come to my house because they have children they need to get to bed. After no one seems excited about my job, I go to town and buy a bottle of vodka to celebrate alone. Monday morning will be here before I know it. With no congratulations from my friends, my planned celebration soon turns into a pity party. I begin thinking of all the miscarriages. I wonder whether other women who have had miscarriages feel as I do. After four miscarriages, I am beginning not to feel like a woman. Self-pity consumes my mind.

I think, *"If I was a real woman, wouldn't I be able to carry a live baby? No woman ever keeps having one miscarriage after another. I don't even feel like a woman anymore."*

I decide I will masturbate in hopes it will satisfy me for a while. I look at my quart of vodka and it is half gone. Ahh…enough for Saturday and Sunday…and I pass out….

Before Noah left for Viet Nam, he assumed I would not be using the cars much, since I was pregnant. He left for Viet Nam with bad tires on the car I usually drive. On the way home from work, I have a flat tire. Someone stops and helps me change it. When Saturday comes, I head for a local tire store intending to buy a full set of tires. Before I reach the store, another tire goes flat. I park the car and walk on down to the tire dealer. As I enter the dealership, the attendant asks if he can help me.

"I sure hope so. My husband is in Viet Nam. I had a flat a couple days ago, and now another has gone flat in the alley before I could get here to buy new ones."

The manager comes from the back of the store and begins talking to me. He tells the other attendant he will take care of me. After I get the tires bought and on my car, John, the manager, begins a conversation. He asks, "Have you always lived in Statesboro?"

"No," I tell him. "I grew up on a farm in middle Georgia. I love the country and farm animals."

"Have you ever seen honey bees and beehives?" he asks.

Puzzled, I tell him, "No."

"I raise honey bees." John wants to know if I want to go with him to see his beehives.

I am excited; I like everything that grows in the country. I have heard people talk about their honeybees, but have never known anyone who owned any. It never occurs to me that this is a come-on. When John starts down a dirt road and reaches over to put his hand on my thigh, I realize this is not about bees or honey.

I have no self-esteem, and I hate myself for not being able to have a baby. Having lost my fourth pregnancy does not help my feelings about my self-worth either. Neither does it appear that Noah loves me. If he did, I believe he would have come home when I needed him. I have already decided that, if he doesn't treat me differently when he comes home, we should discuss divorce. It is too hard living with him, and not being able to have children, especially when he shows no love at all to me.

John parks the car and says, "Let's get in the back seat."

"But where are the honeybees? I wanted to see them."

John laughs, but we are at the same time moving into the back seat.

Sarah closes her eyes and sees before her the image of the "almighty vengeful God" that her mother promised hundreds of times would punish her for her sins. She cannot tolerate this situation she has caused herself to get into.

I can feel my body change from Sarah to Susie. I have no control over the next few minutes. John takes Susie's hand and places it on his erection, which is huge. It causes her to tremble beside him. Her mind wanders back to the time she sat on Daddy's lap and he touched her where John is touching her now.

John says, "I have never felt anyone as wet as you. It feels like a river."

"I need you. I am hurting so bad."

His thigh moves to part her legs and Susie scoots under him. Her body is alive now, yearning for him. As she raises her pelvis to welcome him, his thrust is hard and deep. A shudder runs full length of her body. Then his thrusts became slow and measured. Susie contracts her vaginal muscles and arches her hips to meet each thrust. She wants it to never end, but even now, she feels an urgency growing in him. With each deepening thrust, she trembles. Then the earth falls away, and she goes with him to that place of rapture, utterly consumed.

John and Susie continue seeing each other weekly, and sometimes they go dancing at a little spot outside Hunter Air Force Base in Savannah. I (Sarah) know there is another side of me. For a long time I sometimes hear voices in my head. I know sometimes the other part of me wants to do things I would never do. I know that other side of me is "Susie." I don't always know what Susie does, but sometimes I know more than I want to know.

I know now Susie is doing things with John that are wrong. I feel horrible about this. I am so afraid because Susie is a part of me and I am terrified her sin will keep me from going to heaven. I wish I could die.

The closer it gets to January, the more my guilt feelings grow. I must get away from John. I fly to Ohio to spend the Christmas holidays with Noah's family. While there, I develop a high fever and spend most of the time in bed. Since I am so depressed, being sociable is not high on my list of priorities. I arrive back home two days before school reopens. I had planned it that way on purpose. I have sworn I will not see John again; I can make it now until Noah gets home. It will only be one more month.

Susie does not feel the same as Sarah. She sees John more than she did before Sarah went to Ohio, because she fears she may never get to be with him again after Noah comes home. John is sensible…and wonderful. He promises if Noah learns about their relationship or if they separate, he will take care of me.

Noah returns from Viet Nam the last week of January 1968. First, he goes to the doctor who did my last D & C to hear first hand what he thinks is causing the miscarriages. The doctor explains our chemistry does not match. He tells Noah we could both be married to different people and may not have any problems. I am thinking, *"All the more reason to get a divorce."* He suggests artificial insemination.

Noah says, "Absolutely not. If our baby can't belong to both of us, we will adopt."

After this consultation, there is no question in Noah's mind about adoption. This act makes me reconsider discussing divorce. We go to the state welfare office the following day and file an application for a baby. I cannot wait. Our caseworker's name is Mrs. Black. She tells us it usually takes nearly the same amount of time as a normal pregnancy. They try to match the baby to the family based on education and family genes.

I throw my entire life into my lesson plans. I continue my

weekly nail and hair appointments. With everything in me, I practice mind-control, trying to get over the pain of missing John. He is a real gentleman; he knows Noah is home so he has not tried to contact me.

Working toward being like Mrs. Ledder, my high school Home Economics teacher, takes a lot of time and study on my part. I extremely adore the girls I work with. Many of them come from financially disadvantaged families like my own. I explain to them if they can obtain enough cash to go the first quarter of college and make good grades, the finances will come for them to finish, even if they have to use student defense loans. We do fundraising activities so the girls can go to the Future Homemakers of America Convention in Atlanta in the spring. Even though I am afraid to drive in Atlanta, I receive excellent directions. We go to the convention and have no traffic problems.

Teaching Home Economics was one of the highest points in my life, while, in contrast, the last miscarriage was the lowest point in my life. Noah disapproved of my standing weekly hair and nail appointment at the beauty salon the rest of the year while teaching Home Economics. It is unfortunate I did not continue treating myself with special rewards all through life. When it was time for signing contracts for the next school year, I asked the principal not to renew my contract, because Mrs. Black told us a baby would come before another school year began. As much as I loved my job, I wanted a baby more. I have been trying for five years to have a baby.

It is now time for the new school year to begin and we have heard nothing about a baby. I call Mrs. Black and ask if she knows why we haven't heard anything. She tells me she will call the Atlanta office.

During preplanning week, an elementary school in the same county as the high school where I taught Home Economics calls me and asks me to consider taking a position teaching sixth grade. This school is fifty-five miles from our trailer park; I only drove forty-five miles to my previous job. Any job is better than sitting at home, since we don't have the baby we thought we would have at this time. I tell the principal I will accept the position on one condition.

He asks, "What is that?"

I tell him, "My contract must contain a written clause that I have permission to break the contract when we receive an adopted child."

The principal agrees to my request. I begin work the following day. These sixth graders are so disobedient and out of control. I have a hard time managing this class. I almost wish I had not accepted the job.

Noah receives papers assigning him to go away on temporary assignment again on October 27. I call Mrs. Black to tell her, because we cannot receive a baby without both of us present. The TDYs are three months now instead of two. She cannot reveal all she knows about the baby they have been considering for placement in our home. She knows the baby is past due for placement and she initiates more pressure on the state office to find out what has happened to this infant. The state office begins researching the files.

The woman from the state office asks Mrs. Black, "Did we not offer the family a baby back in August? Our records suggest we did."

Mrs. Black speaks into the phone, "We were expecting you to, but we haven't heard a word from you."

When the conversation is over, Mrs. Black says to us, "Normally, the State requires parents to spend the night before making a decision. Since you are leaving to go TDY tomorrow and it is our mistake, she said we will make an exception in your case. You may check into a motel, visit with the baby for a few hours, make a decision, and drive home."

Noah asks, "What happened? What caused the mistake?"

Mrs. Black answered, "He went to a foster home after a ten-day stay at the hospital. The Atlanta office files indicate that you and Sarah accept him as yours upon his dismissal from the hospital."

Immediately, I resign my contract. Noah takes leave a few days early, and we leave to go see "our new baby." While waiting, I am a nervous wreck. I am worse than any father waiting for his wife to deliver. I get diarrhea and vomit—all from nervousness. I am so excited. The moment finally arrives. The baby's caseworker brings him to our door. He is so tiny, and he looks like he will break if I touch him. I tell Noah to hold him first. The caseworker asks if we are comfortable with him before she leaves. Then she goes, leaving us to make our final and most important decision.

We feed him his bottle and change his diaper. He is two months old and already recognizes the name Nathan. There is no question about whether we want him. We leave and go by the office to sign the necessary papers. A history of the parental backgrounds on both sides of his family, his feeding schedule, and a bag of clothes and diapers, and a baby seat come with the baby. The parental history is limited on the father's side. Nathan cries most of the way home, which upsets me. I feel I am unqualified to give him the necessary "Mother's touch." I check his diaper continuously, but nothing helps.

On Sunday I stop a moment and think, *"Thursday I taught school, Friday we drove to pick up our baby, and Saturday Noah left to go TDY. WOW! What a change in my life."*

For the next few weeks, Nathan keeps me busy. I even stop eating, as there is not enough time in the day. My military friends flock to my house constantly to see my new baby. (See Figure 6.2) They all want to teach me how to take care of him. My parents and Noah's parents drive down for the first time ever to see our baby, see where we live, and to visit.

I believe having a child will make me so happy that I will be content and will feel like a woman now even though I did not give birth to the child. Maybe our marriage will become stronger. Unfortunately, it doesn't work out that way. I have a hard time communicating my feelings and my needs to Noah. (I probably would with anybody, though.) My life has so many scars, and I

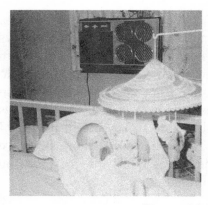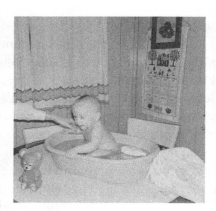

Figure 6.2 Baby Nathan

know of no way to heal them. At this time I know nothing about anti-depressant drugs or therapy, and I harbor everything inside. The older I become, the more depressed I stay. When I try to talk to Noah about my feelings, I burst out crying and no words will come.

When Noah has been gone about six weeks—half of his term— we decide to meet at my parents' home in Alabama. While traveling to take Nathan to meet his dad at my parents' home in Alabama, the Alabama State Patrol pulls me over less than a mile from their home. He reprimands me, stating he has been trying to catch me for miles. I am passing on a yellow line when he catches me, but it is a third lane near a bridge, and I thought I could see far enough ahead. He notices the baby in the floorboard of the car and fusses at me more.

He tells me, "We want you to visit Alabama, but only if you are going to drive safely. Neither you nor your baby is going to reach your destination safely if you don't slow down and drive within the speed limit."

The state patrolman asks if my name and address are correct on my license. They aren't. I suppose he notices how upset I am becoming. Maybe he thinks he has warned me enough, because he stops and tears up the ticket he had started writing. I am so thankful.

After getting to Mama's house, we have time to rest for a while before Mama has to be at work. Nathan is running a fever. His temperature is high enough to cause me worry. I tell Mama, "Mama, I'm scared. It appears Nathan's temperature is rising. I wish you didn't have to go to work."

Mama answers me, "He will be okay. All babies run high fevers when they get sick." She continues to get ready to go to work. As she goes out the door, I follow her and I am crying. "Please, Mama, don't go. I'm so-o-o afraid he will die."

His temperature continues to climb until it reaches 105 degrees. Mama calls to check on him, but she does not believe me when I tell her how high it has gone. I begin crying frantically, and I tell her, "See, he is going to die, he won't even keep his eyes open."

Mama doesn't ask whether she can get off work, she just tells them she has to go home. Daddy walks across the street and gets the chiropractor to come help. The chiropractor and Mama both get there at the same time.

I give Nathan to them and I go to Mark's room, slam the door, and throw myself across his bed, sobbing. When I can cry no more, I pray, *"O God, you have been telling me I am unfit to be a mother when I aborted all my babies. Now I have gone against your wishes and adopted a baby. Dear God, will you let him die just to punish me? Oh, merciful God, it's not his fault. Please don't punish him for my sins."*

I truly believe Nathan will die because of my sins. After what seems like hours to me, Mama and the chiropractor bring Nathan back to me.

Mama lays Nathan on the bed beside me and tells me his fever has gone down a degree; it is now 104 degrees. She asks, "Don't you have some juice we can give him in a bottle? He needs some fluids."

I jump off the bed and get apple juice and pour in one of his bottles. At first he turns his head sideways; he is still burning up

147

with fever. I keep moving the nipple around in his mouth and then he begins drinking greedily.

"Tell me what you did?" I ask.

"We bathed him in lukewarm water, and then we poured a little cooler water in the sink with him. We probably need to do it again after a while if his fever doesn't come on down soon," Mama says.

The chiropractor begins talking. "Sarah, you need to take him to a doctor and get his tonsils checked. That is why he is running the fever. While your mom held him in the bath water, I have been rubbing his neck."

The chiropractor then shows me where he has been rubbing on Nathan's neck. He tells me I should continue to do this throughout the night, as that will relieve some of Nathan's pain and help his fever go down. He tells me I should continue giving Nathan fluids and put him back in the bath water, if his fever didn't continue to go down throughout the night.

I keep a lamp on and have juice, water, and the thermometer on the night stand. Throughout the night I sponge off Nathan's body with a cool washcloth. I cry and thank God as Nathan's body gradually cools down. Towards morning, against my wishes, I drop off to sleep. I awake to Nathan's cries.

I am angry with myself when I come fully awake, because I fear his temperature climbed again while I lay asleep. I grab the thermometer but, before it has time to register I can tell Nathan's fever has broken. His temperature is almost back down to normal. I pick him up and pull him to my chest; I cry and thank God for sparing my child.

When Noah arrives later in the morning, he screams at me for not taking Nathan to the Montgomery military base. He humiliates me for letting a chiropractor even touch him. But there was no way I would have gone out at night looking for a military base fifty miles away. I was too afraid of getting lost in a big city like Montgomery.

Today, I wonder why he didn't take Nathan to the hospital himself after he got to Mama's house. I think it was because Noah didn't want to spend his money. He was stingy with his money.

After the crisis with Nathan is over and Noah has gone back to his TDY train, I start crying. Noah has upset us all—Mama, Daddy, Mark, and me. Mama invites me to stay a few days longer because my sister, Rebekah, and her family are coming today for a visit. There is no hurry for me to get back home to Statesboro, so I agree.

Mark, Rebekah, her husband Kenneth and I have been playing cards and having a few drinks, while Mama is at work. Being depressed about Noah and his behavior, I consume more drinks than I should. Later, Mark and I are outside walking in the night air, drinking coffee when Mama comes home from work. She walks up on her porch at precisely the same time as Mark and I do.

I look at this "self-appointed keeper-of-my-soul"—this person who has played judge and jury over all my actions until I have internalized her and now she is inside me. I look her squarely in the eye and ask matter-of-factly, "Who are you?"

Her contemptuous tone and her ominous words sober me. "I am calling the Welfare Department to come and get your baby. You are an unfit mother. You don't deserve to have any children." Then she slaps me across the face as hard as she can.

After that visit, it is a long time before I go back to visit my parents. When I tell Noah about the incident, he says, "If she is so perfect, why does she let that woman in her basement apartment stay there? She knows the woman is having an affair with the married chiropractor who lives across the street."

Mama does know because she has discussed it with us. She tells us the woman will have to suffer for what she does. I have told Mama, "But, Mama, you are condoning it by allowing her to rent from you."

Noah is not completed with his TDY in time for Christmas; however, he still drives the long trip home because of the amount of time the military gives them off. With Nathan being only four months old, I hardly know it is Christmas. Noah never has been one to celebrate Christmas. The New Year rolls in quickly and

Noah is gone again to finish his last thirty days of TDY. The military informs Noah that he will be going back to Viet Nam in February. His reenlistment comes due in February so he goes ahead and tells them, "No, I am a family man now. I won't be reenlisting." When his time is up, he goes to Atlanta to find work and a location for us to live.

In a couple of months, we pull our mobile home and move north of Atlanta about forty miles. He gets a job as an avionics technician at a large airport. Civilian life is different; however, it is wonderful to know my husband will be around when Nathan and I need him.

One evening, out of the clear blue sky, Noah says to me, "Perhaps you should try sex with another man...or maybe you already have. If you have, you can tell me, because I will understand.

> NOTE: Noah said he would understand, but he didn't mean what he said. I should have known he was setting me up. I was too sick at the time to know he was setting me up just to find out if I had ever had extra marital relations.

The affair with John has been eating away at me, and I decide I should tell him now. I decide it is my chance to get it off my chest.

> NOTE: Telling Noah about my affair with John was the worst decision I ever made with Noah. He never forgave me. He said he did, but he didn't. While our life together went on, I could see that he too was sick.

We have had Nathan now for three years. It is time for me to go back to work. We live in such a large school district it is easy to find a job. I begin teaching seventh grade mathematics in a middle school. It is also my first experience at teaching in an integrated school. Until now, school integration has not started in the southern part of Georgia. I thought I would be afraid to teach Blacks. As it turns out, some of them are my best students.

I love having Nathan, but I still feel as though something is missing in my life because I did not give birth to him. I would feel more like a woman if I could give birth to a baby. Tentatively, I approach Noah, "Would you be willing to try one more time to have a baby? If I miscarry again, I have Nathan to come home to, and perhaps I won't get as upset. You will be here with me too. If it doesn't work this time, I won't ask you to try it again."

"Sure, I told you in the beginning I want to have a dozen children."

I become pregnant the middle of March 1971. June—that dreaded third month—comes and goes. God is watching over me because the fourth month and then the fifth month pass. In this school, once a teacher starts showing, she has to stop teaching. I guess they want to protect the students from knowing teachers lead normal lives like everyone else.

I don't want to be in the classroom now anyway. A miracle has happened in my life. I feel life inside me. I know my baby is alive. A woman has to experience that feeling to know how precious life is. I love being home with Nathan and planning for our new baby. I have never been happier in my life.

In the midst of my happiness, Daddy's doctor says the cause of his severe headaches is because he has several pea-sized tumors on his brain where the optic nerves cross. Mama is forced to quit her job to carry him to Columbus, Georgia, for brain surgery. Following surgery, Daddy develops encephalitis, and it is necessary to admit him to a nursing home near their home in Alabama, until he recuperates enough to care for himself at home.

There home is approximately four hours drive from where we live. I don't enjoy going over there and don't go often, especially since Mama reported me to Welfare when I first adopted Nathan. I go about once every two months just out of respect and to see Mark.

Daddy stays in the nursing home about three months before he is able to come home. He is angry with Mama because he believes Mama could have taken care of him at home. He forces her to promise she will never put him in a nursing home again. While he was in the nursing home, she obtained power of attorney, claiming he was legally incompetent.

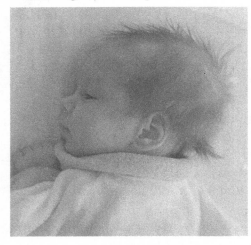

Figure 6.3 Bonnie at birth

"Thank you, my dear precious Lord." On December 6, 1971, I become the proud Mother of a five pound, six ounce little girl. (See Figure 6.3) She is so, so precious to me. It is not a hard decision to make when the doctors ask about breast-feeding.

My decision is a definite, "Yes, I want to breastfeed her."

It makes me feel even more like a woman for today I have overcome the label, "Habitual Abortor."

When Bonnie is five months old (Figure 6.4), she becomes allergic to my milk. She has diarrhea constantly. Her pediatrician makes me keep her off my milk. I have to use a breast pump to relieve my pain and I try feeding her sugar water with a spoon. As the diarrhea slows, I try to breast feed her again on my milk. The diarrhea immediately returns. I call her doctor back and tell him what I did all the while crying on the phone. I am upset with myself for trying my

Figure 6.4 Bonnie at five months

milk without the doctor's permission. Bonnie and I are both upset and she is hungry. She will not suck a bottle. Finally, she gets hungry enough and she learns to suck the bottle.

Mark has called to tell us of wedding plans. He is marrying his high school girlfriend. They want me to be their matron-of-honor. It seems every time I go to my parents' home in Alabama, something bad happens. I am not looking forward to this trip. It proves to be no exception.

Since I love to water ski, and I don't go to visit them often, I ask Mark to take me water skiing on the morning of the wedding. Not wanting to get my hair wet, I assume I can come in by the dock and sit down on top of it the way Mark does. Unfortunately, for me, it doesn't work the way it does for Mark. I come in too fast and my thighs hit the dock. My right leg hits first. In addition, my hair gets wet. The accident damages the muscle in my thigh, and today I still have an indention in my right leg; however, I am thankful the femur was not broken.

For the school year 1972-1973, I decide to go back to work. Noah wants to put all the money we can on the house we purchase ten days before Bonnie is born. With both of us working, we do pay the house off in five years. I also know I will be better to my children if I have them only in the afternoons. I have a wonderful friend with school-age children of her own, who lives about two miles away and who keeps children during the day. She agrees to take care of mine. It will be a different school from the one I taught in before, but I will still be teaching seventh grade math.

I received my certification in elementary education before leaving Statesboro, but I am required to go back periodically to take staff development courses, or be working on a Master's Degree. Soon, the state will require middle school certification of all middle school teachers. So, I begin classes in the evenings through Georgia State University. Sometimes the University offers courses off campus close to my home, but usually I have to drive to the stadium downtown and ride a bus back to the college.

In February of 1973, I see my gynecologist for my annual

checkup. He says, "You need to have a hysterectomy."

When I tell Noah what the doctor said, he says, "No way. You finally had a normal birth. Now I want that dozen babies."

I call the doctor back and tell him my husband wants more children. The doctor explains that, in that case, I will have to have a uterine suspension, because my uterus is receding out through my vagina. We go ahead and schedule surgery for March during spring break. I am grateful Noah did not consent to the hysterectomy.

When I go back to the doctor for my six-week check-up following the uterine suspension surgery, I tell the doctor I think I am pregnant.

He looks at me with his clear, observant eyes and says, "You better not be, because I told you not to have intercourse until after this checkup."

I smile as I say, "You don't understand. I haven't had intercourse since my surgery. I must have been pregnant when you operated."

Neither my doctor nor I knew about my pregnancy. The doctor seems to be upset with me when he says, "I hope the baby will be normal."

I try to encourage Noah to go to Lamaze classes with me because I want to have this baby by natural childbirth. Noah refuses and says, "There is no way I could watch the birth of a baby. The nurses would be taking care of me instead of you, because I would be passed out on the floor."

Now that I have faith in God again, I know he guided the hands of the surgeon as his needles suspended my uterus. *"Thank you, almighty God, for I have felt life inside me again."*

I am growing normally, and my breasts have developed properly, also preparing for the birth of a newborn. In these past two school years, policies have changed about pregnancies. During December, taking my last course on my Master's Degree in Middle Grades, teaching full-time, and having two babies at home is taxing on my energy. I have arranged to have a substitute for the first twenty school days in January because my baby is due January 4. It is a school policy that a teacher can lose her job if she is absent more than twenty days in a row. The last day of school before Christmas holidays is on Friday, December 22.

Bonne's second birthday, December 6, comes and goes quickly. She is precious. I hope I will soon have a little brother to bring home from the hospital for her. Bonnie laughs and says, "Baby," when I allow her to feel the movement in my stomach.

It is the morning of Christmas Eve and I am getting Noah's breakfast before he leaves to go to work. I usually eat breakfast with him; however, I tell him, "I don't think I should eat. My stomach is queasy. I'm also having pains. I think I'm starting labor pains."

Noah seems unconcerned, so I sit down and drink coffee, but I don't eat any food. Then Noah leaves for work.

About two hours later, my pains are worse so I call my doctor. Of course, he is not in on Christmas Eve, so I tell the answering service I think I am in labor. She takes my message and says she will have the doctor call me. Two more hours pass, and my doctor doesn't return the call.

Now I am sure I am having labor pains. I call my doctor's number again and a different person answers the telephone. She asks, "Did you tell them you think you are in labor?"

I feel the pressure and pain in my lower back; however, I don't want to be rude. I answer, "Yes ma'am, I did."

She says, "I will have him call you shortly."

It is an hour before someone returns the call. The doctor tells me to go to the hospital and have the nurse check me. He says the nurse will call him if necessary. I have Bonnie and Nathan to think about too. I call Noah at work and tell him my situation.

He says, "Wait for me to get there and I will take you to the hospital."

Noah is about a forty-minute drive away from home. While I am waiting, I take Bonnie and Nathan over to Mrs. Peck's home. Thank God, she has agreed to care for them until I get back home.

When Noah gets home, I am in so much pain I hardly speak to him. I carry my overnight bag with me to the hospital, assuming they will admit me. When I enter the backdoor of the hospital, I recognize the head nurse, because she is the mother of one of my students.

I breathe a sigh of relief as I beg her, "You aren't going to make me fill out paperwork before you help me, are you?"

Her face lights up in a great big smile as she says, "No, your husband can admit you."

Noah asks her, "Are there any Christmas babies here yet?"

She laughs at him and answers, "No, yours will be the first."

Then, thank God, she whisks me away in a wheelchair. I am happy when I am finally lying on sterile, white sheets. Then I breathe a sigh of relief as I feel my baby is safe. The last few hours have been intimidating.

The nurse comes in to measure me. She leaves and comes in a second time, and then everything happens so quickly, my doctor does not have time to get to the hospital. At the beginning of the pregnancy, I had expressed a wish to Noah to have this baby by natural childbirth. My wish comes true. Hospital documents state my admission to the hospital is 12:05 PM. Allen's birth certificate states he is born at 12:18 PM, thirteen minutes after admission. I am thankful a train was not coming when Noah and I cross the local railroad track. Noah would have been delivering our baby. Allen weighs six pounds, one ounce.

Each of my children holds a special place in my heart. Nathan is the first and Bonnie is the only girl. Allen is special because I helped bring him into the world. The birth of Allen tears loose all the repair work done when I had the uterine suspension. There will be no more babies, and I think my family is complete. I have always wanted three children. My delivery was so easy without anesthesia.

I ask to go home the same day but, of course, they wouldn't let me. I hate missing Christmas with Nathan and Bonnie, but now I have given birth to a second healthy baby, and in time for a tax deduction to boot. I know I cannot breastfeed Allen because I have to go back to teaching the last week in January. What a joy it would have been to celebrate Christmas with "all my children."

Allen and I have been home from the hospital only one week, when Noah starts pressuring me to start taking flying lessons where he works. It is something he wants, so I let him persuade me to begin the lessons. He watches the children on the weekends, while I spend a few hours in training. Rental on airplanes is half-price, since he is an employee at the airport. I begin flying lessons using the Piper Cherokee 140. After several months, I begin flying solo. Before the new school year, 1973-1974 begins; I have earned my pilot's license.

Later, I have another instructor check out my flying skills in a Piper Cub. Those experiences of flying the J-3 Piper Cub over the North Georgia Mountains and riding the mountain switchbacks with Noah on our motorcycles when we were young will never be forgotten. The fall scenery passing by was particularly gorgeous, and we rode until night swooped over the valley below us.

When flying over the Chattahoochee River, I often waved at people in rafts. What a breathtaking view I had of the pastoral countryside God has created, and I am reminded that I am only a tiny speck in this immense universe.

The Cub has to be hand propped, so if I fly alone, I have to ask someone to start my engine for me. I usually fly the Cherokee 140, a much safer airplane. I sing "Top of the World" to the top of my lungs when I am up in the plane alone.

I truly feel close to God as I sing "Top of the World." I had enough faith at that time that God would take care of me. First, my children are at home waiting on me, and I know Noah can't raise them. Second, I feel I need the time away from Noah and the children for introspection. I don't feel guilty, because it is Noah's idea that I fly. Noah said I am his "ultra ego." He says he always wanted to be a pilot.

Wilderness should have been my middle name. I feel at peace and full of serenity when I am sitting or walking beside a stream, hiking up and down mountain trails, listening to the wind whispering through the trees, or observing wildlife, as it reproduces, and protects its young.

I finally have the hysterectomy the doctor tried to persuade me to have before I adopted Nathan. Noah and I decide the best time to have the surgery is the week of spring break during Easter holidays. Mama offers to take care of Allen during my surgery and recovery. With each surgery, the doctor keeps removing the old scar, and pulling the skin back together. With this, being the fifth surgery,

Figure 6.5 Allen at sixteen months

my stomach should be getting tighter and tighter. Allen (Figure 6.5) is looking for Easter eggs.

Every summer we drive to Mansfield, Ohio, to visit Noah's family for our vacation. His parents are good to our children and me. Noah's mother, Marie, always cooks my favorite foods, takes Nathan to play the pinball machines, and buys toys for the other two kids. When we leave to go back home, Marie quietly slips $400 in my hand and tells me to use it on the expenses for the trip. I grow close to Noah's mother, even more so than I am to my own mother.

A big garden keeps me busy, and I use it to help me give the children a sense of responsibility. They are older now and the older two are good at shelling beans and pulling silks off the corn. We make a game out of it. Raising my children brings me so much joy and such a wonderful feeling of fulfillment.

When Nathan is in the first grade, he begins having some

problems. I ask the school psychologist to observe him. The psychologist reports to me, "Nathan has his teacher wrapped around his finger. He misbehaves so she will keep him in at break. Then Nathan will get her undivided attention. He doesn't want to complete the work and go outside, because it is more fun to stay with her than it is to be outside with the other kids."

The psychologist offers suggestions for responsibilities at home, and suggests I try to ensure Nathan gets positive attention from both Noah and me. Noah is a strict disciplinarian; however, and he disagrees with the idea of positive attention. He believes the belt solves all problems. I have sworn to support my husband in his decision about the disciplining of our children, because my parents never agreed, and it was so hard on me. Noah locks the children in their bedroom at 8:00 PM, telling them it is bedtime. It doesn't seem to bother Allen and Nathan too much, because they have each other. However, little Bonnie gets on the floor with her fingers reaching under the door, crying her heart out.

I feel as if it is tearing my guts out and I say to Noah, "It is wrong...what you're doing...letting Bonnie lay on the floor, crying like that."

He glares at me from the top of his eyes, "Stay where you are. You cannot let her out."

It seems forever before the crying ceases and I know Bonnie has tired herself out. I stay where I am a little longer, then I get up and go to Bonnie's door. I ease the door open because she is asleep on the floor behind the door. I kiss the tears, which are still wet on her cheeks as I tuck her in bed.

When Nathan is in second grade, I encourage him to join Cub Scouts. He enjoys scouting. He goes camping with several of the boys and their fathers. I help all I can, but a mother can help only so much. Since I am having a hard time understanding the position Noah has taken concerning Nathan and his behavior, I decide to write Nathan a letter. The following is a copy of the letter I have saved all these years.

Dear Nathan,

Today, on your seventh birthday, my mind wanders back over many years. As a child, I often dreamed of getting married and having children.

Your father and I met when I was a senior in college and he was an airman in the Air Force. We were married after two months of dating. We spent our honeymoon in Ohio, where he was raised, on a big farm at the top of Winding Hill. I met your grandparents for the first time when we were on our honeymoon.

We were not married but three months when I learned I was pregnant. I was so happy and excited. Your father left on a two-month temporary assignment for the Air Force when I was two months pregnant. The joy of my childhood dreams turned to sorrow, while I was being transported to the hospital. The following morning the doctor gave me an operation. I had lost my baby.

The months that followed were sad and lonely. Your father and I were separated for six months, because I took a teaching position away from home. The Georgia State Teacher's Scholarship I used to pay my college tuition required me to teach in Georgia for three years. I was forced to take the only job I could find.

During the following four years, I had three more miscarriages that were similar to the first. Your father was in Viet Nam for a six-month's tour when I had the last one. The Red Cross notified him of my condition; however, he felt obligated to stay there instead of coming home. He didn't realize how sick I was, physically and emotionally. In my heart, I thought I would never again try to have another baby. After your father was notified, he wrote in his next letter, "Be strong."

My letters to him asked him to let us apply to adopt a baby when he returned. He wrote back, "We will talk about it then."

Noah returned home in late January and we made our first visit to the welfare office in March. There were several visits to make and we had to take shots at the welfare department. Mrs. Black, our caseworker, had to make visits to our home. She asked about our backgrounds, our hobbies, our jobs, our religious preferences, and other questions. One question was,

"Does the sex matter?"

We told her, "Yes, we want a boy."

Late one afternoon in October, she called and said she had a two-month old baby boy she wants us to see. We were so excited. I could hardly sleep that night.

I was up before the alarm clock rang. I awoke your father and we left on a long drive. On arrival at the town where the baby boy was staying, we checked into a local motel and called the welfare office. The baby's caseworker said it would take her about an hour before she could get to our motel. That hour seemed like ten. Your father and I were so nervous, knowing we were about to become a mother and father for the first time.

Finally, the caseworker arrived with a little bundle in her arms. That little bundle was you, Nathan. She introduced us to you and told us to keep you for at least two hours while we made the decision between ourselves whether we would accept you. I knew from the moment I saw you, we would accept you. My childhood dream to have children would soon come true. While I changed your diaper, you looked so petite. You were crying and I tried to give you a bottle; however, you continued to cry. As I held you close to me and showed you security and love, you stopped crying. After two hours, we carried you to the welfare office and signed all the necessary papers to make you ours.

The trip home was hard for all of us. We were not accustomed to driving with a crying baby in the car. We stopped to get dinner after several miles. I fed you and you gave up and went to sleep. On arrival at your new home, neighbors came to see our new baby. They all knew how badly we wanted children.

I resigned from my job as a schoolteacher to stay home and take care of you. Your father left the following day to go off on a temporary assignment with the Air Force. Friends and relatives came for miles around to see you. Irene, the military wife who had four children of her own, loved you dearly. She came every day to check on you. If you were not awake, she would stand by your bed and talk loud enough to wake you. I lost ten pounds the first week I had you because I did not have time to eat for trying to take care of you and see all the visitors who came to see you.

When you were two years old, your father decided to leave

the military. He said, "I am a family man now."

Because of you, I risked one more time trying to carry a baby. I was successful and that baby is your little sister Bonnie. Two years later...well, you know what happened then. If I had not adopted you, I would not have had the courage to try another pregnancy again.

Not long ago, you became depressed because I scolded you. You said, "Nobody loves me."

I took out the scrapbook and showed you the many pictures we had taken of you. You saw yourself playing in a little blue bathtub; you saw me feeding you; and you saw your grandparents loving you. You saw your first Christmas pictures; you saw yourself wearing your Daddy's military shoes and hat, and you saw many more pictures. It took only a few moments for you to change your mind about being loved.

Your blue eyes were sparkling when you said, "You do love me, don't you?"

Oh, Nathan, I love you so much.

I am sure there will be more times when you get depressed; maybe even after you are a grown man. If you should get depressed, get out this letter and read it. You will remember there are many people who care about you, especially your mother.

Love,
Mama

School starts back and before I know it the holidays are on me. I am so excited. I can hardly wait. Allen is two years old now, Bonnie is four, and Nathan was seven in August (See Figure 6.6). It is hard to believe he has been with us for seven years now. He and my other two bring me so much joy.

During the summer, after Nathan completes the second grade, Noah forces Nathan to begin a business of mowing yards. He makes him write on three by five cards, "Have Mower, Will Travel" with his name and telephone number. Nathan has to complete fifty of them and pass them out to neighbors. Noah buys the lawn mower. Nathan is not tall enough to see over the handlebars, so he looks below the top part. As Nathan earns money, Noah takes it all but $1.00. He applies this toward the cost of the mower.

Noah's discipline gets worse. If Nathan does not move immediately when Noah speaks to him, or if any of the children utters a word back to him, Noah sees it as cause for physical punishment. In my opinion, Noah abuses all three children physically and emotionally—Nathan more physically than the other two. If Nathan doesn't have enough lawn mowing jobs lined up, Noah forces him to go out and ask his customers if they have other odd jobs

Figure 6.6 Christmas

for him. If he is unsuccessful in that endeavor, Noah makes him make up more cards and pass them out to new people. I give Nathan as much positive attention as I can. Nathan continually asks me why his biological Mama and Daddy threw him away.

Nathan continues to be a discipline problem at home and at school. Noah tells me, in Nathan's presence, to take him back to the welfare department. Noah says he does not want a kid as terrible as Nathan out on the streets carrying his name. Of all the emotional abuse Noah has inflicted on our children, I know this is the worst. I know it will be hard for Nathan to get over the words Noah has just said.

The school suggests we take Nathan to a psychologist for testing. I make the appointment and afterwards, the psychologist tells me Nathan needs individual therapy. I contact an adolescent psychologist recommended to me. Even though Nathan is only eight years old, this doctor agrees to accept him.

On some of Nathan's therapy sessions, I wait for him in the

conference room, and sometime I see the therapist alone. I try to be as honest as possible in talking about our family dynamics. I want to help Bonnie and Allen too.

The weatherman announces gusting winds and a low of nineteen degrees temperature this morning. The high is expected to reach the mid-thirties. That night the temperature dropped down into the low teens. Our bedroom is above the outside door leading into the basement. The basement door beating against the house back and forth repeatedly wakes Noah and me during the night. Noah wants to know who left the door unlatched and I tell him I have no idea.

After breakfast the following morning, Noah asks the children who was in the basement yesterday.

Bonnie answers, "Allen and I played in there."

Bonnie is wearing only her panties; however, Noah opens the door to the concrete patio and pushes her outside. As he closes the door, he says, "Now maybe you will remember to close the basement door the next time you go in there."

Bonnie wraps her arms around her bare chest and begins crying. Noah leaves her outside in the weather that is still hovering in the teens for at least ten minutes.

Another cruel punishment I discussed with the psychologist involved Allen. He disappeared and we couldn't find him. Sometimes he sneaks over to our neighbor's house. Mrs. Peck always gives my kids an apple or a cold biscuit when they come to her house. All three of my children love going to Mrs. Peck's house. It reminds me of how I felt as a child about going to the Michaels' house. After finding Allen at Mrs. Peck's house, I delay a few moments to visit with Mrs. Peck. Noah arrives and takes Allen from my arms. Right there before Mrs. Peck, Noah pulls down Allen's pants and spanks him hard on his bare butt. Then Noah took Allen and left.

After Noah left, Mrs. Peck begins crying, because she loves my children. She tells me, "Sarah, he ought not to whip those children like that."

NOTE: Later, after Noah and I were divorced, I continued to visit with Mrs. Peck. She cried each time I visited her. She always mentioned how cruel Noah was to our children. Finally, I stopped visiting her, because my visits were reminding her of Noah whipping our children. She died a short time after I stopped visiting in her home.

Nathan has probably had six sessions with his psychologist alone when the doctor requests that his clerk schedule extra time with the next visit for him to discuss Nathan's progress with me. At this visit the psychologist explains the depth of Nathan's intelligence. The psychologist informs me of several comments made by Nathan:

➤ "Since no money was paid for me, that means I'm no good."
➤ "Nobody gives anything away that has any value."
➤ "My mother gave me away, therefore, I am useless."
➤ "Mama has promised to help me find my biological parents when I reach eighteen. I intend to show them how rotten I've become, because they threw me away."

I leave the psychologist's office and go to my car. I hug the steering wheel with my arms and lean my head on my arms. Then the tears come—tears I have kept inside for too long. When they start, I can't stop them. I have a horrible feeling in the pit of my stomach that I have failed my child. So many issues too painful to face…. Where is the line between when it is right to support your husband's decisions, and when to intervene when you think he has crossed the line into abuse?

"Dear Heavenly Father, I come to you one more time. Please help me to help this special, needy child of mine. And, please give Noah a more understanding heart where our children are concerned. Amen."

When Nathan reaches the sixth grade, I ask for a transfer to the county middle school that Nathan will attend. The middle school in our town has an awful reputation. By now, I have become a strong teacher and a firm disciplinarian. I believe I can help make some changes for the better in this school. I want this school to be the best in the county, since all of my children will be enrolled here. Fortunately for me, the county office hires a strong principal to take over this school the same year I begin teaching here.

The entire county is growing fast, but especially right here in our town. Allen is starting first grade, Bonnie is in the third grade, and Nathan is in the sixth. The elementary school is so overcrowded the county decides to move the first graders to the middle school building. Both Nathan and Allen are in my school. I never see either of my boys, but I know Nathan is assigned to two of the best teachers in the school.

After my brother Mark married, he and his wife Sunny move to Georgia. Then my parents sell their home on the lake and buy a small home in middle Georgia, which is closer to all of their children. I still live north of Atlanta, and I never see much of the family except at Christmas.

Daddy does well for several years; however, he grows steadily less able to care for his personal hygiene. His brain tumor has returned and the doctor will not operate again. Even though Mama promised not to put him back in a nursing home, the time comes when she can no longer care for him at home.

Two years pass quickly now since all my children are in school. Nathan is in eighth grade now. With me being the only eighth grade math teacher, and math being Nathan's worst subject, it makes it hard on both of us. His disrespectful behavior and my unexplained loss of eyesight toward the end of this school year are taking a toll on my nerves.

Before school opens this year, I have my annual eye exam. In December, I schedule an appointment with my gynecologist who prescribes prednisone for the pain I am having in my lower right side. He says it is caused from the scar tissue left because of my numerous surgeries. From January to March, my vision grows noticeably worse day by day until I can no longer read the numbers in my Mathematics book.

I schedule another appointment with my ophthalmologist. I complain to him of going blind overnight. He dilates my eyes in order to see down into the lens well. He says, "Well, those tiny cataracts you had last fall have almost covered the lens now."

"What? You didn't tell me about any cataracts. I wouldn't forget something like that. Only old people get cataracts." I cry hysterically, right there in front of him.

He said, "What have you done differently? Any new drugs?"

"Yes, I just finished two rounds of prednisone."

"Well, prednisone intensifies the growth of cataracts."

"See there, do you think I would have taken it if you had told me I had cataracts?

He insists he told me and that I just didn't know to tell the gynecologist.

When I leave the doctor's office that day, I am extremely upset. Both my eyes are dilated and already I can't see because of the cataracts, but now to make it even worse, I am crying like a baby. I am so young—only thirty-eight years old. The doctor said he told me about the cataracts last fall, but he *did not*. How could anyone forget something that serious? I see only through a blur and I feel myself going away.

Kristen is the alter who plays the least role in Sarah's life; however, she always comes when Sarah or Susie is in life-threatening situations or other crises. She tries her best to keep them safe. Kristen takes control of the car now because she fears Sarah will have a wreck. She safely drives the car through Atlanta's congested traffic and doesn't let Sarah take back control of the body until they are safely back at home.

I have enough sick days accumulated to take off the rest of the school year, six weeks. I apply for long-term disability, and find a substitute to complete my school year, since I cannot even see the numbers in the math book.

I find an ophthalmologist who is retired military. The date for surgery is set and it is my last day of school for the year. Nathan is in my class and he is misbehaving. He is seated three rows from me. I know how important it is for Nathan to learn math. I want so much for him to understand the principles of math and I know this is my last opportunity to teach him so I move him up to the first row. Nathan continues to talk and turn around in his seat. With my anxiety, I reach and slap him across the face. Immediately, I am sorry, and I know I have made a mistake, but it is too late.

Other children cry out, "Sue your Mama, Nathan. Sue her."

I have always been teased about having four eyes since I wear glasses. I wanted to wear contacts when I could afford them. Doctors tried to fit me for contacts, and they tell me the shape of my eye is too steep and will not allow for fitted contacts. My eye surgeon says I should be able to wear the extended-wear lens, since they are much larger around than the average contacts.

At this point in medical history, the oldest implant in anyone's eye is twenty years old. I am only thirty-eight; therefore, the doctor removes the entire lens and fits me with an extended-wear lens. Cataract membranes are growing back at a rate faster than normal because of my younger age. The only YAG laser used for removing cataract membrane is located in Baltimore, Maryland. Noah and I fly there and have the YAG laser used on my eye and fly back the same day.

Adding to my stress, the following day on March 20, Mama calls to tell me Daddy has not been doing well. Mama never calls because of the cost of long-distance phone rates. I fear Daddy is dead and she doesn't want to tell me over the phone.

Over the past few years, when I've gone to visit my parents, Noah has insisted he and the children stay home. His excuse is, "Your father is sick and you can enjoy your visit better if me and the children are not along."

It takes days to get our lives back to normal after I return, because of Noah's physical and emotional treatment of our children while I am gone. I had hoped, possibly, Noah might go with me this time, but he doesn't.

The next morning everyone has gone from Daddy's room except me. It hasn't been long since the nurses have picked up

Daddy's untouched breakfast tray. Adam left to buy some breakfast for himself. Other members of the family are in the waiting room having coffee. We all fear this will be Daddy's last day. I hold his hand as I gaze into his little blue eyes. Each blood pressure reading is lower than the last. I don't handle death well. Daddy is no longer able to speak; however, I feel he is trying to communicate with me with his eyes. I believe he is asking for forgiveness as he squeezes my hand.

I lean down toward him and say, "Daddy, I forgive you." Then he takes his last breath. I leave the room crying and I tell the family I don't understand how the soul leaves the body. Auntie's dying while I was in her room comes to my mind. I was only seven years old then. Death is so strange to me. Daddy died March 21, 1981, at 9:57 AM.

Accepting Daddy's death was hard for me, and it was years before I overcame it. I had so many immediate problems with Nathan and with my own health that I grieved much longer than I should have. And, I had no time to deal with the dreams his death triggered—dreams of the little child who was molested by her father. On waking, I rushed to the bathroom and splashed cold water on my face. Then I pushed the memory back down into my subconscious and would forget it until the next dream came about the little girl who, all her life, had a love-hate relationship with her father. Now that he has died, a storm is brewing in her inner life.

That storm is brewing all kinds of emotions. It is playing havoc on my life and those around me. I've almost gone blind at age thirty-eight. I'm home alone all day as I have the rest of the school year off (April and May) because of my eyes, and now my childhood perpetrator and father is dead. I turn to alcohol to cope.

Two months pass before the surgeon operates again to remove more of the membranes. At the same time, my eyelid is inflamed from the contact.

In high school, Nathan's problems with Black students get worse. When the Black students flirt with White girls, it makes Nathan angry. I try to tell him it is possible the White girls might be flirting with the Black boys first. At any rate, it is none of his business.

Nathan is the shortest boy in the school; but, at the same time, he can run faster than almost anyone can in his school. Students tease him by calling him, "Shrimp."

Bonnie, on the other hand, is exactly the opposite. She has her homework completed precisely as the teacher requests. She is a perfectionist; she is in the gifted program at school; and she makes straight A's. She craves her daddy's praise. One day she shows him her excellent report card, expecting him to congratulate her. Instead, his comment breaks her heart.

In a cold, sarcastic voice, he said, "Well, you ought to have perfect grades. You never help your mama with anything around here. All you ever do is schoolwork."

I believe Noah enjoys inflicting pain on others. I think much of the emotional pain he causes Bonnie, he does because he never forgave me for the affair I had while he was in Viet Nam. She wasn't even born then, so she doesn't understand why he is so mean to her.

The greatest goal I had set for my life was to be a good mother, but, in spite of all my good intentions, I see the problems in my children and I know I didn't protect them. I failed to be a perfect mother. My life is closing in on me. My nerves are getting worse. Horror of all horrors...I am losing blocks of time when I don't know what happened during that time. Sometimes I bring groceries home and I don't even remember buying them. What if something happened to one of my children during one of those blocks of time? Dear God, this stress is killing me.

In the summer of the following year, I undergo surgery on my left eye. I use the same ophthalmologist who did my previous eye surgery. He implants the plastic lens inside this eye, because the right eye is still giving me problems wearing an extended-wear lens. About three months passes and he suggests I have the YAG laser used on this eye also. Fortunately, we have one in Atlanta now. Before the end of another school year, I have surgery for a secondary implant on my right eye.

NOTE: Today, I am thankful modern medicine has made it possible for me to see, even though my eyesight is not perfect.

Bonnie stays after school with me to practice drums. I am extremely proud of her as she is one of the best drummers in the middle school band this year, and the two years that follow. Her academic teachers always have wonderful things to say about her. Because the school is so large, teachers never realize Nathan and Bonnie are both my children, thus teachers are not making comparisons between them and for that, I am thankful.

Allen stays busy with his scout work. I take him to his meetings in the evening. A scout's parent bakes a cake to sell at every meeting to make money for the organization to have for campouts and other needed supplies. Funds from the sale of cakes are minimal, because no one will take responsibility for the sale of the cakes. I volunteer to be in charge of getting parents and other volunteers to make the cakes and finding creative ways to sell them. I decide to sell chances. Since many of the parents know me through the school, I can persuade them to buy many chances. Everyone begins calling me "The Cake Lady."

Sometimes I bring a group of the scouts to our house to help them with a project for their scout book. It is rewarding to work with the younger boys and occasionally have a break from the middle school kids. Allen has a great personality. All his friends like him, because he is willing to help others when they need him. Mothers cannot go on the camping trips, but I help his scout group in other ways like the cake sale.

Nathan's lawn mowing business has grown. He has now paid for his mower so he starts a savings account. It grows fast. He uses some of his money for brand name tennis shoes and clothes, so he can be well dressed like the other students.

Nathan is always in trouble at school. As a teacher, I have seen many children with discipline problems. Previously, I have always thought, if the parents would address the problem at home, we would not have as much trouble with the child at school. Nathan changed my belief on that issue. I have done my best at home with Nathan, and he still causes trouble at school. One time he shows a friend the switchblade he carried to school. The friend waves the switchblade around before others, because he knows Nathan will get in trouble.

The teacher takes the knife and asks, "Whose knife is this?"

The student says, "Nathan's."

Nathan is suspended for the rest of the school year, but the principal allows him to return during the post planning days to take his finals.

School year 1983-1984 begins and I am ready to get out of the house. I have overworked myself this summer in the garden and freezing and canning vegetables for the winter months. I enlist the children's help in pulling weeds, hoeing the garden, snapping the beans, and washing the vegetables. It keeps them busy and helps me too. Nathan is a junior in high school; Bonnie is in the eighth grade; and Allen is in the sixth grade. Now I have two sets of school activities and not three to keep track of. This helps me.

Bonnie starts dance when she is in the sixth grade. This year she takes four classes, but is not allowed to start Pointe because of weak ankles—a genetic trait that runs in my family. The instructor is afraid the extra stress will damage her feet. Bonnie is upset and many nights she cries because of her instructor's decision.

Finally, I go to see a therapist for my nerves. I talk to him about Bonnie, and he suggests I allow her to get involved in outside activities that take her out of the home, and away from her father as much as possible. The more Bonnie is around her father, the more stressed she becomes.

Bonnie is now continuing her drums with the middle school band, and taking four dance classes. The dance instructor asks her to perform in the company, which is the final dance of the recital.

Allen begins strings when he starts in the middle school. He plays the violin and does a beautiful job. At the December PTA meeting, the orchestra and the band both perform. Any mother would think so, but I believe my children are a great contributing reason the orchestra and the band both sound so well. Noah never goes to watch our children perform. I cannot understand why any parent would miss seeing their children perform.

I give Allen less attention than the other two. He appears to never want or need any. If he cannot help himself, he simply does without. He is a stable child. He plays alone and finds ways to entertain himself both inside and outside. He also entertains his friends when he has company without needing me to find entertainment for them.

Bonnie, on the other hand, worries about what the other children at school think of her, and she strives for perfection in everything she attempts. She needs approval after a task or job is completed. She enjoys being a helper.

Everything was going smoothly for Nathan during his junior year until the second week of December when I receive a call from the principal. He says, "Nathan will be going home until after Christmas."

"What?" I ask. Whatever the reason, I know I cannot leave Nathan roaming the streets alone until I get out of school for the holidays.

NOTE: The decision I make is a bad mistake, but I decide never to let Nathan go back to that high school again.

The principal knows me well by now and offers to keep him until I can finish my school day. There is a county close by, which does not have any Blacks. Nathan has wanted to live there for a long time. Since he and his dad have never gotten along, and Noah will not help me with any of Nathan's problems, I see no alternative but to let Nathan move to that county and go to school there. I locate a family willing to accept Nathan, and I sign temporary guardianship over to them. I think perhaps our marriage will get better if Nathan is not living with us.

The only transportation Nathan has is a motorcycle. The county, being farther north, has a great deal of ice and snow on the ground in the winter. I worry about his having an accident on the road.

Noah's mother, Marie, knows the problems I have with Nathan. She allows me to call her collect from the school when I feel I need to talk. I just can't hold all my anger in any longer. She knows Noah doesn't help me with the problems concerning Nathan. After I find Nathan a car, she sends me money to buy it. Nathan hasn't had the car long when, on a trip home to visit, I suspect something is terribly wrong. Nathan isn't talking right. His speech is slurred and his eyes are bloodshot.

After Nathan is gone, I begin making telephone calls, first to the school. Most of his teachers report he is in class daily, but is sleeping in class, almost every day. I call the restaurant where Nathan works. His supervisor tells me Nathan and several other employees have gone on a vacation to Florida and will not be back for a week. From all the information I learn, I fear Nathan is on drugs.

I check with a local rehabilitation hospital to see if they will admit him. They tell me it will be about two weeks before a slot is available. When I finally get Nathan admitted into the hospital, he is rebellious and uncooperative. I lie to Nathan to get him home so I can take him. I tell him he has an orthodontist appointment. The lie and then wondering if I am right about him being on drugs make me so shameful. I cry everyday at school after admitting him. My teaching goes to hell for awhile. Bonnie is in my Algebra class at this time. The hospital helps Nathan with his high school credits; however, he still fails eleventh grade English.

Once a week we attend family counseling. It appears Nathan is angry with me. He makes nasty comments to me, telling me I have no modesty.

He is hunched over hugging himself, but he looks up to stare at me. His eyes glow with a savage inner fire as he spews out the words at me. "Every time I walk down the hall, the bathroom door is open, and there you are sitting on the toilet, peeing. Why don't you close the door when you go to the bathroom?"

NOTE: I understand now why I didn't; we were never allowed any privacy as children.

Nathan's words hurt so much that I begin to wonder whether I have made the wrong decision in placing him there, not because he has hurt me, but because he isn't focusing on his problems.

Before Nathan gets out, he learns the system. If he does what they want him to do, he will start getting privileges. Therefore, that is what he does. Nathan is in the hospital for six weeks.

Nathan is out now, and I am worried again. If he wants to graduate from high school on time, he has to drive to a county school offering summer classes to get his eleventh grade English. On the first day, he meets his new cocaine friend. Two days out of the hospital and he is back on drugs. He drives to another school closer to our home for his senior year. The same cocaine friend goes to this new high school. Nathan graduates on time; however, he is only seventeen.

While Nathan is in summer school, Noah receives a telephone call from his dad, who explains his mother has had diabetes for a long time. Since she neither took care of herself nor ate properly, she is deathly sick, and the doctor has placed her on complete bed rest. Noah's dad wants him to come visit his mother, and see her condition for himself.

While Noah is visiting his mother, he calls me. Marie asks him to let her talk to me. After speaking into the phone, she starts crying. I can hardly believe my ears when, this woman who has always been gentle and soft-spoken in my presence, becomes so upset she is almost screaming into the phone.

"Sarah, John and Noah aren't taking care of me," Marie cries. "They ignore me when I call. They refuse to give me anything I ask for. I know you are busy, and I wouldn't ask this if I weren't so sick. Please, Sarah, I need you to come up here."

She continues to cry into the phone.

Noah takes the phone away from his mother and tells me, "No, you cannot come up here. We are doing everything for her that she needs. Your place is there with the children."

"But Noah," I tell him, "she wants me. Won't you drive to the Columbus Airport and pick me up? I have friends who have offered to keep the children while I am gone."

"No," he says, and he hangs up the phone.

If I weren't so afraid of getting lost—one of my major fears— and so afraid of Noah, I probably would go anyway. I had just had knee surgery though and it was swollen twice the normal size. I think I had caught staff infection in it, but I still wanted to go.

NOTE: I later told several people about this incident, and they all asked why I didn't go anyway. I never forgave Noah for not agreeing to meet me at the airport so I could see Marie once more. I never saw her again.

Marie gets a little better, and then gets worse again, which is typical of a Type B diabetic who has never taken care of themselves. I receive two telephone calls from Marie before she dies. During each call, she begins crying as she tells me Noah's dad is mistreating her.

The Christmas break has ended and school has reopened when Noah gets the call from his dad telling him his mother has died. Because school is back in session, Noah refuses to let the children attend their grandmother's funeral. I am hurt and angry, for myself and for my children. She called out to me for help, and I didn't help her. Now I am forbidden to even attend her funeral. I hated Noah for not letting me attend Marie's funeral, but I hated him even more for not letting me go to her when she asked me to come when she was still alive.

I loved Marie even more than I loved my own Mama. She was a gracious woman and I learned much from her. She helped me financially; and she loved me like a daughter. I didn't know when my marriage to her son Noah would end, but now I knew for sure it wouldn't last.

I know I need to increase my salary as much as possible, since retirement is based on the last two years of annual salary. The only way I know to raise my salary is to obtain a higher degree, so I begin work on my Doctorate in Administration and Supervision at the University of Georgia.

My statistics course is so involved and time consuming that, when it ends, I know I have not understood it well enough to do the dissertation for my doctorate. My self-esteem is so low, I am not even sure I want to be a principal. However, my course is set and I drive myself, loosing all track of time, using coffee to keep me awake so I can study late into the night.

I complete all my course work for the doctorate but after talking to my counselor, I settle for a Specialist in Education for Middle Grades and a Specialist in Administration and Supervision. I breathe a sigh of relief as I am glad the stress of studying for school work is gone. However, I feel rewarded too. I accomplished my goal and it will show in my paycheck…and the final reward— in my retirement funds.

Nathan has a full-time job now at the same local burger facility where he has worked since he was fourteen years old. He works late hours and does not come straight home. Our home has only three bedrooms. He and Allen have to share a bedroom. Allen never complains, but I know it is interfering with his sleep because Nathan gets on the phone in their bedroom and talks loudly to his friends. Sometimes Nathan's loud voice on the phone even awakens me.

Bonnie is still in the gifted program at school. When she starts high school, she stops dance classes and band. When I ask why, she tells me it is because she won't have time to continue those activities and complete all the schoolwork she will have assigned from five classes.

I remember Bonnie saying the other girls were better than she was in dance class. It is possible they are better than Bonnie because they have been in dance since they were three years old. In my opinion, Bonnie has done great in her three years of dance classes.

Allen is growing fast. He is taller than anyone in middle school. I can look down the hall and spot his head above all the other middle school students. When time comes for Allen to enter eighth grade, I don't tell the administration Allen is my child, because they will avoid scheduling him for my team.

I have to teach Nathan math because our school has only one team of eighth grade teachers. When Bonnie reaches eighth grade, I am the only algebra teacher. Now there are two teams of eighth grade teachers. The other two children have not presented problems being in my class. My team has the best set of teachers, especially the language arts and math. Allen is randomly chosen for my team. Now I have taught all three of my children their eighth grade math.

Three months after Nathan graduates, he turns eighteen. Noah tells me we are no longer responsible for him.

He says, "Let's go pick out an apartment close to where he works, pay his first month's rent and tell him he has to move."

I tell myself I have no choice in the matter, and I go with Noah and we choose an apartment for Nathan. My worst nightmare comes true when I learn Nathan's drug habit has skyrocketed. He not only spends his entire check on his drug habit, but he pushes enough drugs to support the rest of what he needs. Unknown to us, Nathan is transported to the emergency room several times over the next few months. Deep down, I feared Nathan was suicidal long before he ever left home. Noah had previously removed the clips from all the guns and locked them in a small pistol cabinet.

A cold wind is whipping against the house one evening when Nathan comes to visit. He is wearing a long heavy coat. I don't think it is unusual for him to be wearing the coat because of the weather. I tell him to come in; I have to go to the kitchen a moment to take something off the stove. When I return I want to hold Nathan in my arms—the Nathan that was my little child before he got so hurt and so messed up on drugs. I wonder how much of Nathan's problems are Noah's fault. And how much of his problems are my fault for not intervening? I shut my eyes while my children were being abused the same as my mother did. Oh God, I did the same thing my mother did, didn't I?

Nathan looks terrible. His hair is long, and his face is clammy and devoid of all color. I am sick with worry, but I believe there is nothing else I can do for him now. I have spent much time in prayer; however, I think it is now up to Nathan.

NOTE: I am unaware that while I was in the kitchen Nathan took his daddy's 57 Magnum, a box of bullets, and hid them under his coat.

Nathan leaves and about thirty minutes later, he returns. He and I are alone when he shows me the gun. He tells me he does not know how to single load from the chamber.

I am too emotion-filled to speak as I hug Nathan. I feel as if this may be the opportunity I have been praying for. Finally, I am able to get words out. "Nathan, please sit down and talk."

Nathan sits down with me at our kitchen table and he tells me he is dying, and he wants help. He says, "I want to go back to the hospital on the adult unit. I want to admit myself."

I cannot stop the tears that are blinding my eyes and choking my voice. I am overjoyed at his decision. I tell him, "Nathan, I am so proud of you for deciding to go back into rehab. You don't know how much I love you. I want you to live. Tell me how I can help, Nathan, and I will."

Nathan stays in the hospital four weeks, including Christmas. While inpatient, he tells me, "Mom, I would never have had the nerve to admit myself if it had not been for the stay while I was in high school. I would have been too afraid."

NOTE: Nathan's admission picture stayed on his dresser for several years. He wanted it to remind him of how bad his life had become. He never touched crack or cocaine again.

I keep the promise I had made to him when he was nine years old. I had promised that, when he reached eighteen years old I would help him find his biological parents. As soon as he is released from the hospital, I hire a lawyer to open his case.

The lawyer informs us how it will work. The state will call his biological mother to see whether she is willing to meet her son. If she is receptive, the state obtains her personal information, telephone number, and address and gives it to Nathan. Then Nathan calls her to introduce himself.

When Nathan tells us he has received the call informing him his biological mother wants to see him, I watch the changing expressions on his face. I know he must be feeling a gamut of emotions. He looks at me with his intelligent blue eyes, which are now flashing with spirit, as well as uncertainty. I have never loved him more.

Nathan calls her to introduce himself and is astonished to learn that she lives only four miles from his apartment. He couldn't believe it—only four miles. His mother becomes so excited she starts crying. They arrange a time to meet.

She tells him, "After you were born, I married, but I never had other children."

I loan Nathan his baby book to share with his biological mother for several weeks. At the meeting with his mother, Nathan inquired about his father; however, his mother would only tell him, "You don't need to know. He was a sorry man."

NOTE: She and Nathan stayed friends up until three years ago. Nathan is a true friend with his sister. I don't know if they will get together again or not. He lets me know I am his "real mother." He calls me often and writes messages in his own handwriting in my birthday and Mother's Day cards.

I thank God I still have him when my thoughts wander back to the day he stole Noah's 57 Magnum. Nathan is still cocaine free today, has fourteen years in Alcoholics Anonymous, joined the Marines at age thirty-two, has been to

Iraq and back safely, and intends to make the Marines a career. What more could a mother ask for?

Allen begins playing basketball in high school. His height is an advantage. Many of the other boys' parents let them play little league sports; however, Allen has not had as much sports training as the others. He enjoys the practices and friendship with the other boys even though he sits on the bench through most of the games.

I feel as if our family counseling is intensifying the pressure on me because Noah and I later quarrel about what transpired during therapy. Family counseling does not seem to be helping our marriage. Noah continually tells me we cannot divorce because we were married in the Catholic Church. He says, if we divorce, neither of us can ever marry again. I feel the anger building in me because, if he believes in the Catholic Church so much, then why didn't he help me raise the children in the church as he promised before our wedding? I had to get another Catholic couple to assist in Bonnie and Allen's baptism, because Noah wouldn't fulfill his responsibility. They were ages two and four before I had them baptized. The priest had told me I should not wait any longer. He said I should go ahead and do it by myself.

One of the teachers where I work tells me about her trip to Medjugorie, Yugoslavia. She has recently returned. She says I will get all my answers about my problems related to my marriage if I can afford to take this trip. When I go to a travel agent to inquire, the only trip available during the summer following the school year ending 1989 has the Rome extension. I sign up for this trip, and purchase the ticket.

This trip gives me the opportunity to have many hours of internal communication. It is wonderful to have time to be away from the tensions of home; where I feel Noah is constantly watching every move I make. I have time to pray and to listen to what God may want me to hear. I have decisions to make and the decisions will affect not only me, but the lives of my children too. I pray for the Lord to guide me. I expect to hear all my answers distinctly while away on this trip.

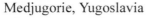

Medjugorie, Yugoslavia   Sarah with friend

Figure 6.7

The church in Figure 6.7 has priests, speaking ten different languages hearing confessions, around it day and night. The five teenagers hear the Blessed Mother of Jesus, Mary, speak to them daily on Apparition Hill. My friend and I are on the path leaving our guest home on the way up to Apparition Hill in the picture on the right. (See Figure 6.7)

We leave Yugoslavia by boat, cross the Adriatic Sea, and go by bus up the west coast of Italy. We stop in Bari and visit the home of Father Padre Pio, the priest whose hands bleed like Jesus' hands. From there, our bus travels into Rome where we spend three days and nights. Our group gathers in Vatican City to say the

Figure 6.8 Vatican in Rome, Italy

Rosary together and meditate until 10:30 PM when Pope John Paul's light goes out the same time each night. His bedroom is on the top floor, the third room from the right end. (Fig. 6.8) We visit the Sistine Chapel and the Holy Stairs. We have to go up the stairs on our knees as we are told it is Jesus' blood on the stairs.

The last day we are invited to hear Pope John Paul II speak. I am one of the fortunate ones in my group who is close enough to shake his hand as he exits the building. (Figure 6.9)

Unfortunately, the trip does not provide me all the answers to my marital problems as I had hoped. When I return from my trip to Medjugorie, Noah refused to talk to me. He gives me the silent treatment.

Figure 6.9 Pope John Paul II

In a therapy session, when I am there alone, I tell the counselor, "I love Noah, and he loves me."

The counselor screams at me, "Love, love, love! What you two do to one another is not love."

The session ends shortly after because I don't know what to say after that. I feel so hurt, confused, and brokenhearted.

A member of the church wants Bonnie to live with her to finish her last year of school. I find myself considering that option to allow Bonnie relief from the tension in our house, when all at once I recall, *this is exactly what I did with Nathan. Don't make the same mistake with Bonnie.*

I am chronically depressed (See Figure 6.10) and I lose more weight daily. I realize something is wrong when I am willing to let my children leave home to make it possible for me to live with Noah. I pray long and hard, and I decide it is time for me to leave. Noah has scared me into staying long enough. I thought he could not survive without me. I thought I could not survive without him.

Figure 6.10 Depression

Perhaps the counselor's remarks are correct after all. Maybe what Noah and I have isn't love.

I am out of town visiting Mama, who is in the hospital, when I get a telephone call from Bonnie. I hear a tremor in her voice when she says, "Mama, I won't be here when you get back. I'm leaving. If you're not going to leave Daddy, I will leave by myself."

I ask Bonnie not to leave until I get home. She knows it will take me two hours to get home. I stay at least two more hours crying, and talking with my brother Mark, seeking his advice.

I ask questions like, "Who will light my furnace in the winter? Who will maintain my car? How will I know when it is time to buy tires?"

On my two-hour drive back home, my mind was in turmoil. I dreaded facing Noah, and I dreaded facing Bonnie, who expected me home two hours ago. I knew I had procrastinated as long as I could; it was time to file for divorce. Pieces of our lives came to filter through my mind.

Coming home late from mass one evening, Noah questioned my tardiness, "Where have you been?"

"I stayed a while to talk to Father Chris. I love him so much."

Noah used this statement against me in our divorce. He indicated Father Chris and I may have had sexual intercourse with each other.

Noah expects me to have his supper on the table at 4:30 PM when he comes in from work. The children and I arrive home from school at 3:30. One afternoon my best friend stops by for a visit soon after the children and I get home from school. This friend is my children's Godmother and her husband is their Godfather. She doesn't visit often, and I don't want to start cooking while she is visiting.

When Noah comes through the door, he says in a grudging tone, "Where is my supper?"

My friend stands up quickly, "Oh Sarah, I'm sorry; I forgot you eat supper early. Why didn't you tell me?"

NOTE: My friend left and she *never* came to my house again. When we met, it was either at her house or at church.

Noah would occasionally get off work early, come to my school, and follow me around. I believe he never forgave me for my infidelity while he was in Viet Nam. Telling him was the worst mistake of my life. A priest once told me at a confession that a lie is better than the truth if the truth will hurt someone. I have thought of the priest's advice many times since that day.

Noah knows I am about to file for a divorce and he gets the divorce filed first. The last night we stay together, I have been drinking too much and that gives me the courage to talk to him. "Noah, you have lost Nathan and Bonnie's love, but maybe you haven't yet lost Allen's love. If you start now treating him differently, he may learn to love you."

Noah appears to be in a pensive mood as he says, "I have no complaints about you as a mother. I wish you had taught me how to love the children like you have."

With tears flowing down my face, all I can utter is, "I tried."

NOTE: Before Noah and I married, I had not told him of the emotional, physical, and sexual abuse I encountered as a child. He used the fact that I had not told him as grounds to get our marriage annulled, even though it was twenty-six years later.

   The sad and unfortunate part was I allowed Noah to inflict many of these same abuses on our children. Noah mostly neglected Allen, but he physically and emotionally abused

Nathan and Bonnie.

Divorced life is different; the children and I no longer feel we are walking on eggshells wondering when the bomb is going to explode.

A card comes in the mail to my new house and it offers a free facial. After giving it some thought, I decide I need a facial so I call for the appointment. I like the woman and the cosmetics so much; I decide to start selling their products.

Following the facial, I have my hair styled and I update my wardrobe. I begin feeling better and my self-esteem improves. I am meeting many different types of people.

It is late one evening at a nightclub after I have had a few drinks that Susie breaks through to again take an active role in my life. Although Sarah has been unaware of it, Susie has been influencing her behavior for weeks. This evening Susie has control of the body and she is euphoric. She forks out several hundred dollars to join a club where women preview men's profiles on video and vice versa. Then, after previewing a video, if she finds someone she wants to date; she writes that person a letter. And the person chooses whether he wishes to respond. Someone tells her it is similar to the dating services on the internet, only safer.

The remainder of the school year flies by...and with it both Allen and Bonnie.

Part IV
Living with Multiple Personalities

"And no one knows you better than your angels know you, dear.
For every day that you have spent on earth, they too, were here."
- Angels Are Always There, by Leigh Engel

You Love Your Daddy, Don't You?

Chapter Seven

Searching for My Lost Childhood

Shame, fear, depression, loneliness! What awful feelings I have as I go about trying to find the childhood I never had. After all, I am only forty-six when I get my divorce. *"I deserve to have a little joy and freedom now. I have played the saint, and stuffed my feelings too many years."* Those are the words Susie plays over and over in Sarah's head.

My divorce is final on December 18, 1989, while Bonnie is still a senior in high school. Allen is a sophomore. I have rented a house for the three of us in the same county as our previous home, but it is about twelve miles from our school. When the holidays begin, we go to the north Georgia Mountains and rent a cabin for a few days vacation. I have always wanted to own a cabin in the mountains. While there, I find a lot marked for sale on a large mountain called Screamer Mountain. It is beautiful and, on a clear day, you can see for miles. Many nearby lots have signs with names I recognize as people who live in Gwinnett County, the county where I live. The price seems to be reasonable and the mountain has townhouses built at the top. Many homes are built there. I decide to buy a lot on this mountain.

I had no furniture when I rented this house. The judge made it clear the children's bedroom suites went with them. That helped, but now I still have to purchase a sofa and a dinette set. I will shop for these items after Christmas, when I get another paycheck.

Noah comes on Christmas Day to bring the children their presents. We have to sit in the floor. I am nervous. I look at Bonnie and notice she is twisting her hair around her finger.

The children open their presents and tell their father, "Thank you."

I am aware Bonnie is becoming increasingly uneasy under Noah's scrutiny, as he engages Allen in small talk...while watching Bonnie from the corner of his eye. Awkwardly, Bonnie clears her throat.

This is the sort of behavior I want behind me. Suddenly, I feel anxious to escape Noah's disturbing presence. I am glad when he says he has to leave.

I keep a half-gallon of bourbon under the kitchen sink and I have a few drinks every day when I get home. The bottle goes fast. I wonder whether Allen and Bonnie are sipping it; however, I never catch them.

So many of my close teacher friends know how long I have been depressed in my marriage. Many of them encouraged me to divorce long before I did; however, they remained supportive of me in my inability to decide sooner than I did. They have now organized a surprise party for me to celebrate my freedom. (See Figure 7.1)

I start attending mass in the local church, which has activities for singles. We meet with another Catholic Church singles group to play softball. This allows me to meet new people. I become a good friend with Beverly. The following summer, Beverly and I decide to jointly buy a house. The house is farther away from the school where I teach—thirty miles instead of twelve.

Allen plays basketball, and transportation to and from practice becomes a problem for me, so he asks whether I mind if he goes back to live with his dad.

"Besides," he says, "all my friends live there too."

Noah promises not to charge me child support if I agree to let Allen come back to live with him. I realize I will not be receiving the $500 per month anymore from Noah for child support, but it is best for Allen to be in the same town with his friends.

I tell Noah, "All right, if that's what Allen wants."

As soon as Allen moves back to Noah's house, Noah hires a lawyer and files for child support. He forces Allen to sign the papers to help him receive the support. I never received any

Following my divorce, my friends gave
me a party to celebrate my freedom!

Figure 7.1

support for Bonnie because she was already eighteen before our divorce was final. I now have to pay Noah $400. The difference of $900 less for me a month really hurts my pocketbook and payment on the new house.

Simultaneously, Bonnie leaves to go live on the Oxford Campus at Emory University. I now have no children in my home. Bonnie is having her own problems with addictions, which I know little about at the time. She too knows little about my internal problems or my growing dependence on alcohol. We only know we love each other, and I miss her tremendously.

> NOTE: The "empty nest syndrome" throws me in a cauldron of self-pity until I hear Susie talking in my head, "You're free, and you are finally, truly free. Now is the time to begin the search in earnest. Now we will find the childhood that was stolen from you so long ago—the childhood you never had.
>
> There is little I remember about my life over the next two or three years. I changed from one alter to another, depending on my current life situation. I lived in a survival mode.

I join a group called "The Solo Singles." We have a dance at a hotel nearby each Friday and Sunday night. Cathy, a friend I met at the church singles group, and I take turns driving to this dance. Cathy is fun to be with; she has a great personality and sense of humor. She dances well and is on the floor for almost every dance. Cathy runs the computer at a hospital, and works seven days on and seven off. When she is unable to go to the dance, I begin going alone. In the first few months, I don't get serious about anyone in particular; I date different men.

Then, Jim and I begin seeing each other regularly. Jim and I both drink too much when we are together. Sometimes the following morning I cannot remember what happened the night before. An old problem—losing blocks of time—has come back to haunt me. And, another old problem—the voice in my head—has also returned.

Sometimes it isn't me who is with Jim; it is my alter, Susie. Jim tells Susie she is the only woman he has ever dated who can out-drink him. I stay with Jim at his apartment every Friday night after the dance.

Jim and I eat breakfast on Saturday morning on the way home. I enjoy being with him. When Jim goes to China on business, he leaves his family's names and telephone numbers with me, and he gives his family my phone number. If anything should happen to him, he expects his family to stay in touch with me. While Jim is in China, he buys several small, unique gifts for me.

After another couple of months, Jim tells me, "If we keep seeing each other, I will marry you, and I know I shouldn't get married again. I have been married four times."

I feel a huge, painful knot rising in my throat; however, at his request, we stop seeing each other.

One year later, Jim calls me and says, "Guess what? I'm married." Then he tells me he wishes he were married to me instead of the person he married.

Into the phone I say, "What do you expect me to say?"

Nathan has been doing well with his job at the burger facility. The boss has promoted him to supervisor. He is engaged to a girl who works there. They plan to marry in June. After learning about her pregnancy in March, they move the wedding date up to April.

I begin seeing a man who has recently been divorced. He misses his daughter. He is still angry with his wife. The first night I go to his house, he massages my feet for at least half an hour. It feels wonderful. When I return to the sofa from the restroom, I stumble over his coffee table and hit my head. The next day at work, my head hurts so much I fear I may have a concussion. I call my doctor to schedule an appointment. At the doctor's office, the doctor asks me how much I drink and how often. I am not honest with him. The X-ray's show I have a fracture on my skull.

I see this new man several more times, and later, he becomes merely a dance partner. I have chastised myself repeatedly for drinking too much when with him. I think, possibly, he would have made a good partner if I had controlled my compulsion for alcohol and sex.

Nathan's baby is born in the fall. He is angry with Noah and me. He says, "All my childhood, you and Daddy talked about divorce and now, when the happiest time of my life comes, you finally get divorced, and we can't all be together to celebrate my baby."

Nathan's baby is one of my happy moments, too, because I

believe babies are God's little blessings. I am happy for his family.

On Friday evenings when Cathy is with me, we go to a little bar after the Solo Singles dance. It has a jukebox, and sometimes we dance all night. The men from the General Motors Plant come over when they get off work. The man who massaged my feet works at this plant. On two separate occasions, Cathy and I stay out all night on a school night. I go home to shower and then go straight to work. The first time, I feel terrible, but I get through the day. The second time, I don't risk doing an inferior job of teaching my students or worse—falling asleep in class. I send a student to the office to tell the administration I am sick and need a substitute.

Nathan has been having marital problems but he hasn't let me know. He is spending much of his money on beer for him and his friends. His wife tells him, if it doesn't stop, she will leave him. When it happens the third time, he comes home and she and Dianne are gone. Nathan believes if he gets sober she will come back. He begins an outpatient program the same day she leaves and never touches alcohol again.

Figure 7.2 Dianne

NOTE: Nathan's wife took Dianne back to New York where her family lives. Figure 7.2 shows a picture of Dianne the first summer she was in Georgia after her parents' divorce. I only see Dianne two or three times a year. She is sixteen now and she was the only grandchild I had until December 4, 2005, when Allen and his wife gave me a grandson.

I have been going steady with Tom, who has only one arm. He behaves as if it doesn't bother him, but I later learn it bothers him emotionally. However, he manages well with only one arm. I met him at The Solo Singles Dance.

When my roommate and I throw a going-away party for Jack, a member of the church group, we learn Jack lives in the same complex as Tom, the man I am currently dating. So, we invite Tom, also. When I offer Tom a mixed drink, he refuses and accepts tea instead.

I drink more alcohol than anyone in this group or at the dances. I think often about what Jim said to me. He said I out-drank any other woman he has ever known. I know alcoholism runs in my Daddy's family. I use it as an excuse to have sex. It numbs my senses, and as a result, my personality switches and I lose blocks of time. Since my divorce, I have been with many men, many more than I have written about.

NOTE: Years later, after being hospitalized at Women's Institute for Incorporation Therapy in Hollywood, Florida, I understood I was not Sarah, but my alter Susie, when I engaged in sexual affairs with men during the months immediately following my divorce. Switching to Susie protected the core personality, me, from the guilt and shame of the sexual affairs, thus making it easier for me to live with myself. My addiction wasn't alcohol, but sex.

However, psychologically, my need went deeper. Unconsciously, it wasn't sex I was searching for; Susie was still trying to get her Daddy's love, and she was going about it the only way she knew how. At the age of four, on her daddy's lap, love and sex had become scrambled—almost synonymous.

I had become wise enough to know I had been robbed of my childhood. Now I wanted it back; however, I had no notion of what real love was. I was afraid if I stopped drinking, I wouldn't get any more love. I learned in the hospital I had the definition of love all confused. My Alcoholics Anonymous sponsor gave me a book entitled *Is It Love or Is It Addiction?*

Knowing Nathan is attending Alcoholics Anonymous meetings now, I decide to call him and invite him to dinner. He answers, "I'm sorry, but I can't. I have to go to ninety meetings in ninety days. I cannot miss one. Why don't you come go with me?"

What a coincidence. That is exactly why I called him. I wanted to talk to him about going to an AA meeting. I tell him, "Okay." I meet Nathan about four miles from where I live and we go to the meeting in his truck. When we enter the room, I am shocked. There in front of me sits Tom.

I later learn Tom has thirteen years in Alcoholics Anonymous. He begins "thirteen-stepping" me. That means he does not allow females to invite me to go to meetings with them. He wants to help me get to know the program, and he starts taking me to the meetings himself. I pick up a white chip that night, which means I will try not to drink alcohol for at least one day.

Beverly, the girl I purchased the house with, lost her job. She can no longer help with the house payments. I try to pay the house payment alone, because it is a gorgeous home. The payments are $1,200 a month, and a single teacher's salary with child support payments cannot afford those house payments. Houses aren't selling well at this time, but I list it anyway. The third couple who looks at it buys it. Beverly and I haven't been in the house but eight months, but we break even. I sure am thankful. I buy a townhouse in the same complex where Tom lives. I am on the backside and he is on the front street.

Tom tells me he owned land where the Pocono's Mountain Resort was built. He says, instead of paying him money, the owners exchanged it for several free weeks of timeshares. Tom has also said he had timeshares in Florida. My son, Allen, waited until the last minute to ask Tom to find him a week in Florida. He and his friends wanted to celebrate graduating from high school. Tom had promised to give him a week, but now says he can't find one available.

I confront Tom on several of the things he has been telling me; things I have learned that others believe are not true. I want him to be honest with me; however, I break up with him when he declares his statements *are* true. Then he writes me a letter, in which he asks me to let him come to my home, and he will explain his behavior.

I decide to let him come. Tom tells me the truth about everything, and promises he will never lie to me again. He asks me to marry him. We start eating together almost every night. He enjoys cooking; I wash the dishes. After we eat, we go to an AA meeting. This is our life for about two and one-half years. On Friday nights, people from the AA meeting come back with us to Tom's house. We play penny poker until midnight.

We have already been to the Bahamas together. Tom loves to travel, especially on a cruise ship to the islands. Frequently, I am painfully reminded of Noah's cruel prediction that no one else would ever have me. Thoughts of marrying Tom are exciting, because he wants a big wedding, and, being a gourmet chef, he wants to prepare the rehearsal dinner and reception himself.

Before I tell Tom for certain I will marry him, I get a commitment that he will go to a counselor—one different from the one I am seeing, but within the same group. He agrees and goes at least three times. His counselor tells my counselor there is nothing wrong with Tom.

The big wedding plans, and Noah's prediction that no one else will have me are the reasons—granted the wrong ones—I marry Tom. I want to show Noah another man will have me. I thrive on the excitement of the big wedding plans, all the presents, and the rehearsal dinner.

The wedding is wonderful with our six adult children all taking part in the wedding—three his and three mine. It is a beautiful wedding. My gown, cake, and one arrangement of flowers are shown in Figure 7.3. Nathan's daughter, Dianne, was the flower girl. All of the wedding gifts were gorgeous.

A seven-day cruise follows the reception. We visit Judy, the youngest of Tom's daughters. She studies Oceanography in college. After her BA degree, she was hired by a company to

Figure 7.3 Sarah's wedding

research conches in the Caicos Islands. Our visit with her on the island is the most fun I have while married to Tom. She teaches me how to snorkel. While under water, I see all the beautiful sea life. It is like another world. Then we travel by four-wheel-drive jeep to the most northern tip of the island to see the Tiki huts where many of the underwater movies are produced.

The honeymoon ends all too soon. Tom has a trait that upsets me; I have to schedule an appointment to talk to him. When he walks in the door, he turns on the television. If I need to talk to him, there is never a convenient time. Of course, I can interrupt him; however, he asks if I can wait until the sitcom is over.

We stay married only two and one-half years. I sell my townhouse and move in with Nathan. I stay sober for seven years. I live with Nathan for nine months, while I spend time searching for my perfect retirement home, even though my retirement is still another year away. I am so proud of Nathan. He purchased his own home and began his own landscape business about one year ago. It is located in the county I allowed him to move to when he was an adolescent in high school.

I find the most perfect spot. The lovely rolling mountains around northern Georgia lay in the distance as you drive down my driveway. (See Figure 7.4)

Figure 7.4 Sarah's dream home in Dawsonville

On approaching my house, you see a spring-fed lake with two decks built over it, the lower picture. The house has a fireplace in the great room with a cathedral ceiling—all so romantic. It has everything I have ever wanted, except for a garage, or at least a carport, so I have that added. I also have a sign made to attach to the mailbox and the gate to my walkway that says "Sarah's Paradise."

Nathan's neighbor across the street calls the police about her husband, Pete shortly after I move. She tells the police Pete hit her. The police take Pete to jail. Both the man and his wife are friends of mine. The only location to launch Nathan's boat is behind their house, so we have talked often with them in a neighborly way. I visit Pete in jail the next day. One of his adult daughters posts his bond. Since his wife restricts him from the home, he goes to his daughter's house near Atlanta. He has equipment and trucks as he owns his own tree service business. He needs somewhere local to stay where he can park all his vehicles. Not foreseeing a problem, I offer my yard and home to him. I tell him he can rent from me. I see it only as extra money in my pocket.

I am still teaching, but I also begin work with the tree service on the weekends doing all the clerical work, payroll, and bookkeeping. With my teaching job and the money I am making with Pete, I am making more money than I have ever made. He and I are having a blast in other ways too.

I honestly had not intended anything to develop between us other than a work relation. With both of us being lonely, we allow a love-sexual relationship to begin. The chemistry is there from the first day. He doesn't like being in bed alone. For six months, we have a great time and I have the opportunity to do everything I was denied as a child, meaning the fun things, not the sexual things. This is definitely when I find my "Lost Childhood."

(Clips from my "Lost Childhood" days are shown in Figure 7.5.)

Pete and I go camping. We take our bikes to the mountains and ride the trails. We ride inner tubes down the Chattahoochee River. We rent a log cabin up on a mountain, cut firewood for the fireplace, turn the lights down low, eat cheese and crackers, and

After a day of hunting and fishing, "Nature",
as God made it, is so peaceful!

Figure 7.5 Searching for my lost childhood!

drink beer (oops, I lost seven years of sobriety) while we sit by the fire. We take off walking the next day; I wear my fanny pack and both of us carry a fishing pole.

We catch bugs, tadpoles, worms, anything on the ground that moves, to use for bait. Soon we arrive at a big lake. It has some empty bottles lying around. We empty my fanny pack into the bottle so the bait won't die. We begin fishing. After catching several fish, we go back to the cabin, clean them, and cook them for supper.

Now, I ask you, "Is this not what all children look forward to at one time or another in their lives?"

I never had it. I always had to be at home milking cows and feeding animals, or hoeing in the garden, or trying to prevent Mama from seeing Daddy put his hands on me.

Gosh, I am having the time of my life, and the fun is not over yet. Many more good days are ahead. We go deer hunting. I climb to a tree house and sit in the dark to watch for deer. I watch him and his cousin dress their kill for the day. While at his cousin's house, we build a bonfire, roast hotdogs and marshmallows with another couple, and then we sleep in a bed outside under the stars.

Pete and I sit in the bathtub together and soak our tired bodies, when we come in from a hard day of work with the trees. When we get out, we make wonderful love together. We fish right off the deck from my own private lake. Our largest catch is a four pound, six ounce large-mouth bass, which Pete had mounted. On it he had engraved the words *Caught at "Sarah's Paradise."* Right now I feel this is the best time of my life. Pete goes to arm wrestling competitions. It is fun to go with him and watch him compete. He has won many trophies in the past.

While he and I are living together, I make the choice to give up my seven years of sobriety. We only drink beer, and we never drink on the job. We take beer with us when we are camping. The tree service takes a great deal of time making calls, finding properties, and going to give the estimates for the jobs, then scheduling the jobs. While I am still teaching, this work is done after I come in from work.

I am only fifty-four years old when my thirty years of teaching are finished. Since I have Pete living with me now, and he needs me with his work, I decide to retire younger than I would have normally.

A retirement party is given for me for an entire day so all the teachers can come to visit during their planning periods. I appreciate this effort so much. Seventeen of my thirty years were in this one school.

After I retire from teaching in 1997, God leads me to what I feel, at the time, is my purpose in life. This is to work as a volunteer with the CASA Program. CASA is an acronym for Court Appointed Special Advocate. Being a Court Appointed Special Advocate requires I receive forty hours of training and a monthly meeting with my leader to discuss cases and any problems I experience. Foster parents meet with us too. Advocates provide input to judges, which assist them in making decisions concerning children's placements. We visit parents to see they are following court orders. Sometimes we visit inmates in jail, visit children in foster or group homes, and write reports.

Most of my cases were adolescents; because that is the age group I extremely love. Many adults are afraid to work with adolescents. Four of the children on my caseload were living in group homes. Two of the four completed high school while living in the group home, one went on to college, and one ran away. Two brothers were placed in the home of a paternal grandmother. They were never allowed to return to their parents, so their grandmother adopted them. Two other brothers were placed in a home where parents were unable to have their own children. Eventually, the foster parents adopted these boys. It was a wonderful time in my life, but also stressful. It was rewarding to see children removed from dysfunctional families and placed in homes where they were nurtured and loved. Children are my first love, and it should never be forgotten; they are our future.

I give so much of myself to my cases that I sometimes get too involved personally. Two brothers are taken from their home, and I find myself comparing the home environment they were leaving to my own childhood home environment. My heart goes out to these boys when I realize their situation is much worse than my own. Concurrently, I met with female inmates in the same county for a weekly Alcoholics Anonymous meeting.

Twenty-six of the thirty years of my teaching were in the same county. While teaching, I was elected for a seven-year term as one of a seven-member board on the Finance Committee to make decisions about teachers' retirement funds. I was selected as one of the "Teachers as Leaders" and I published my own math book, *Using Your Sense to Make Dollars*.

> NOTE: I have related the entire above, not to brag, but to clarify how well I was able to compartmentalize my life. Most people would view my adult, public life as that of a competent professional educator.
>
> William B. Tollefson, Ph.D., explains in his book, *Separated from the Light*, "Compartmentalization provides the dissociative self greater areas in which to hide the core and store the person's 'normalcy' for later retrieval. The construction of storage areas allows the victim to hide what is overtly or covertly forbidden. It safely stores away qualities and traits (emotions, behaviors, feelings, sexuality, thoughts), which are self-deemed forbidden."
>
> Until this point, in my public life, I was able to stuff down (or compartmentalize off) all the pain and shame I carried from my childhood, and from my two failed marriages.
>
> Now that my responsibility to my children is over, my life takes a drastic downward spiral from this point, until my final breakdown when I finally find the help I need.

In my final two or three years of teaching, I teach Physical Education all day. My healthy physical condition is another reason I am so much help to Pete on the job. Besides my intelligence, especially my knowledge of computers and money, and the aid I provide in keeping his books and taxes, I tell myself I am an asset to Pete.

> NOTE: The only person I am fooling is myself, but I didn't know it at the time. I had myself convinced Pete really needed me.

Pete and I continue bringing in good money with the Tree Service business. It is hot during the summer months. We begin to drink more beer after we finish work for the day. We save all the large hardwoods and use his log splitter to cut them for firewood. In the fall, we sell it by the truckload and make more money on the side when the other part of the business is slow.

Pete is good at climbing trees. I stay on the ground and pull on the rope ensuring the tree or limb plummets in the direction intended. If the job includes clean up, we have to take all the limbs and feed them into his chipper. Many of the limbs whip back and catch the shinbone on my legs. They look ugly and scarred. My body is strong and I can perform as much work as a man. I even learn how to use the small chain saw to cut small firewood. I always have been an outdoor person. I enjoy working with Pete, but I probably should not stress my body as severely as I do. I pay myself well since I do payroll and bookkeeping. I keep all the records and file income taxes at the end of the year.

To reward ourselves on Saturday nights, we go to a nightclub with a live band, drink mixed drinks and dance. I do most of the drinking since he has to drive home. For some reason, I don't think I can dance unless I've had a few drinks. My feet stay glued to the floor unless I have at least three before the first dance.

Sometime during September, Pete's high school has a class reunion. Since my retirement in June, we have been together day and night. I know I will get lonely this weekend, but I also know he is not mine, and I have no right to try to control his time. I abhor having to be without him on this weekend.

The weekend of the reunion arrives much too quickly. At the reunion, Pete talks to a girl who knew him when he was in high school. She remembers him, as he was one of the lead football players. He attended a small boarding school. He does not remember her, as she was much younger than him. They spend the rest of the weekend together. Pete lies to me about his relationship with this girl on upcoming weekends. He tells me he is meeting several of the old friends from his class to play ball. On the

205

weekends Pete is away, I stay home alone and drink more than usual.

My children come to see me, sometimes unexpectedly, and detect I have been drinking. They know I had been sober for seven years before meeting Pete. They don't understand the change in me. Sometimes, I cry unexpectedly in front of them, not meaning to.

Then the girl Pete is seeing has a bad car accident and breaks her hip. Pete begins staying away from home much more now. Then he tells me about her, about her accident, and how he is trying to help her.

Even though I knew about her, I'm not prepared for the anguish that stabs my heart the day I come home from buying groceries and find Pete and the girl in *our* bed together. I stand, silent and defeated, not understanding why Pete has brought her to my house. I feel myself shriveling inside as I move all my belongings out of our bedroom and go to the other bedroom. I intend this as a temporary situation until I can arrange for Pete to move out of my home.

Now I am tormented by his presence. My misery is like a steel weight. I found my "Lost Childhood," even if it was for only six months. And oh, how sweet it was. I do not regret the months I had with Pete, even though he hurt me so badly. He continued to stay on for six more months before I got him out. I was alone in my home that year for Christmas—no tree, nothing, knowing Pete was in a motel room with his old high school friend. I cried and drank most of the day. How could one more hurtful Christmas alone be so bad after all the many painful Christmas days I had already experienced?

While I was teaching his friend how to keep the books for the tree service, she and I talked about Pete, and we learned he had told each of us lies about the other. She wanted to believe Pete, and after Christmas, they moved into an apartment. They married shortly after, but it lasted for only a few months. She went back to her family in Hawaii. Those six months Pete and I were together before his reunion occurred are the most treasured moments of my life. The last six months he lived in my house were some of the most painful I ever had to endure. Pete took advantage of me, because of the help I was giving him with his tree service, and I was too naïve to know it.

Chapter Eight

My Mental Breakdown

Depression and alcohol almost kill me before I get back into Alcoholics Anonymous. This wonderful twelve-step program does for me what it has done for millions of people like me, who are hopelessly trapped in addictions, have hit the bottom, and have no where else to turn.

I have the most wonderful children. They call me often and ask me to eat out with them. Nathan has his own landscaping business. During the summer months, Mary's grandson, Keith, comes to live with Nathan, and Keith helps Nathan with his landscaping business.

It is July 4, 1999, Bonnie, Keith, Nathan and I decide to go out on Lake Lanier in Nathan's boat. Since I rarely have the chance to water ski, I decide not to miss the opportunity. The lake appears to be a hot tub turned to its fullest capacity with more boats than usual stirring the water, making beautiful, but dangerous waves. The fourth of July is the most popular day on the lake. I jump the waves, back and forth again and again, until one of them catches me between my legs and splits them open, oh…oh, so far. I have no choice but to let go of the rope and go down. I feel extreme pain, but have no idea what the extent of my injury is until later. When the boat comes around, Nathan asks, "Do you want to go again?"

I tell him emphatically, "No."

I have lost one ski. When I try to turn over in the water to help look for the lost ski, it hurts too badly. My children decide to help me get into the boat before looking for the other ski, because it has floated so far away. When I lift my right foot to get in, I find I cannot use that leg, so I switch to the left foot. The bottom rung is missing on the ladder, and using weight on the left side hurts too, because the step is so high. My children drag me into the boat.

Nathan drives fast after we pick up the second ski. "Nathan," I cry in a harsh, raw voice. "Stop the boat. You are going too fast and bouncing over the waves is causing me too much pain."

Nathan stops the boat to let me talk and my children stare at me. I remember how far our launch site is from Nathan's house. I know there is no way I can walk back to his house from the boat ramp.

I cannot prevent the grimace of pain on my face. "Something is broken," I say. "You won't be able to get me out of this boat. You need to call an ambulance to pick me up somewhere."

Bonnie calls 911 on her cell phone and explains my condition. She is given the name of a boat ramp that will be the best meeting place. I grit my teeth as the boat travels through the rough waters to the first dock to let Bonnie out in order for her to go pick up her car. Then we travel to the dock where the ambulance will meet us. I think Nathan cannot imagine how much pain I'm in, or he would slow the boat down to lessen the motion of the boat as it hits the waves. When we arrive at the boat dock, the fire truck is already waiting. Using emergency medical skills, they begin trying to remove my body without causing further injury.

One of the emergency medical technicians takes scissors and begins cutting off my new shorts. I am glad I haven't lost my sense of humor; I tell him, "You can't see anything, because I have my bathing suit on under my shorts."

The ambulance arrives, I am lifted into it, and we are off to the hospital. Finally, I can lie down; however, it does nothing for the pain. "Please give me something for the pain," I ask one of the attendants riding with me in the ambulance.

"I'm sorry," he answers. "We can't, not until we know what is wrong with you."

When we arrive at the hospital, the pain is so excruciating I don't have any humor left. They take me directly to the X-ray department; however, it is forever before they start taking pictures.

When the technician finally begins, she tells me to move my body first one way and then another.

I tell her, "I can't."

"Well, drop your arm down out of my way."

"I can do that."

When she finishes taking a few more X-rays and checking them, she comes back into the emergency room where she left me and says, "No wonder you are hurting. Your hip bone is broken."

Bonnie is standing in the doorway and she sees me when I begin to cry. I am thinking to myself, *"Only little old ladies with osteoporosis break their hips. How will I ever relive my childhood since this has happened to me?"*

Bonnie, too, begins crying and then she disappears. She and Nathan come back to see me together. A nurse finally comes with a wheel chair and a shot for pain. I remember nothing else about that day.

The following day someone tells me if the attendants don't come to take me to surgery before 3:00 PM, the surgery will be postponed another day. I am in severe pain. I have a morphine pump; however, it doesn't control the pain. I want the surgery done today. Shortly after 3:00 PM, attendants come to take me to the operating room. The surgery lasts more than four hours. The surgeon uses metal plates and screws to repair my hip.

Time passes so slowly from day to day. I have to learn how to walk again. My insurance doesn't normally approve the hospital the ambulance carried me to, but, because it was an emergency, they cover my charges. After a week, it is time for physical rehabilitation to begin, and I am moved by ambulance to another hospital located twenty miles further south.

Before my dismissal date, Nathan sets up my daybed in the den so I won't have to turn all the corners to get from my regular bedroom to the kitchen. He brought my Boston terrier, Daisy, and his Boston terrier, Dixie, over to me for company. In Figure 8.1, you will see them on the bed loving and kissing me. Daisy is showing how much she missed me while I was in the hospital.

An occupational therapist comes to my home to help me learn to accomplish my household chores. A homecare nurse comes once a week for four weeks to check my blood. The physical therapist comes for several months before I can get into my car and drive myself to physical therapy.

Watching television seems to become my only pastime. I read some, but it isn't my favorite thing to

Figure 8.1 Boston Terriers

do after six years of college. I become depressed, because it seems I'm not getting any better—worse if anything. I still hurt badly in my groin area and now the right knee feels damaged too. My physical therapist encourages me to go to another orthopedic doctor to get my knee checked.

When I see the second orthopedic doctor in October, I explain to him where I am hurting. He takes X-rays first in his office. He shows the X-rays to me and says, "It looks as if the bone is not growing together properly, where the other doctor joined the hipbone together with plates and screws. I will give you orders to take to the hospital to get an MRI done on both your knee and hip. It will show exactly what is going on."

When this second doctor receives the results, he calls me and asks me to come in to his office to talk. He tells me I have a torn meniscus in the right knee. The hip is not growing together and the pain in my groin is a bone chip floating around left during the first surgery.

I want to numb out, but something tells me I need to hear every word this man has to tell me.

The doctor says, "Let's get your knee fixed first." He schedules the knee surgery for November of the same year. In January 2000,

I have a total hip replacement, seven months following the first hip surgery. I never remove the daybed from my den. The incision is much longer this time, extending the first incision on both ends. What a way to start a new year. I spent half of 1999 in the hospital, in rehabilitation, therapy at home, and now at least half of this year will be spent the same way because of that one accident on the lake.

> NOTE: Susie does not allow us to stay tied down six months this time. My body heals faster and besides other medical problems arises within the next two months.

Nathan fulfills his lifelong dream to become a marine. He leaves right after my surgery to go to Parris Island for his basic training.

I cannot explain what happens to me after this. I change. I react to my disability and isolation by hardening my heart and erecting barriers of anger. I consult a lawyer about filing a lawsuit against the first doctor. He informs me the doctor had to try the method he used first, and I will get nowhere in a lawsuit, so I drop the idea. I have lost almost a year of my life and I want…I need…to make up for it. I cannot go out alone so I start spending time on the Internet.

I was bored, and I entered sites on the Internet that beckoned to Susie. I have always known there was another part of me. Sometimes it seemed I heard chatter in my head, but I have always tried to keep the other side of me stuffed down. It was the "sex-addict" Susie. I didn't want to be like her and I tried to pretend she didn't exist.

Now I'm tired of being the professional, straight-laced Sarah. I am tired of lying in this bed with nothing to do. There is nothing wrong with psyching out. There is nothing wrong with going away and letting the other side of me have a little fun. This body sure isn't going anywhere.

Susie says, "Sarah, I'm sick and tired of this life you're living. Did you think you had buried me forever? I know how to liven it up around here. I'm becoming a member of 'Adult Friend Finder.' You stay there in your bed. This is definitely *not* your game."

I isolate myself from friends and family; I don't allow anyone to know what is happening in my life for I am embarrassed. Later, when I am admitted to the hospital at the Women's Institute for Incorporation Therapy, I learn this is the time that Susie, my sexual alter reappears and for the third time plays a major role in my life. Soon another alter, Faith, who has been dormant for a long time, will reappear, and inappropriately give away my money. My third and last alter, Kristen, will come to rescue Susie when she gets herself into trouble.

When I have recuperated sufficiently to leave the house, I buy a new 2000 Honda, because it is rough for me to get up into the Ford Explorer, which is the vehicle I now drive. My new car and the exciting letters from the men on the Internet give Susie a false sense of pride. She assumes it is all right to drink, and she causes Sarah to lose a little more than two years of sobriety.

Susie starts out being smart. When she meets a new man she has contacted through her fantasies, she makes a habit of exchanging several emails, having several telephone conversations, and seeing pictures of him before she considers meeting him. The first meeting is always a neutral location, like a movie theater or a restaurant. If she doesn't like him, she can simply go home and he can go his own way.

Susie's carelessness leads to problems. On many of the occasions, she puts herself (and vicariously, also Sarah) in danger by letting these men follow her home. One man begs Susie to go with him to a local nudist camp. Susie doesn't know how popular they are now. She thinks he is crazy; however, she is having a ball. Meeting new men is becoming an addiction.

Susie goes with a man to his home and while there, Sarah returns and sees evidence the man is married. Sarah objects to being with a married man, and the man tells her he and his wife are planning to divorce.

This sort of behavior is what her daddy did to her mother. This is why she feels as if her whole life is stuffed down somewhere inside her and she doesn't know what it is that's stuffed down there. She only knows she feels like a time bomb about to go off.

Sarah doesn't feel so nice towards this man; however, she tries to be nice. "I'm sorry, but I wouldn't like it if I were in your wife's shoes."

NOTE: I later learn about the Dissociative Continuum and how it applies to my life. It seems the greater the trauma to the individual, the higher up the scale the dissociation will be. Multiple personality disorder is at the extreme end of the Dissociative Continuum. In Dr. William Tollefson's book, Separated from the Light, his highest three stages are (5) Fragmentation Reaction, (6) Multiplicity Reaction, and (7) Severe Multiplicity Reaction.

I am not a psychiatrist; therefore, I cannot diagnose myself. I think, probably, I do not fit at all times into the seventh category. If I understand the scale correctly, severe multiplicity reaction—the seventh category—means a total separation of the alters from the core personality. I believe I did not fit always into the seventh category, because I sometimes heard Susie talking in my head. Most of the time, when Susie had control of my body, that time was lost to me; however, sometimes I remembered what she had done. For example, I remembered the man mentioned above had once spent the night at my house.

What I do believe is no one—not even psychiatrists—can predict or guarantee with certainty what will happen in the mind of victims, who are abused when they are small children, especially sexually abused, and the injury is worse when it is inflicted repeatedly by family members they love.

*Dr. William Toffefson, mentioned above, is director of the hospital, Women's Hospital for Incorporation Therapy, at Hollywood, Florida. I write about my stay at this hospital in Chapter Ten. Dr. Bill, as patients at the hospital call him, performed a ceremony at my request called incorporation. I describe this beautiful ceremony in the chapter entitled, "My Spiritual Journey." I love the staff at this hospital, for I believe they saved my life. In naming the chapter, "My Spiritual Journey," I do not mean to imply the hospital is spiritually oriented, or affiliated with a religious organization. The naming of the chapter was a personal expression for me. I prayed for healing...I prayed before my incorporation...I prayed as I had never prayed before. I prayed for God to use Dr. Bill to help make my incorporation a success. I felt God's presence during the process, and I will never again doubt my God is real, and he does perform miracles. My only regret is I waited until so late in my life to seek help.

One of Susie's greatest fears is getting lost. It is a fear born of an incident when Susie was five years old, and her mother walked up a flight of stairs in a department store leaving Susie on the floor below. Susie became hysterical when she could not find her mother. Now Susie's wish to meet a new man and her fear of getting lost constantly do battle in her mind. Susie does frequently get lost. Susie may be precocious and sexually active, but she is still a little girl, and she cannot remember directions well.

Later, Kristen becomes the chief rescuer, but, at this point in Susie's life, it is usually Sarah who reappears to figure out where they are and continue the journey or turn the car around to go back home. As these type incidents increase in frequency, and I become more aware that Susie is taking more risks, I become afraid. I realize my life is becoming chaotic and I am losing control.

I see little of my family and friends. Susie continues her nightlife; however, I continue my cases with the CASA program during the day.

NOTE: For each of the three years I volunteered with the Court Appointed Special Advocate program, I was awarded a certificate. (See Figure 8.2) Some of the children, and their situations, bothered me more than others. The more similar their situations were to my own childhood situation, the more stressful it was for me. I wish I had been able to work with the CASA program longer; however, I finally, painfully, accepted that I needed healing.

Certificate of Appreciation

presented to

Sara ████

CASA Volunteer

on December 13, 2000

for outstanding dedication and effective advocacy
for the children whose lives you have touched.

Pamela Collins, Executive Director
CASA for Children, Inc.

A child's voice in court.

"How wonderful it is that nobody need wait a single moment before starting to improve the World."
- Anne Frank

Figure 8.2

On one occasion, Susie allows, for the sake of a name, I will call him Andy, to persuade her to meet him north of Nashville, Tennessee. He has to be in Nashville to do some volunteer work he committed to with his message therapy business. Susie meets him at a motel. They go out to dinner and then return to the motel.

We are both anxious to experiment with sex. As soon as the motel door closes behind him, he walks up to Susie and begins undressing her. His fingers fumble with the buttons of her blouse. Susie unbuttons his shirt, unbuckles his belt, and soon they are nude. As she presses against him, she feels his impatience. He moves against her, fanning the sparks of arousal.

Suddenly, he takes her by the shoulders and throws her backwards onto the bed.

"Wow," thinks Susie, as her excitement level rises. *"Maybe he isn't Mr. Fumble Fingers, after all."*

This man—tall and dark—hovers over her slender body. His

216

black penetrating eyes bore into Susie's, which gaze back eagerly.

Susie reaches down to encircle his penis, and she finds that he is huge. She lifts her hips in sensuous invitation and guides him to the mouth of her vagina. His naked body claims her, and the sound of sex is the only reality in the room.

Susie feels the incredible power of his surging body, and fire bolts of desire arch through her. A shudder runs full-length of her body. Susie caresses him with the instinctive movements of a woman who knows how to please a man. She feels the strength of his body possessing her in ever quicker, deepening thrusts. She arches upward against him and the moment of ecstasy explodes all around them.

Afterward, they lay in silence. Susie crawls into his arms, snuggles there, and they sleep. Later they wake, and engage in rough, raw lovemaking again.

The following day they go to play golf. The next day they go to the Grand Ole Opry Hotel simply to view its beauty, while they talk. Susie is attracted to this man, and she thinks he is to her; however, all fairytales must come to an end. At the end of two days, his business in Nashville is over. Susie is genuinely sad to see him go and as his car pulls away, her gaze is clouded with tears.

It seems no two men Susie meets on the Internet are the same. Another young man, who she often emails, is from Raleigh, North Carolina. They continually discuss meeting. First, they arrange for Susie to fly to Raleigh, and then they change their minds and plan for him to fly to Atlanta. Final arrangements haven't been made when he stops communicating. Susie doesn't hear from him for four weeks. When next he writes, it is Sarah who receives the letter—not Susie. He writes that he has been to his brother's home, and he had to go into the hospital. Because of the four-week period and his story of the hospital, I conclude he may have been in a rehabilitation center.

When next he calls, I answer the phone, not Susie. I tell him, "If you have a problem with alcohol, you need not be ashamed. I understand and I, too, have a problem with alcohol, and have, at one time, had seven years of continuous sobriety."

The man finds a way to hang up quickly, and I never hear from him again.

I (as Sarah) have seen a few local men. I am impressed with one of them whose name is Ralph. His home is near mine. He has a son and daughter-in-law living with him, but he is moving to Louisiana where he builds Chinese restaurants. He plans to let his son and daughter-in-law move into his home permanently, because his son's employer has transferred him from Florida to Georgia. Ralph lets me treat him like a big brother. I feel free to call him any time I want to talk.

All types of men are listed on the matchmaker site. At first, it was only Susie who responds to ads, but recently I have responded to a few ads I could tell were posted by gentlemen. Susie is more prone to pick the unsavory men.

I must confess the matchmaker site fascinates me. I meet Allen and he doesn't have all the baggage some men have. Allen has a son still in high school and a daughter in college. He has pride, and he doesn't smoke or drink. I stay at his home some and sometimes he stays at my home. After we are together a while, Allen tells me he loves me, but that's too hard for me to believe. *How could he, as sick as I am?*

I know I am sick, because I am learning more about Susie's activities. I saw one of the trashy men she brought home to my house. It is my house, not Susie's. Allen appears so healthy emotionally compared to the men Susie dates. It is hard to understand why he is on "Adult Friend Finder." I know I am sick, because I am beginning to hear Susie more in my head, and I know she is making a game out of the matchmaker site. Susie is seeing three men at the same time, and none of them knows about the other. Susie has no loyalties, and she has no boundaries. Susie knows every type of sex act, and she prefers being the aggressive partner. With her, anything goes. She thinks life should be one big party.

Susie and I now sometimes carry on conversations with each other. That's how I know for sure I am literally going off the deep end. Yesterday I said, "Susie, this has to end. You will get us both killed."

She talked right back to me. In fact, she laughed at me. "You can't pretend any longer you don't know what's going on. You can't play innocent and say you lost the hours. You know when I come out. In fact, you know why you're so tired and feel like you're falling apart. You know it's because I'm spending twenty or more hours without a break on the Internet. All those hours I'm talking with men making plans to meet them. I only get a few hours sleep. That means you only sleep a few hours too. How can you *not* know?"

I hear a voice in my head say, "It's okay; you deserve to have a good time."

I wonder if it is the voice of Satan. I cannot explain my behavior if my life depended on it. I know I am not myself. I know what I am doing is a compulsion, but I cannot stop myself. Who is this person? Who has taken over my life? Is it Susie, or is it Satan controlling my life?

Mama's voice comes in my head. "God will punish you for your sins." She would kill me if she knew what I am doing, and yet I am so angry with her. I feel she neglected me, and her neglect caused me not to get my needs met. Her denial allowed Daddy's sexual abuse to continue throughout my childhood and teen years. She should have protected me from Daddy and she shouldn't have made me sleep with Adam. Why didn't she ask questions when I told her there was blood in my panties?

I feel alone. I hate the chatter in my head. Sometimes I sit with my arms crossed over my chest, hands tucked under my arms, rocking back and forth with my eyes closed. Sometimes I cannot stop the humming sound in my head. Then I grit my teeth and feel nauseated. My energies are wasted from fighting the turmoil within. In despair, I gaze at the stranger in the mirror. Often, in desperation, I take a handful of Tylenol and cry until I fall asleep.

A person from Florida named Joel Hinson emails Sarah. Susie answers his email. Before I know what Susie has done, she has invited him to drive to Atlanta to see her.

When I first see him, I think, *"Oh no, what has Susie gotten me into?"* I want him to turn around and go back home.

A voice in my head says, "It is too far to send him back home." This is the voice of my alter Faith.

> NOTE: I wish I had had the foresight to send him back home at that time, because my whole life is about to change because Susie has invited Joel into our lives.
>
> My core personality is fragmented at this point. My other two alters, Faith and Kristen, are about to once again become active in my life. Faith is the eight-year-old child who emerged when Sarah's family spent the desolate, impoverish winter in the old shack near the Smoky Mountains of Tennessee. Faith empathizes with others she perceives to be in need of money or food. She tries to take care of them and gives them her own money. Kristen emerged last and she is intelligent. She is also the energizer and protector of the others.

After Joel takes off his dark glasses and combs his hair, Susie decides he doesn't look so bad. She sighs and takes a deep breath, thinking the awkward moment has drug on too long.

"Okay," she says, "let's go to the house and unpack."

As he is following Susie to Sarah's house, Susie is thinking about how different he looks than she had expected. His slightly overweight body doesn't thrill her at all and he only stands five feet tall. They arrive at Sarah's home and Susie helps him unload his car. When the car is unpacked, Joel asks, "How far is it to the closest hardware store?"

Susie doesn't know where a hardware store is located and she is about to panic when Sarah comes to the rescue.

"Sure, I know where there is a hardware store. It's about fifteen miles from here."

"That's not bad. I need a few things. Why don't we go there?"

We leave and stop by the hardware store and he buys something, and then we stop by the grocery store. We were there only two minutes when he reaches in his back pocket and says, "Oh, I left my wallet at the hardware store. I'll be right back."

He leaves quickly. When he returns, he says, "No one reported finding it. I have no license, no money, and no credit card."

The following day Joel's Buick breaks down. The local Good Year cannot fix his Buick. Faith empathizes with Joel. He is stranded away from home, without money, and his car has broken down. Faith pays for Joel's car to be fixed at a Buick Dealer in a town nearby.

"Joel," Faith tells him, "you should call your credit card company and cancel the card."

Quickly, he replies, "Oh, I have insurance on my credit cards, so don't worry."

Sarah's alters have an uncanny ability not to recognize con artists.

When Joel is ready to leave, he asks for cash to get home. Faith gives him four hundred dollars, which was more than necessary.

When Susie drives down to Florida to see Joel, he persuades her to spend the evening with him at a nudist camp. As soon as they enter the gate, Joel pulls off Susie's shirt. Looking around, Susie sees many nude people. She wonders if she will get used to this lifestyle. Joel's second car is a Sebring convertible and, on this day, they are in the convertible. Susie loves the excitement and the new way of life.

Joel says, "This is the way to live. You are retired and you need to go ahead and find us a house near this nudist resort. We could both find jobs nearby, maybe here at the resort."

"But Joel, I don't even love you. This is just for fun."

"We don't have to love each other. That will come with time as we stay together."

On the entrance to the little store at the nudist resort, there is a sign, which says, "No Shoes, No Shirt, No Problem."

The strangest feeling to me, while I was staying in one of the motel rooms was when I was getting ready for bed after I showered. I thought, *"You don't have to worry about closing blinds here, because everybody has already seen you nude anyway."* Another strange feeling is sitting on the front porch in the nude eating lunch.

While at the nudist camp, Susie's sight in her right eye becomes totally blind. It scares her badly because it has never happened to her. They are at a dinner party when it happens. She asks Joel to go outside with her to walk around, so she can tell if she can see when she is outside. She still can't see from her right eye when she goes outside, but it returns after about fifteen minutes.

Susie and Joel find the dream house before they leave town, and Susie leaves earnest money. When she gets back to Georgia, Sarah has returned and naturally knows nothing about the incident with her eye until it happens again a week later. Susie's whole trip to Florida begins registering in my brain like some kind of movie. First, I remember Susie went to Florida with Joel and my eye went blind while they were in Florida. Then I remember about the house. Dear God, I cannot believe Susie has put my money down on a house in Florida with plans to move in with a total stranger. The visit to the nudist camp and the conversation about getting jobs in Florida come back to mind.

I am terrified at this point. Susie has gotten me into some crazy situations before, but this is insane. I recall the man who wanted me to go with him to our local nudist camp, and I thought he was insane. Now, look at what I've done. I spent the night at one. I think I am bordering on insanity. I close my eyes and feel blessed, peaceful nothingness...

Susie gets ready to leave the home in Georgia and move to Florida. I have been dating three local men about once a week and talking to one in Nashville, Tennessee, when this terrible affair with Joel started. Two of the local men present no problem. Ralph is moving to Louisiana. Allen is so involved with his business and his two children that he doesn't seem to care.

Vince, the third man I am dating at the time my affair with Joel starts, has previously lived in Manhattan. He does not know that I have already put money down on a house in Florida for us, just that I am considering it. He gets extremely upset that I would even consider it and writes me a two-page letter explaining Joel's type. He mentioned that Joel is a con artist, only in it for the sex and the money, and I am making a grave mistake. Everything else he warned me about came true within the first few days of being in Florida after I bought the house for Joel. He says, "You haven't been around like I have, and you don't know what you are getting into."

And I have been making plans to meet Jeff in Nashville. We are still communicating by emails and phone. He begs me to come see him before moving to Florida. He thinks he can change my mind about Joel. With what I have told him, I guess he, too, knows I am making a grave mistake.

All this time, Joel and Susie are still making plans for their Florida home. Susie sells both of Sarah's cars to have a twenty percent deposit on the house in Florida. Joel says his two cars are better.

NOTE: Sarah later learns Joel's big Buick belongs to his aunt and has more money owed on it than it is worth.

It is the day of my appointment with the technician in Atlanta whom Dr. Amy Barfield sends me to about my eye. I am nervous and irritable. Dr. Barfield sends me to have a carotid arteriogram and scan done. After the completion, the technicians will not allow me to leave the office until they speak with Dr. Barfield on the phone about the results of my tests. The main technician tells me he is afraid of the danger I present, both to myself and others if I drive on the highway. The tests reveal the right carotid artery has a ninety-nine percent blockage. I am forty-five miles from home. She explains the necessity for me to schedule surgery immediately. Dr. Barfield recommends a vascular surgeon in Gainesville,

Georgia.

The technician explains that, if it had not been for the warning the day my eye went blind, I may have eventually had a stroke.

I schedule the appointment with the vascular surgeon that day and I have four days to wait.

On the day I am scheduled to see him, Joel is here from Florida.

When we start to leave the surgeon's office, he reminds me to stay close to home.

Joel says, "We have to make a quick trip to Orlando before the surgery."

The doctor interjects, "You would be taking a big risk."

I think, *"No one in his right mind would take such a risk."*

Joel disregards the warning and takes me to Florida anyway. I'm sure your thinking, "Don't I have a voice? Can't I speak up and say no? What can I say? I guess I don't. At this point, I can't even blame it all on Susie because I am Sarah most of the time after I learn about my eye problem. I am tired and stressed out. I do what he tells me to do. We go to Florida and sign final papers on the house. He wants to finish the closing by Federal Express immediately after the surgery. We make the trip in three days and it is time for my surgery.

The surgeon explains he cannot put me to sleep, because he is going to remove the stretch of artery, which is clogged and he needs to know I am alert.

He says, "I will ask you to count to ten or wiggle your toes, so I will know you are aware of what is going one."

I begin coughing during the surgery and cannot stop. Someone tells me to try to stop coughing. She says I am slowing the surgery and losing too much blood.

When I finally stop coughing, I begin mentally talking to myself, *"Oh Lord, please let me pass from this earth. Forgive me for all my sins and now take me home. I am tired and I don't know how to get out of this mess I'm in. Please, Lord, let me die."*

All I can think about are the words in the letter I received from

Vince warning me of Joel's type and what he is doing to me. I know he is probably right. I truly hope I will bleed to death on the operating table.

Joel plans to take all the furniture from my house down to Florida tomorrow. Susie has gotten me into a situation I feel incapable of reversing. I would never make these stupid decisions. I don't remember half of what led up to this mess. Unfortunately, I don't die. (See Figure 8.3)

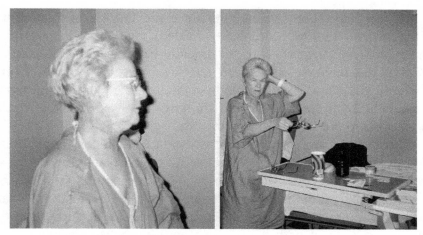

Figure 8.3 Carotid artery surgery

Joel is out in the waiting room planning to take me home as soon as the twenty-three hours the doctor requires for my stay are over. When we get home, Joel goes into town to find some day laborers he can pick up tomorrow morning. He needs them to help him load the U-Haul, because he plans to head to Kissimmee, Florida. My doctor told me not to lift or drive until after my two-week checkup.

I explain to Joel that the closing on the house is not scheduled for several more days; however, he refuses to listen to me. He has taken control and I feel powerless. The following morning Joel loads all my furniture and heads out toward Florida. Now my home is bare.

The closing papers on the house arrive and Susie opens them. She drives to the bank to have them notarized and sent back to the realtor, even though Sarah was given strict orders not to drive. I have no idea what Joel has done with my furniture and the U-Haul, since the closing was not scheduled to occur for several more days. However, I find the closing papers Susie has brought back from the bank, and I realize the money due for the closing is much more than I had expected.

It has only been two months since my last hip replacement. That surgery has not completely healed, much less this carotid artery surgery. Nevertheless, I frantically begin cleaning the house hoping the realtors, who listed it, may come to show it. Even though I pay a couple of people to come help me paint the interior, carpet the living room and hall, I am now totally exhausted after all my efforts to prepare the house for sale.

I am too ashamed to tell anyone what I have done. My children do not know the extent of my madness. I have isolated myself for a while, and everyone thinks I am spending time with others including my children. Both of my boys are too busy to know what is happening in my life. Nathan is in the marines at Parris Island, and Allen is busy with his job in Charlotte, North Carolina. My daughter Bonnie stays in touch and lives nearby, but I have been lying to her about my happiness. I tell her I know what I am doing, and it is right for me. Besides, she has her own problems facing her now.

On the day of my two-week checkup with the vascular surgeon, there is a terrible storm. The vascular surgeon tells me everything is fine, and he releases me. One of my friends warns me not to leave for Florida because of the storm. There is no furniture in my house—the mat I have been sleeping on and all my personal items have been packed in my car, so I ignore her advice and begin the drive to Florida. I tell myself I cannot afford a motel, and besides my friend from Valdosta is expecting me tonight.

I drive for about two hours. The rain is heavy, and I can hardly even see the road. I drive slowly and continue. About three hours later, it lightens up a little. My friend's name is Martha and her house is about halfway. It is after dark when I get to Valdosta. I cannot see how to get to my friend's house, so I stop and call. She comes to meet me and I follow her to her house.

Martha and I met on the Internet, and we are the best of friends. We have visited each other several times. After I get to her house, I confide in her. I tell her I know I have made a terrible mistake. She gives me the courage to do what I know I have to do. When I leave her the next morning, I leave determined to do what I know must be done.

On the highway my alter Kristen comes out. This is the first time she has come out with this much force in an effort to protect Sarah. She says, "I am turning this car around. Sarah, you shouldn't be going to Florida. You know Joel is a con artist. When he left Atlanta, why did you give him your credit card? Are you completely stupid?"

Susie says, "No, we are headed to the sunshine state. We're goanna have a ball. It's about time we had some fun. This car is going straight ahead."

Kristen says, "Sarah, don't listen to Susie. You should know by now she only gets you into trouble. Haven't you learned anything yet? You and Martha worked it all out last night. Now stick to the plan. Let's turn around and go back home."

Susie says, "You are a party pooper."

When I arrive about noon at my newly purchased house in Florida, I see my neighbors are out in their yard so I speak to them. I have a cigarette in my hand. Joel hates for me to smoke. As soon as he sees my cigarette, he goes into the house. When I go inside, he will not talk to me.

I am tired and I finally have had enough of his attitude. I tell him, "If you are going to act like this, you may as well go back to St. Cloud and try to get your old apartment back, because you are not living here with me. I am exhausted from my surgery and cleaning the house in Georgia, when I should not have been doing any physical labor. I'm tired after this long treacherous trip in awful weather and here you are acting like a baby."

We don't speak for the remainder of the evening. When it gets dark, Joel gets a blanket and goes to sleep on the living room sofa and I go to bed. When morning comes, he is gone before I get out of bed.

I go to talk to my neighbors, and I learn he made a nuisance of himself when he first arrived with the furniture. He forced the realtor to open the house to let him in, so the owners charge him— actually, me on the closing charges—seven days of the mortgage payment for him to move in before the house closed. This explains the extra cost reflected on the papers, which I couldn't understand on closing day. They arrived in Georgia from a Federal Express person and a bank representative notarized them after Susie signed them and returned them to Florida.

The neighbor who I paid to help Joel with some interior painting now tells me he saw Joel lying in bed with the woman whom Joel has told me was his aunt.

The neighbor says, "You don't lie in bed in the position Joel and that woman were if she is your aunt."

I then remember a phone call I received from Joel while I was still in Georgia. Joel must have realized the neighbor saw him in bed with the woman, because he called me and told me he was sick. He said his aunt had come over to see his new house, and she was taking care of him. Now I believe it was a woman who was in on his con game to cheat me out of my money.

After talking to the neighbor on the left, I go to another neighbor who had been friendly to me when I was down on an earlier trip. I confide in her, telling her the entire story about Joel being a man I met on the Internet. She is sympathetic with me. Later, her husband helps me resolve the crisis, and prepare the house for me to leave.

When Joel comes back to the house the next day, I tell him to get all his stuff and leave. He takes his belongings and more. He took my credit card when he left Georgia with my furniture. Now I learn he has charged many household items to my card. He has charged two bicycles—one for himself and one for me. He has bought many new shrubs and a grill for the deck. He charged a new refrigerator-freezer, trashcans, towels, and other household items. Joel takes his bike and many other items, which were charged to my card, for example, a massage table and all the oils and other supplies that go with it. He steals Nathan's $400 down comforter. I do, however, get my credit card back before he leaves.

I call the realtor who sold me the house and tell her I want it back on the market.

I explain to her what has happened and she says, "You know, I never liked him to begin with." She is sympathetic.

I begin matching items with tags, and taking purchases back to stores to get credit on my card. I even dig up some of the new plants. Lowe's agrees to pick up the new refrigerator-freezer. I lose several hundred dollars in the carpet because we special ordered it before we left Atlanta. Installation of this carpet occurs while I return other items. I am still driving one of Joel's cars. Once the men finish with the carpet, I drive to Joel's apartment. The plan was for Joel to have supper prepared for me.

Instead, he is angry with me for being late and says, "We don't have time to eat." He brings me a drink and says, "Get in the car. Let's go."

I gladly take the drink. I am tired. I have been running the entire day trying to return all the items I possibly could while I still had a vehicle. Yet, I needed to be at the house to keep it open for the men who were laying the new carpet.

Joel drives straight to my house. I expect him to drop me off and leave immediately. He doesn't; he wants to get into the hot tub with me. We fix another drink, leave our clothes inside, and get in the hot tub. After several hours, we get out and try to go back inside. The door is locked…and we have no keys and no clothes. Our only choice is to break a window in the door.

Joel prepares us another drink. The bed was disassembled so the men could install the carpet. Now Joel pitches the mattress on the living room floor.

Suddenly, my head is spinning. I realize alcohol alone has never given me this kind of "high." I realize Joel has put something other than alcohol in my drink.

Joel is cruel as he drives himself savagely into me. He is angry and he is punishing me. His sadistic attack goes on and on. He hurts me and I cannot stop him. He rapes me, over and over, throughout the night. The following morning he brags about his sexual ability to satisfy women. He says I will miss him if I force him to leave. In an effort to ignore him, I log on to the Internet. I am not aware Joel is standing behind me watching when I enter my pin number to open my email.

While I'm reading my email, he says, "If you won't pay me any attention, then I'll leave."

I tell him, "The sooner, the better, buddy."

Joel leaves shortly after.

Before leaving, my neighbor helps me change the locks on the doors and fix the broken glass in my door. When these jobs are completed, he drives me to the airport.

Susie thinks, *"Gee whiz, what a bummer; I really screwed up. I owe Sarah big time for getting rid of that rat for me. I didn't think she had that much guts. I'll be more careful next time."*

Susie is flying into Nashville to meet Jeff, the man who begged her to come before she went to Florida. He sells used cars at a local car dealership. She had called him the day Sarah first asked Joel to leave, because she knew they had to buy a car.

The used car salesman had told Susie, "A couple traded for a new car last week, and the 1993 Buick they were driving is still available."

Susie had met the car salesman on the Internet through "Adult Friend Finder," which is also where she had met Joel. I wish I *had* gone on to see him.

While in flight to Nashville, Kristen comes out. Her stomach is churning with anxiety and frustration. In her seventeen-year-old voice, she says, "Sarah, we are in serious trouble. I know my job is

230

to save you, but Susie is out of control. If you don't stop her, I'm afraid I won't be able to save you."

I'm not listening, so Kristen calls Sarah's brother, Mark, at his home in Alabama. She tells him about meeting Joel, about the home in Florida, and about what happened there. She tells him they are on their way to Nashville to buy a car.

When Susie arrives in Nashville, Jeff meets her at the airport. We go to his apartment and unpack.

Susie thinks, *"Wow, Jeff is the cleanest and best-dressed man I've been with in many years. Nothing terrible will happen with him like what happened with Joel in Florida,"* and Susie leans back on the bed and relaxes.

I come back and remember the phone conversation Kristen and Mark had on my cell phone. Kristen told Mark about Joel and all that had happened in Florida, including selling both her cars to buy the house.

"Sarah," Jeff asks, "are you all right?"

"I'm sorry if I seem preoccupied. I have a headache. My sinuses act up every time I fly. I'll go in the bathroom and take some Tylenol."

In that instant, I had an insight. I had remembered all the lost blocks of time that had once plagued me. I knew that earlier Susie was further cut off from my conscious mind and that explained the lost blocks of time. Now, I know more often what Susie is doing...and her behavior is terrifying me. The headache is becoming a frequent companion.

"Here I am in Nashville," I think. *"Where will this end? However, I do need a car."*

I am resting on the bed and Jeff is sitting in a chair. I think Jeff appears to be a kind, considerate person. I had not been in Jeff's apartment ten minutes when my cell phone rings. It is Joel.

His voice was heavy with sarcasm, "I'll bet his penis is only half the size of mine. I'll bet he can't satisfy you half as well as I did."

I hang up; however, Joel continues to call and call and call—

even in the middle of the night.

The following day Jeff takes me to see the Buick. I buy the car and I enjoy it so much, I drove it for the next six years.

On Saturday, I receive a call from my son Allen. He is in Atlanta and wants to know what is going on. I tell him I am in Nashville, and I'm planning to go to the Grand Ole Opry this evening.

He says, "If you care about me, you will skip the Grand Ole Opry and get home tonight to see me while I am in town."

The remainder of our conversation slips my mind. When I get home, he says, "You cannot go to Florida alone to get your things out of the house."

I am confused; I don't know how Allen learned about the crisis in Florida. I didn't know Kristen called him from the Orlando airport.

Allen continues, "If Uncle Mark can go with you that will be all right, since he doesn't work. If he can't, I will take time off from work and go with you, but you are *not* going back down there alone."

Waiting until Allen can schedule time away from work could take forever, so I call Mark to ask if he and his wife Juliette can help me load some of my belongings from the house. He agrees to help me and we plan to meet in Valdosta.

When Mark begins talking about events that happened between Joel and me in Florida, I close my eyes, and I am embarrassed and speechless. "Who told Mark all these personal details? Was it Joel? No, I never told Joel about Mark. It had to be somebody in my head."

"Oh dear God, I have fought so hard not to accept it...but I can't deny it any longer. What Mary told me is right; I need professional help."

NOTE: Over the last few years, my sister, Mary, had continually recommended literature she thought would be beneficial to me; however, it never has interested me in the least. Years later, I understood I was afraid to read about it.

Back in Florida with Mark and Juliette, we lay boxes in the floor and begin packing. It takes the entire U-Haul for the daybed, the computer desk and all the miscellaneous boxes. While I am there, I arrange for a lawn and pool service.

With my telephone line still connected, I begin receiving obscene phone calls. Joel knows my password and the code to my Internet account. I learn he has changed my account, listing my address and telephone number, and changed my ad to state I like orgies, threesomes, and couples. He even added nude pictures of me to the account.

I feel the blood as it begins to pound in my temples. My younger brother is staring at my computer and the monitor is showing a nude picture of me. I feel my face flush crimson as I shudder in humiliation. In an instant I know it will be a long time before I get over the hurt this man did to me.

I go to the county police to file a complaint against Joel. They are halfway through taking down the information to arrest him for pornography, when they learn his address is in the city.

The police officer taking the information stops and says, "We cannot take his case because he is out of our jurisdiction. You can try the city police."

I go to the city police and an officer tells me, "We can't do anything. You shouldn't have let him get your pin number."

Next, I try my Internet Service Provider and a representative tells me, "It is your fault for letting him get your pin number."

Being upset, I decide to call Ralph, in Louisiana, my big brother friend who I always call in times of stress, especially when we were both in Atlanta.

Simply hearing Ralph's voice causes me to feel better. His deep timbred voice soothes me, "Sometimes, when there is nothing else that can be done, you have to let it go and move on. Get what you can out of the house and leave the rest."

"Thank you, Ralph. I feel much better after hearing your

voice."

My brother, Mark, and his wife, Juliette, are on disability for back injuries. They cannot help me load heavy furniture. I give my realtor two selling options. Sell the house with the furniture for one price or without the furniture for a lower price. I make the first option attractive to the prospective buyer, because my furniture was originally expensive; it is made of heavy hardwood.

When we get to Alabama, at Mark and Juliette's invitation, I decide to live with them for a while instead of going back to my empty house in Georgia. I cannot explain what happens to me next. It seems that, once I realize the immediate crisis is over and I think I can finally calm down, I slid fast into a depression. I begin thinking about suicide.

I receive a letter forwarded from my Georgia address from a woman in Arkansas. I wonder if it is from the wife of one of the men Susie has been making plans to see. When I begin reading the letter, I am shocked. She is warning about the man in Raleigh, North Carolina,—the man I thought may have been in a rehabilitation center during the four-week period I didn't hear from him. The woman who has written the letter had met him, and he manipulated and swindled her out of money in almost the same way as Joel did me. She found my name and address as well as other women's names and addresses among some of his papers and she has written to all of us. Being too distraught to write to her, I pray for her. I believe my situation with Joel was worse than her situation and probably more expensive. When I totaled all my losses, I was devastated; I had lost almost $30,000 because of Joel.

NOTE: In that lost, dim time before my water skiing accident, when I got on the Internet to relieve boredom, I had no idea how much "Adult Friend Finder" would eventually cost me.

My misery is so acute it is a physical pain. Kristen is crying and I can't console her. She feels she failed me. I tell her she didn't; Susie failed us both. Thoughts of suicide will not leave my head. I think of possible ways to do it. I am too tired to figure out how to do it. With Mark and Juliette in the house, how can I possibly do it without them intervening? Dear God, why don't you strike me dead? I remember Mama telling me so many times, if I do this or I do that, God might strike me dead.

"Well, God, I've done worse than Mama could ever imagine, so now will you strike me dead?"

Finally, in desperation, I call my insurance company and ask for psychiatric hospitals and psychologists in the area covered by my insurance. I feel an immediate sense of urgency as Kristen's hysterical cries in my head are making it hard for me to hear the insurance representative.

In a trembling voice, I ask the representative to repeat the information several times. The woman is patient and she gives me several names. One of the hospitals is located in Columbus, Georgia. One of the therapists is in Auburn, Alabama.

Having made the decision to get help, I feel a measure of immediate relief. Kristen's cries in my head also end. I make a quick trip to Georgia to check on my empty house and my bank account. I also go by Dr. Barfield's office, the medical doctor I first saw when my carotid artery was blocked. I tell her I need some Prozac.

Dr. Barfield says, "Aren't you living in Alabama now? You need to find a doctor there."

My whole body begins to shake as I wrap my arms across my chest. "Please," I say, "as I begin to rock back and forth."

"Sarah, are you suicidal?"

"I don't know."

"You need to check yourself in the Medical Center of Georgia in Gainesville."

Dr. Barfield gets angry with me, but she writes the prescription anyway. I know Mark will help me get to the hospital in Columbus, so I leave with the prescription and head back to Alabama. On the road I alternate between crying and praying. I ask God to help me get the house in Florida sold. Until I get it sold, I will be making mortgage and utility payments on two houses. All my money is disappearing. I feel hopeless. I cannot see a reason for me to live. I would be better off if I were dead. I begin thinking about all the sins and the shame and guilt I feel. All my teachings from my childhood come back to me. I begin to cry again.

I think, *"I can't die in this sinful state, or I will go straight to hell."*

Susie asks, "Why are you being so hard on yourself? It wasn't your fault you were born into such a dysfunctional family."

I begin praying and I ask God to help me get my life straightened out. Most of the drive to Alabama is a blur in my mind. I am in a fast-food restaurant and I don't recall how I got there. I pay for my food and go back to my car. I see no landmarks that look familiar. I approach a man sitting in his car with his window rolled down and I ask, "Can you tell me the name of this town?"

He looks up at me, clearly surprised I would ask that question. "You're in Newnan, Georgia."

"Can you tell me how to get back to Highway 34?"

The man gets out of his car because he has realized I am lost and all confused. He gives me directions to get to Highway 22. He tells me to turn left on Highway 22 and stay on it until I reach the Alabama line. Then he tells me Highway 22 changes into Highway 34 when it crosses the state line.

When the man pulls out of the parking lot, I lean my head on the steering wheel and cry. I knew everything the man told me. How did I get lost? How did I get so confused? I look at my watch. My hands are shaking so badly I can't hold my watch still. Where has all the time gone? There are many miles still to go before I get to Mark's house in Alabama. I crank the car and drive on, trying to follow the directions the man gave me.

I cross the state line and I am on Highway 34. My mind wanders and I try hard to refocus on the highway. When I hear noise in my head, I shake my head, blink my eyes, and breathe deep. I don't want anything to distract me from the highway. I don't want to get lost again. Before I know it I am pulling into Mark's drive.

Mark tells me the realtor from Florida called today. When I return her call, she tells me someone made an offer on the house. I hold my breath, waiting to hear what the offer was.

"Sarah," the realtor says, "the offer was $10,000 less than your asking price, and the prospective buyer wants the furniture with the house."

I hesitate, disappointed, telling the realtor, "I need time to think, crunch some figures, and I will call you back."

I have to consider the cost of the trip to remove the furniture and storage of the furniture, or taking it back to the Georgia house. I have to think about the expense of the lawn and pool service, the expense of utilities, carrying the loan for more months, and not knowing when I will get another offer. Considering my emotional and financial condition, I call the realtor and tell her I will accept the offer. We finish closing the final papers. The sale of the house in Florida provides a feeling of closure for me to all the sickness that went on with Joel. I feel I now have a chance to put all that behind me. For a few days I think I am better, and I procrastinate about going into the hospital.

A week after the closing date of the house in Florida, the realtor calls me again. "Sarah, you will never guess who bought your house?"

I answer, "The papers list the buyer as a woman from New Mexico."

"Yes," the realtor says, and then her voice rises with excitement, "but when I carried her the plant, which we carry to all new owners, Joel answered the door."

I am silent as my mind races. The realtor, also, says no more. Finally, I hang up the phone. I am remembering Joel was working in New Mexico when we first met. I suspect he called back out there to a wealthy woman and conned her into buying the house I had bought for him.

Anger...rage...humiliation...I know all those emotions

intimately. I lose all my sanity after that telephone conversation. I cannot understand why the realtor felt the need to tell me that bit of information. I am angry with her. Now Joel has my furniture. I especially resent him having my bedroom suite. I would never have agreed to let the house sell at any price to Joel.

Ralph calls and wants me to come out to Louisiana to be with him. I want to go, however, I explain to him who purchased the house in Florida, and I tell him it has made me sick. I describe my suicidal feelings, and I tell him I must get therapy before I can come.

Then, immediately, I call the hospital in Columbus. I am told to come for an evaluation. Mark agrees to drive me there.

At the hospital, the evaluator asks me many varied questions about the possibility of hurting others or myself.

I tell him, "I can't handle everything anymore. It is too much, I am too tired, and I might kill myself to end it all."

The young man doing my evaluation recommends I admit myself into the hospital.

I tell him that is what I want to do, because I don't know what else to do.

Chapter Nine

Living as Faith

Since my son Allen knew about my involvement with Joel, I know he will try to contact me. I call him to let him know I have admitted myself to a psychiatric hospital. Allen is pleased with my action.

When I enter the hospital, I am naive about what to expect. I am stressed out and I want to rest. And I think, when I'm not allowed to rest, that I will receive psychotherapy from a psychologist or psychiatrist. I want the hospital personnel to help me gain some insight into the noises in my head. I want them to help me make Susie stop doing what she does with men like Joel. They are the professionals, I am the patient. I came to the hospital for rest and treatment.

I get little rest. The program is fast-paced and works on the twelve-steps of Alcoholics Anonymous. We patients go to AA meetings daily and have group therapy. We have classes on understanding addictions, we have recreational therapy, and we each have a personal therapist.

While I am a patient there, I recall some of the events leading up to my affair with Joel. Everything leads back to two words, "sex" and "money," the excitement, the frills, the promises, the lusts and "no love." As far as I can see at this point, I never had a part in that life, and neither did Kristen. It was all Susie and Faith—Susie for the erotic sex and Faith for empathizing with and giving my money to Joel.

At the end of five days, Susie convinces the doctor she is fine, and he dismisses her. I have seen my therapist only twice and my psychiatrist only once during my stay in the hospital. I don't believe the hospital stay has helped me at all. Possibly, I am a little calmer.

I leave the hospital and return to Mark's home. He and his wife, Juliette, have a surprise party for me when I return. (See Figure 9.1) It makes me feel welcome.

Figure 9.1 Welcome home

Since I know I am addicted to sex, Mark helps me find a Sex Addicts Anonymous meeting in a nearby city and I begin attending. I attended one several years earlier while teaching, but couldn't (for some unknown reason) become attached to that group. The one I begin attending here in Alabama makes me feel welcome. I am the only female, but all the men are professionals, and they practice anonymity, as all twelve-step groups should. The men give me support from a man's perspective, and I give them support from a woman's perspective.

I schedule my first appointment with Dr. Crystal Kelley, the psychologist in Auburn, whom my insurance referred. She is wonderful. I feel more confident with her than any therapist I have ever been with. It takes a while for her to understand my background, but then I think she has good insights into my personality and what is happening in my life. I tell her about the SAA meetings I attend on Monday evenings.

While living with Mark, I pay rent, and I work hard each day helping Mark build a new section onto his house. I am Mark's little gopher and construction assistant. He had been paying his daughter $5.00 an hour to help him. She now has a job in town and is no longer available to help him. Without realizing, I allow Faith to take control of my life. She becomes extravagant in the financial help she gives to Mark.

During the summer months, a friend I meet in AA offers me vegetables from his garden if I will come pick them. I gratefully accept his offer. Juliette and I freeze some of the vegetables. Faith buys Juliette a canner because she does not have one, and they can the rest of the vegetables in jars.

Faith gives Mark and Juliette all the tools and some other items I had brought from Florida. Some they can use and others they can sell at flea markets. Faith could not see where Sarah had any further use of these items. Faith is grateful to Mark and Juliette for coming to her and Sarah's rescue and taking them into their home. She becomes compulsive about giving them food and money.

This is my sixth week with Dr. Kelley. I explain my feelings to her. I am allowing Mark and Juliette to mistreat me. I work all day with Mark outside on their house and still they want me to cook at least twice a week in the evening, thus giving Juliette a break. She never gives me a break helping her husband building their house. She takes a nap daily after lunch, even though there is fresh corn which needs to be shucked. Mark is also trying to control who I see by telling me this is a small town, and everybody knows everything that is happening. He hates it when I go out to Louisiana to see Ralph. I discuss with Dr. Kelley the possibility of getting my own apartment. I feel more stable now, and I think I should get out on my own. She agrees, and I commit to finding my own living quarters.

Following one of my AA meetings, I talk to the friend who gives me the vegetables. He shows me some apartments near his home. When I contact the manager of the apartment complex, I learn the rent is only $345 a month, plus the utility bill, which includes city water, electricity, and sewage. Other than my telephone, that will be all my housing expense.

When I tell Mark I want to move into my own apartment, he tells me quickly I will mess up his budget. "Sarah, I've grown used to the extra money from you in my budget, and there's no way I can manage without it."

Immediately, Faith comes out and feels guilty. She saw one of his payments recently and saw that, even though he sends in $62 each month as payment on the credit card, the balance only drops by $4. The rest of the $62 is going toward finance charges. He has three other similar cards. Faith has no idea the balance on the four of the cards totals several thousand dollars. Faith tells Mark about a card Sarah has, which is available at 3.7 percent annual percentage rate for six months. She asks Mark if he would like to transfer the balances from all his four cards to Sarah's card. Of course, Mark jumps at the offer. Sarah's credit limit on that card is $48,000 so it ought to be enough for his four.

Sarah learns what Faith has done but it is too late; the transfers have already been made. Sarah tells Dr. Kelley about the credit card and about Mark not wanting her to move out.

Dr. Kelley tells Sarah, "You don't have to feel guilty. He made it before you moved in; he will make it when you move out."

I can hardly stand the pressure or the guilt I feel about moving out of Mark's house, and yet, I cannot stand to live here any longer because he tries to control my life.

NOTE: It was while I was hospitalized at Women's Institute of Incorporation Therapy that I learned about abuser values. In my childhood, I had let family members victimize and take advantage of me. Mark was not one of my previous family abusers, as he was younger, but he was family, and I was allowing him to take advantage of me.

Because of Faith's trust in Mark, she believes he will continue to pay on Sarah's one credit card the same amount he had been sending to the four cards. I had allowed the statement to continue going to Mark's address, since he would make the payments instead of me. Therefore, it was some time before I saw the statement sheets again. I later learn Mark not only made the minimum payment of $50, but he made the payment late some months.

Susie decides there is no harm in having a drink occasionally. She drives to a package store and buys a bottle to keep at home.

One of the men in SAA begins to stop by her apartment to see her. Sarah struggles to keep control. Susie tries desperately to take over her body. Kristen overpowers her, and starts talking about how uncomfortable it will be for Sarah and the man to have to pick up new chips Monday night at the SAA meeting.

He says, "Yeah, you are right, it would be uncomfortable to have to start our time over."

Thankfully, nothing happens sexually.

He stopped by other times, too, and we never allowed anything to happen that would cause either of us to have to pick up a new chip.

At the same time, the guy with the vegetables is stopping by to teach me steps to the waltz, so I can dance with him when we go to the VFW dances on Saturday nights. I master the steps and enjoy a few dances with him. I believe if I had not belonged to SAA, and had not worked so hard with Dr. Kelley, I would have given in to the urge to let Susie take over my body. I longed for love and attention. Thanks to my program, I never had to pick up a chip.

My beautiful apartment boosts my self-esteem. (See Figure 9.2)

Once again I feel like a human being. I have stopped going to AA meetings; however I still go to SAA meetings, and I am still in therapy with Dr. Kelley. Up to this point, Dr. Kelley believes I love Ralph, and I do. Mark is bitterly opposed to my seeing Ralph. Dr. Kelley cannot understand the loyalty I feel I must give to my brother, Mark. She tries to help me understand why I feel so loyal to him.

On my last visit with Ralph, he has plans to go to Baltimore to one of the Mayo Clinics to have prostate surgery. He has a sister living in Baltimore where he can stay while he recuperates. I told him I would be happy to go with him. He thanked me and said, "No this is something I have to do alone."

I am hurt Ralph will not allow me to be with him. Needing time alone, I call Cheaha State Park and reserve a one-room cabin for Friday and Saturday evenings. Allen took me to this state park

Figure 9.2 Sarah and her new apartment

when I went to visit him at West Georgia College. Allen and I had a good time and took many pictures that day. I always wanted to go again. It is such a peaceful location.

When I return, I visit with Mark and Juliette, and I tell them about Ralph's condition. Even though I have my own apartment, I continue taking advantage of the free vegetables offered by my friend, and I share them with Mark and Juliette.

Ralph doesn't call until four weeks later, when he tells me he has recovered from his surgery. He says, "I am back at my sister's house, but I'm still in pain. The doctors won't let me drive yet. I may get my cousin, who is taking a college course now, to drive my truck back to Louisiana, and then pay his airfare back home."

I had composed a poem while resting at Cheaha State Park shortly after he left town for his surgery. I had the poem matted and framed. I sent it to him as a "Get Well" thought. (See the poem and a photo of the cabin in Figure 9.3. Notice the first letter of each line spells the name of the park.)

Mark begins telling me what I believe are lies about Ralph, trying to turn me against him. Without understanding my own feelings, and not knowing whom to believe, I remain confused. Mark says he called the Mayo Clinic, and they reported to him that Ralph had never been a patient there. Perhaps Mark is right. Louisiana is a long way to drive from Alexander City. Maybe I am not meant to stay with Ralph. After what Joel did to me, I hope I can trust family before an outsider. I stop calling Ralph to check on him. I never hear from him again.

In a therapy session with Dr. Kelley several months later, I recall Mark has a hidden motive about my relationship with Ralph. Earlier, he had requested I ask Ralph if he would hire him to work as a laborer in his restaurants, and pay him in cash, since he is on disability. He wanted his pay in cash so he wouldn't have to report it on his income tax report. Ralph told me he couldn't pay Mark in cash because, if he did, he couldn't claim his wages as expenses on his own income tax. When I told Mark, he didn't comment, however, judging by the expression on his face, I believe that was the time he decided he didn't want me to see Ralph anymore.

Well, I have lost Ralph. I enjoy my Saturday nights at the VFW with my friend and his regular dance partner. On Monday nights, I continue attending my Sex Addicts Anonymous Meetings. It seems Susie and I are getting closer. I no longer strive to be the professional, perfectionist woman I presented to the public in Atlanta. Some of Susie's sexual needs are also my needs now.

CHEAHA STATE PARK

Christ is present, he's all around.
He's in the sky and on the ground.
All of God's creatures have their needs.
Echoes come from the trees.
Heaven reaches to the earth.
Awesome flowers show rebirth.

Stars shine in the evening moonlight.
Trees bend and stretch with all their might.
All is well in the State Park tonight.
The chapel waits with open arms.
Everyone present experiences its charm.

People are hiking through the trails.
All are informed to hold onto the rail.
RV's and tents are scattered along the way.
Kids enjoy this scenery everyday.

July 15, 2002
by Sarah Harrison

Figure 9.3 Poem and Cabin

Masturbation is helping partially, but I miss being with men.

Several weeks pass, one day I am outside my apartment with a mixed drink in hand when the maintenance men for the apartments come by. I remember them from the day I moved in. The older man impresses me so I speak to him.

That night, much to my surprise, the doorbell rings. It is the older maintenance man with a teenage boy. "Hi," he says with a huge smile on his face. "If you don't have any cheese, I'm not coming in."

I begin laughing. "I don't know. Come in and let me check." I learn quickly that he loves cheese, so I begin keeping cheese in the refrigerator.

The man's name is Wayne and his fourteen-year-old son's name is Ray. I cannot believe he is living with his dad instead of his mom. Wayne is paying on his own house around the corner from where my apartment is located. Wayne has been working for the owners of these apartments for several years. I begin seeing him every day on his break at 10:15. He has an incredible sense of humor and that is what attracts me. It is hard to believe we've known each other for such a short time; we spend all our free time together.

Wayne's son, Ray, loves playing on my computer, because his dad does not have one at home. I try to be good to him, because, having been a middle school teacher; I realize how much children this age need to believe someone cares about them. When I visit Wayne in his house for the first time, I am impressed with the size and the way he has taken care of his home. He and Ray's mother were separated for four years before their final divorce, which was one year before we met. In the beginning, Ray's mother received the house, but she couldn't keep up the payments and almost lost it. Wayne's boss financed it for him, and now Wayne is having $50 each week taken out of his paycheck to make the payment on his house.

My sister Mary had been so excited about my relationship with Ralph. Every since I broke up with him she is angry with me and

Mark for interfering. We have been communicating by email for several months now. She is happy I am in therapy with Dr. Kelley. Several weeks ago, after Dr. Kelley and I talked about Mary and some of the hard times she had growing up, Mary mailed Dr. Kelley some of her journals and other information concerning her therapy hoping they would help Dr. Kelley better understand our family background.

I enclose a page from my journal dated July 30, 2001.

I had a marvelous discussion with Dr. Kelley today. She is the first therapist I have ever had that I feel comfortable enough with to tell the truth. I know she won't ridicule or laugh at me. Today is the first time I have ever told a therapist about that harrowing experience that happened in the only upstairs bedroom in the home on Lay Avenue in Knoxville, Tennessee.

Today, memories that still lurked in some secret place in my mind come pouring out of me as I covered my breasts with my arms and rocked back and forth.

I told Dr. Kelley, to this point in my life, all I could remember was my fourteen-year-old brother put a lamp under the sheet. Both of us put our heads under the sheet so we could see what he was doing. He took his "thing" with one hand and pumped it up and down, while he played with my bottom with his other hand. I remember it felt good and then, a bunch of white stuff started coming out of his "thing." I thought the only liquid that came from there was his pee. It scared me so badly. I thought something terrible had happened to my brother.

Today, I remembered he had convinced me he wasn't hurt, and it felt good to him. The next night we did it again. Until we moved away from Lay Avenue in Knoxville several months later, to the old run-down shack, I don't recall how often it happened. I do remember I did everything I could to keep from going to bed.

After this, I remember how much I like to push pencils or anything I can find into my vagina. Carrots out of the refrigerator made me feel good too. Afterwards, I put my panties on and they pushed on the object, holding it into my vagina. It hurt, but I liked it. I spend several hours some nights after lights are out feeling of myself and playing with different objects.

Dr. Kelley sits quiet as I continue pouring out the demons from my past. I have dredged up these memories of depthless neglect and abuse, and I cannot stop the flow of words from my mouth. Dr. Kelley lets me go over my time.

I close my eyes and the grimace on my face shows the pain I feel. The voice of a small child speaks as her knees rise to meet her chin, and she wraps her arms around her knees. "Mommy, something terrible is wrong with me. There is blood in my panties."

Mama never even turned around from the stove. She said, "Don't worry about it. You probably fell on your bicycle."

Mama and Daddy bought an old house on a hundred acre farm in Georgia. We were all still under the age of sixteen. It was my job to milk the cows, help churn the milk, and mold the butter. Afterwards, Mama set out to peddle the dairy products. My older sisters had to take turns going with Mama to drive the truck. I liked staying home alone, because I could masturbate and no one would know.

Why was today my day for confronting demons from the past? Today I had flashbacks of events that caused me to feel nauseated. My daddy behaved, at times, in a trashy manner, and at those times he caused me to feel trashy too. Today I remembered that, whenever Daddy was out of work, he lay in his bed exposing himself every day when we came in the side door on our way home from school. I always wondered why Mama didn't see him and cover him. He always pretended to be asleep.

I want to understand why I became sexually promiscuous, and why my compulsion to travel to meet one man after another was so great, it overrode my fear of getting lost.

A con artist talked me into leaving my home in Georgia and buying a house in Florida. The house in Florida was only ten miles from Cypress Cove, a clothing optional resort.

We visited Cypress Cove together and I decided, "This is for me."

I wouldn't have to take off men's pants in my mind any more. I can look and see everything, because everyone was nude. Everything was so free, open, and noncompetitive. We were planning to become members so we wouldn't have to pay every time we entered the gate.

I strongly believe my curiosity about the size of a man's penis is because of seeing my father and brother's penises, and so many others during my sexual addiction.

On this visit with Dr. Kelley, she told me she had returned Mary's journal and other information to her by mail. She didn't reveal the contents of Mary's material; however, she bragged on her writings, saying it was obvious Mary had been a good mother to her children, unlike our mother. Even though our mother had worked hard to feed and clothe us, she failed to protect us from our father and brother.

Wayne and I continue to enjoy each other's company. He has two stepchildren, sixteen and eighteen, whom he helped raise from ages three months and two years old. The man Ray's mother left Wayne for is Black. The sixteen-year-old stepdaughter has a Black son and is pregnant with another child. The father is awaiting court trial for possession of stolen goods.

Wayne keeps me laughing. He has such a great sense of humor. I haven't dated a man like him in a long time. I am at ease with him. Ray is happy to see his daddy excited about life again. We build bonfires out in his back yard. We roast hotdogs and marshmallows and drink beer. I am reminded again of the childhood I missed.

Wayne, Ray, and I are sitting around a fire in Wayne's back yard and Wayne has grown quiet after his usual spill of antics. We three are comfortable with each other. I have heard from others that Ray can be a real troublemaker but I have yet to see it.

"Ray," I tell him. "Look up." I point to the majestic blind whirl of the Milky Way.

After a while Ray grows tired, or bored, and goes into the house. Gazing up at the heavens brings a tear of sad joy to my eyes. The moon is cold, full, and watchful.

I move closer to Wayne and he puts his arm around my shoulder and we continue to stare into the flames. In a quiet, tranquil voice, I ask, "Wayne, I have a timeshare week at Still Water Resort. Are you interested in taking a week off from work to go there?"

"I'll make you guess; what do you think?"

I laugh at him again. We have a great week, swimming, relaxing by the pool, and I work out in their gym. We even go out on the lake in a pontoon boat.

We go hiking down a steep hill near Cheaha Mountain, which has waterfalls and a big water hole, where brave individuals jump into the waterhole from a high rock. Wayne was raised nearby, and came to this water hole when he was a child. Many of his trips were to fetch water and bathe.

Faith has learned that Wayne, like Sarah, experienced a dysfunctional and economically poor childhood. She urges Sarah, "Let Wayne experience the childhood he never had. Show him that childhood can be a fun, exciting time."

Faith buys a pop-up camper in excellent condition, so they can camp out all night.

Wayne says emphatically to others, "I'm just country, and I don't care who knows it."

Then Faith buys a beautiful jeep with four-wheel drive (See Figure 9.4) to make it easier to pull the pop-up camper down the steep washed-out terrain into the bottom flatland near the waterhole. Faith talks the car dealer down to $12,000 and then finances it on another one of Sarah's credit cards that she has a deal on at 3.9%. Wayne and I begin talking about marriage.

Figure 9.4 New Jeep

One factor leading to my decision to get married is Mama. She knows some of what's been happening in my life and she talks with my siblings, telling them she is worried about me. She hints that she knows I am living in sin. It appears, at this point, Mama does not have long to live, and I had rather she not know I am living with a man. Wayne is everything I have ever wanted—or so I thought at the time.

Wayne and I stay at my apartment some, and some at his house. His house is cold at night. I like my apartment better. Wayne has space heaters. The house is about fifty years old, but is well constructed. If we let my apartment go, we will have more money to put into improvements on his house.

The owners of the apartments warn me about Ray's behavior. I have already witnessed one incident of bad behavior, but I think, *"He can't be that bad. I worked with middle-school children for twenty-six years."*

One owner of the apartments says, "I just want you to know what you are getting into. One of Wayne's friends left him because of Ray. I don't know all the details, but I do know Ray kicked her in the leg."

I hear one of the owners tell Wayne, "If you want to keep this woman, you better set Ray straight, and use the belt on him once in a while."

Until this point, Ray has behaved towards me. After we move my furniture into Wayne's house, Ray changes for the worse. He beats on the door after we go to bed, saying he is afraid. He doesn't want to go to school, and he gets into trouble at school more than before I moved in. Wayne starts having panic attacks. I fear it is heart attacks, because he is holding his chest.

The panic attacks get a little better so we continue with our plans for a December wedding. Faith hires a contractor to install a central heating and air-conditioning unit. All the ductwork has to be laid and vents installed. The electrical wiring in the house is so old it has to be replaced. Mud from the front yard is tracked into the house, and onto the newly installed carpet Faith had installed. Now Faith hires a contractor to lay concrete around the front of the house.

We invite Ed, Wayne's brother, and his wife over for dinner. Ed tells me, "You are spending too much money on Wayne. You don't know him like I do."

I'm confused; I comment, "You may be right, but I hope you're not."

Wayne and I are both getting nervous, trying to get the house prepared for a home wedding in December. My children and his family, too, begin giving excuses for not being able to attend on the date we have set for our wedding. We set another date, and get excuses a second time, so we cancel again, and go to the courthouse in Dadeville. On December 14, 2001, we have the probate judge perform our marriage ceremony.

Our Christmas together is wonderful, and even Ray shows me more love than he ever has since I've known him. His face beams when he opens his Christmas gifts—lots of new school clothes, which he desperately needed. He cleans the house and washes the dishes. He even washes the cars. I hug him and tell him I am proud of him.

Wayne's stepdaughter has delivered her second child, and the father has been to court, and sent to prison. I never met the father. The two children are so sweet.

> NOTE: In time, we help with these two children, especially, the second one who is a little girl. Then I am happy because I am making someone else happy.
> However, deep down, all I ever wanted was for somebody to love me and take good care of me.

There is not much work available at the apartment complex during the winter months. When there *is* work, the owners let their own sons do the work. Faith tells Wayne he might as well quit the job. Now Sarah has to pay the mortgage and all the expenses.

It is almost an impossibility to force Ray to go to school now that his Daddy is home all the time. Wayne has another panic attack, trying to force Ray to go to school. He says, "Ray, I didn't finish high school, and I want you to stay in school."

This is news to me; I didn't know Wayne hadn't finished high school. After that panic attack, Wayne takes no responsibility for anything. I am forced to use my money to support the whole clan.

NOTE: While in therapy after separating from Wayne, but before our divorce, my therapist told me that she thought I used my money to control men so that I could have the upper hand.

In the spring we plan a vacation in North Carolina. First, we spend some time with Nathan on base at Camp LeJuene. When we leave Nathan, we drive to a scheduled timeshare at Myrtle Beach. While traveling home, we spend a few days with Allen in Charlotte.

Before we leave to go on vacation, Ray informs us at the last minute, he is not going with us. Wayne refuses to make him go, so we made plans for him to stay with Ed. While on vacation, we receive a call from Ed, reporting Ray will not come home by curfew time. He tells Wayne he has told Ray the next time he is late coming home; he cannot stay with him any longer. The following day Ray calls, telling his father that his Uncle Ed has thrown him out. We cut our timeshare short to come home early.

The credit card Faith charged the Jeep on is going back up to ten percent annual percentage rate, as well as the one Mark is using. I call the one Mark used to consolidate his four cards. I learn Mark has recently charged an additional $4,000 to my card without my permission. I am furious. I realize I have been taken advantage of, and I do not appreciate it. I call the company and have the card canceled.

When I call Mark and ask him why he did it, he tells me, "You and Wayne were in North Carolina. I could not reach you by phone. I tried."

When I check the dates, I learn the charge was made two days before we left for North Carolina. Our cell phone is our only telephone. He could have called me, even if I were on vacation.

When I confront him about the dates, his reply is, "I thought you were already gone."

Now his total borrowed is tens of thousands of dollars and the interest keeps adding to the amount.

Since I want a lifelong marriage to Wayne, I talk to the bank about getting a home equity loan on his house. It appraises for $53,000. That gives me enough to pay off my credit card for Mark's loan and a second card for the Jeep. I can also pay off the loan Wayne has with his old boss for $12,000 on the house, since he is no longer working for the apartment complex. It is a balloon note to be paid off in five years, or to be refinanced. It costs me $512 a month. I set up Mark an amortization schedule for five years at nine percent interest. Mark's share comes out to be $290 a month. I ask Mark about meeting with a lawyer to draw up a legal contract, or at least have the amortization schedule notarized.

Again, Mark succeeds in making me feel guilty. He says, "I *am* your brother; don't you think you can trust me?"

I wish I could have trusted him. Mark paid three payments, then an extra $1,000, and then two more payments. Then he stops making payments. When I file a lawsuit against him later, trying to force him to pay me something, he tells my sisters, "Sarah doesn't need the money, she has plenty."

I ask him to get life insurance for the loan amount; however, he is turned down, or it is so expensive he does not buy it. He told me he tried.

Deep down in my heart, I believe he hates me for marrying Wayne. It means Faith is helping Wayne financially, instead of him.

Mark and I live six miles apart. I spend my time trying to understand my relationship with him. I still don't understand why he was so bitterly opposed to my seeing Ralph.

School is out, and Ray has failed seventh grade. Wayne does not punish him in any way.

In July, my family has a birthday party for Mama at an upscale restaurant in middle Georgia. Many members of my family have not yet met Wayne. He is nervous, and begins drinking beer in the morning before we begin the trip to Georgia. It is a three-and-one-half hour drive to the location of the party.

"Since you have been drinking," I tell Wayne. "I want you to keep your mouth shut when we get to the restaurant."

"Have you ever known me to keep my mouth shut? I told you when I married you, 'I am just me.' I'm country and I can't help what I am."

"Well, that's fine, but still, as I said, don't talk, just be seen."

"I'll try. That's all I can promise."

This conversation before helped with his mouth, but not his hands.

When we arrive, the family is waiting in the lobby, and I am trying to keep Wayne behind me. He comes around me and speaks to Mama. Then he sees the receptionist and reaches out to touch her. Without looking away, the receptionist backs out of his way.

I am embarrassed and my voice is stifled and unnatural. "Stop, Wayne. Don't do that."

The receptionist hears me; she realizes Wayne is drunk. We are all escorted to our special party table. I tried to watch Wayne while we were walking to our table but, obviously, I did a poor job because he touched a customer.

While everyone is ordering, my sister Rebekah calls me outside. She tells me, "A member of management came to me and complained about Wayne. If you cannot keep him in his seat, they are going to throw us out. He has bothered some of the staff and some of the customers."

I am embarrassed. While we are outside, one of Rebekah's daughters, who never met Wayne until today, comes outside and says, "Why don't you divorce that man?"

When we go back inside, I tell Wayne what has occurred. I tell him not to get up again. He doesn't order any food so I order a cup of coffee for him. I feel as if everyone at the table is staring at us. I cannot wait to leave. When the meal is over, Wayne goes out to the

Jeep and gets into the driver's seat. The plan was for all of us to go to the activities room at Mama's apartment building for her to open her presents, and have ice cream and birthday cake.

When Nathan sees Wayne in the driver's seat, he comes over and says, "Wayne, I think you better get out and let Mother get in the driver's seat."

Wayne gets out and goes to the passenger side. I hug Nathan and tell him I am sorry for Wayne's behavior, and then we leave. I drive straight home, skipping Mama's apartment.

Nathan and Wayne never got along. Nathan had been to visit us before, and he, like many others including myself now, cannot understand why Wayne does not discipline Ray. After all the problems Nathan had in his own lifetime, he knows where Ray is headed if someone doesn't take a firm grip on him now.

Because Wayne didn't insist Ray go to North Carolina with us in the spring, Ray and his girlfriend now have a child on the way. Ray is only fourteen years old. Wayne will soon be a granddad. That is partly what Nathan had reference to, when he stated someone has to take a firm grip on Ray.

The house in Georgia has made its own mortgage payment for about eight months because I have had it rented for $900 a month. The renters have a daughter in high school. The school had been letting the parents drive her back to her same school since January but now, since it is a new school year, they tell the parents she has to live in the county. They move out, and leave my house vacant once again.

We decide to rent Wayne's house in Alabama, take Ray, and move to Georgia. His house rents for $350 a month. With Mark's $290, we have more than enough to make the payment on the loan; but now I have my Georgia mortgage payment of $998. The amount recently went up because of a tax increase.

While living in Georgia, I use the yellow pages to find a big screen TV technician to have my big screen repaired. The big screen is something else Faith bought for Wayne and Ray, hoping to keep them happy. The technician wants $200 up front to order the part.

When the technician returns a week later to repair the big screen, he has his female friend with him. Both behave as if they are educated and trustworthy people. They indicate an interest in buying the house from me after the contract with the realtor ends.

The technician says, "That way, we can both save money. I am set to inherit $500,000 as soon as the court has settled the estate. Then I can pay you in cash."

We write up contracts, dates, amounts, and go to my local bank to get them notarized. I am so excited and can hardly wait for the contract with the realtor to expire. After all the paperwork is finalized, the technician asks me if I will loan him $3,200 to keep him from going to jail the following day. Just like a fool, Faith comes out to listen to his story. She hates the thought of him having to spend the night in jail for something as minor as failing to appear in court for a traffic violation. She gets Sarah's purse and writes him a check, signing Sarah's name. That was eight years ago.

NOTE: The technician's story about jail was probably just that—a story, or better yet—a lie. Maybe Faith was trying to fix everybody with Sarah's money. That's what my therapist assumes. I don't know; however, it all seems pretty out of character to me, knowing how conservative I am with my money when I am myself. I stayed in touch with this technician through telephone calls until his death with him always promising to pay that $3,200 back, but I never got it.

Ray's enrollment in Georgia schools lasts for one week. Ray cries every night until Wayne lets him have his way and takes him back to Alabama. He gives Ray's mother temporary custody of him, while we try to get the Georgia house ready to sell again. It doesn't sell. At the same time Wayne has applied for disability in Alabama. He is not able to work for more than two or three hours consecutively during hot days. The doctor has given him a permanent disability tag for his vehicle, because he gets out of breath after taking only a few short steps. The government is starting to schedule his doctor appointments. We have his house rented so we cannot move back into it. We are in Alabama seeing one of the doctors when we try to reserve a room at a local motel for the following week.

The manager says, "You don't need a reservation; you have one. It will be here for you."

Wayne asks, "Can't we give you money to hold the room?"

The Native American tells him, "No, you have a place."

When we arrive the next week, the manager says to Wayne, "No, no room. Leave and don't come back."

I go inside to see what is taking Wayne so long to get signed in. I ask the manager, "What's the problem?"

The Native American manager tells me, "Leave; we call the cops."

Wayne and I leave. A few minutes later, seven cop cars pull us over on the side of the highway. Due to my lack of experience with the law, I get out of the car when Wayne is taken in handcuffs to one of the police cars. Apparently, they are waiting for me to step a foot on the ground. As soon as I get out, an officer handcuffs me and locks me up in the back of a different police car. When the jeep has been vacated, the police dump our luggage and steal our camera. We both spend the night in jail—my first ever. Wayne is charged with a DUI and I am charged with public intoxication. Court costs, fines, bail and lawyer's fees cost me roughly $4,000 for both of us.

One of my friends, who is a sheriff in the county, told me the reason the court treated me so unfairly was they learned I was Mark Mahoney's sister. The court and lawyers of the small town are not fond of Mark, so they made it hard for me. Part of my costs was DUI School, and I was not driving. Another part of my costs was bail. They let Wayne out the next morning on his house, but wouldn't release me. The house is in both our names, and we are married. It seems there is something wrong with the city government in that town.

Mark has informed me he cannot make any more payments on his loan. Since I cannot afford a motel, I tell Mark I will use the travel trailer in his backyard to stay in when we must be in Alabama for Wayne's doctor appointments. It is small, and we cannot take showers in his travel trailer, but we have a television, and we can cook our own meals. Mark allows us to use his bathroom for showers.

We find a beautiful twenty-seven acre piece of land out in the country. I love it, and I believe my house in Georgia will sell soon. I have my home in Georgia listed with a different realtor now, one who knows the area and the homes of my builder. Ray needs to get out of the city if he is to grow up and become a decent human being. No one has lived on this land in hundreds of years. It has deer, wild turkey, and other types of wildlife. Wayne and I both want this land so much.

I have been taking Wayne to Tuskegee to get his medications. We have done the necessary paperwork to apply for military compensation for his loss of hearing from his days in the army. It is my hope he will soon be getting disability from social security as well as compensation from the military. In addition, I am in hopes my house will soon sell.

Most of the time I am with Wayne, it is definitely Faith, who takes over my personality. It is trusting, adolescent Faith who loves Wayne. She is the one who supports him. She is the one who hangs in there, long after Sarah would have thrown in the towel and gone back to Georgia.

Faith decides to buy the land. When it is time to sign the closing papers, Faith thinks of Wayne's pride, so she asks the woman preparing the closing papers to list the property in both names. There is much work to be done on the new land. A septic tank has to be dug, the yard has to be leveled, and the land has to be cleared for the electric lines. The waterlines have to be dug and run 900 feet through the woods.

I am aware of what Faith has done—sometimes I learn sooner, sometimes later. I love this land and I think it can provide a new beginning for Wayne, Ray, and me. I find a used mobile home to move onto the land. Since I am in a mess financially, I decide to trade the jeep for the used trailer. All total, I have invested $82,000 in the land, mobile home, and other preparations to the land.

In January, after we move into the mobile home, we begin keeping Alison some for her Mama. She is Wayne's half-Black step-grandchild, who is fourteen months old now. I love her, with all my heart, but it seems that no one but Wayne and I care about her. One grandmother works and the other simply doesn't care about her. Alison's mother, Sandra, often brings her other child for me to keep. Once Sandra brought Alison and, without calling to explain, did not come back for her for an entire week.

Wayne and I work hard to get the underbrush cleared from the land. Just when I think the quiet, serenity of our woods is having a positive impact on Ray; he becomes restless and begins cussing me and his father. Then he attempts suicide by overdosing. We admit him to a psychiatric hospital. I think, *"Ray is crying out. Possibly now we can get to the bottom of his problem and get him some real help."*

The next day when we visit him, Ray cries and cries; he will not stop crying. He wants Wayne to sign him out of the hospital.

When Wayne tells me he is going to sign Ray out, I tell him not to give in to Ray; however, Wayne won't listen to me. Wayne signs Ray out against the doctor's orders.

Wayne and I are both drinking more and more. I thought Wayne and I could leave the house in town, move out here in the country, and have some peace. I did not count on all this other baggage following us.

We aren't the only ones Ray creates problems for, and finally, he is sent off to boot camp for four weeks—a few short weeks to catch my breath. I want to help this child, but he needs more than I have to offer. He is in serious need of professional help, because he has attempted suicide several times. Wayne should have left him in the hospital. To have released him from the psychiatric hospital against doctor's wishes proves to be a big mistake.

When it is time for Ray to be released from boot camp, Kathy, who gave birth to Ray's baby on March 1, tells us she has permission to go to Ray's graduation. It was a lie; she didn't have permission. When we return, she tells us she cannot go back to her grandparents' house where she and the baby have been living.

Then unexpectedly we are threatened with "kidnapping a minor." Further, the authorities say Kathy will be charged with "abandoning her baby," because she didn't take the baby with her.

Wayne wants me to keep Kathy, help her fight for her baby, and all of us stay together here in the country. First, there is no money for a lawyer; neither do I want to go to jail. Second, I am tired; I am exhausted. I have reached my limit financially, physically, and emotionally.

I cannot control Ray; much less raise all these babies. Two belong to Wayne's stepdaughter, Sandra. Now, Sandra often hangs out here too. Kathy, Ray and Kathy's baby are too much. A single wide mobile home won't hold all of us.

Nevertheless, Wayne lets Ray and Kathy move in with us. Ray isn't home from boot camp long when he gets suspended from school for the rest of the year.

When Bonnie calls and asks me to come to her house early to help get ready for Nathan's homecoming from Iraq, I am ready to go. I am sicker than I realize, and I have bruises that my family will later question. I cannot take it any longer, and I am so, so ready to get into my car and leave.

And I never again go back there to live....

* * *

Mary and I though, attempt the beginning of my healing by visiting our old childhood homes on Ulster Street, Lay Avenue, and the shack in Heiskell. We simply ride past the place on Ulster Street because the area has become a dangerous part of town where many drug deals take place. Upon finding the home on Lay Avenue, we knock on the door. Mr. Roberts, the same Black man who purchased it from Daddy fifty years earlier answers the door. We explain to him who we are and he says, "Please come in. If you would like to look around, you are more than welcome to."

I said, "Are you sure? I would like to see so many things in the house. I have so many memories." Daddy's corner cabinet he built looks almost like it did the day we left it when I was eight years old. The maple wood is still varnished to a beautiful shine and not a glass shelf or window appears to be broken.

"Oh, I see you removed the black pot-belly stove." It was strange to not see the coal bucket sitting beside it on the square metal mat which held the claw feet of the stove. I gaze toward the ceiling where the flue pipe extended and went out. It had been filled, not so nicely, with a square of wood and painted over.

Mr. Roberts explains, "Yes, coal got too expensive and after my children left home, it was too heavy for me to carry into the house."

The rest of the kitchen is the same except for minor repairs. I wanted to get upstairs. To get there, you must go through the bedroom Mary and Rebekah slept in. That's also where the closet is I used to hid in and cry. I go over to the closet and open the door.

Kristen, my protector, comes to help me. I cannot take any more of this house as "Sarah". I had to dissociate or die. The closet is filled with junk. She sees Susie hiding behind the boxes crying. Kristen closes the door quickly. "Come on Mary, let's go upstairs."

"Wait, I want to see more of this room."

Mary lingers there, but Kristen slips on up the stairs to the top. Straight ahead is an opening to the unfinished part of the attic where Sarah used to hide her doll Sally, and other toys. Kristen opens the door, but cannot see anything because it is too dark. She looks down the stairway and there at the bottom is Mary. Flashbacks come of the day Sarah threw Sally down exclaiming, "I don't love Sally any more." Her head broke into three pieces. That was the last doll Santa Claus ever brought to me.

Mary comes on up the stairs and we look into the room where Sarah was abused by Adam. Mary says, "Look out the window. See how beautiful it is from up here. You were so lucky to have this room for yours." Sarah didn't answer her. My mind returned to the bed, the lamp, Adam, and the first night Mama sent me there to sleep with him. "Sarah, what's wrong with you?"

This question shakes me up and I quickly revert to Sarah. "I've seen enough. I think we need to leave Mr. Roberts alone. We have used enough of his time."

"You are right." Mary turns toward Mr. Roberts as we go down stairs and says, "Mr. Roberts, we do appreciate your hospitality and allowing us to go through your home."

Then I ask, "Do you mind if I take a picture or two of the house?"

Mr. Roberts reply is, "You can take as many pictures as you would like. I was happy to have the two of you enjoy your childhood home again."

We took a few pictures and then I drive on up Lay Avenue to Mr. and Mrs. Michael's house. Blacks are living in it too. I wonder where the Michaels went or whether they are even alive.

We decide we must find our school and I'm so thankful we did, because we found out it was to be torn down shortly. Seeing friendly home owners nearby, we ask them to take a picture of us standing in front of our school.

Next we travel to Park City Lowery Park where Mama took us when she had the time and money. The white ducks paddling around on the water look like patches of white silk while little blotches trailed close behind. Families are gathered on the grass near picnic tables with Daddies pushing their children on the swings or throwing balls to the boys. I ask Mary, "Don't you wish our family was like those families?"

Depression rises when we leave the park to find our last childhood home, the "old shack" We drive past it several times without knowing it. We find a farm house we remember and judge the distance down the road. I park the car, get out, and we begin our struggle through the briars, bushes, and weeds until we spot the shack in the distance. We reach the front door first, but the porch and steps are gone and it is too high to get up into the house. Then we go around to the side and climb through a window. We took some pictures there also. It was dangerous for us to be in there because the house was in such disrepair. We may have fallen through the floor, but we were determined to see it, even the second floor.

This trip was enjoyable for both of us. We probably experienced more good memories than bad. We drove into Pigeon Forge and stayed two nights before going back home.

As yet I did not know how fragmented my brain, nor how sick my soul was.

You Love Your Daddy, Don't You?

Part V
Healing

"When I say, 'I am a Christian,' I'm not claiming to be perfect, my flaws are far too visible, but God believes I am worth it."
- Maya Angelou

You Love Your Daddy, Don't You?

Chapter Ten

My Spiritual Journey

"When it is dark enough, we can see the stars."
- Charles Beard

Sometime in the early spring of 2003, while talking to Bonnie on the telephone, one of my alters tells her I cannot take it anymore.

Later, Bonnie confronts me, "Mama, what did you mean?"

I reply, "I don't remember saying that, but that's the way I felt. I don't exactly know what I meant except I was tired all the time. My back hurt all the time. Ray talked ugly to me all the time. I didn't let you children talk to me that way, and he sure wasn't going to. He stole my jewelry, my medication, and my coins. I had to keep everything locked tight. I was tired of living in that situation. Wayne and I got along great when Ray wasn't around."

When Bonnie called and asked for me to come help with Nathan's "Welcome Home Party," she had been to the motorcycle races in Virginia the previous Sunday and had a bad accident on her motorcycle.

My first thought about helping her was, *"How can I help you when I feel so bad myself?"*

Never ignoring my children's needs if my body still moves, I take Ray and the step-grandchildren to Wayne's ex-wife. By this time the grandmother has gotten tired of Kathy's baby and told her to come and get it. Kathy is angry with all of us anyway so she calls her mother and asks her if she and the baby can come over to her house.

Wayne lost his driver's license because of a DUI about eight months ago; therefore, I am chief navigator. I am feeling disoriented. I experience two of my three alters coming out within the next few hours.

I know if Bonnie sees me as I look now, she will begin to hate Wayne. I look dead. I have no color in my complexion and no energy. I am sick. I have been to doctors, but none of them can diagnose what is wrong with me. This state of depression is killing me:

➤ Wayne has no job; he drinks from morning to night.
➤ We finally get Ray into a psychiatric hospital, and then Wayne signs him out the next day against doctor's orders.
➤ I am taking care of his stepdaughter's little Black baby, whose father is in prison.
➤ My number one addiction, sex, is getting no attention.

On my trip toward Bonnie's house, I am tired and depressed. I wonder what Bonnie will think when she sees how terrible I look.

I have entered the ramp to I-285 when Susie takes over the wheel. She thinks, *"We cannot allow Bonnie to see Sarah as she looks now."* She takes a wrong exit off I-285, but soon realizes she doesn't know where she is. She gets back on and realizes she is going in the wrong direction. Exiting again, she makes the same mistake. It seems we are going in circles. She is lost.

Susie goes away and I return to head the car back in the right direction. I don't want Wayne to know I am lost because I have made this trip so many times. I am having trouble breathing, so I hold on to the steering wheel and concentrate on breathing as deep as I can. I feel overwhelmed with a wretched desperation and I do not know how to get out of this mess I have gotten myself into.

On arrival at Bonnie's, I try to eat the dinner I bring for us, but I can't. I excuse myself and tell Bonnie I will clean her kitchen in the morning.

I awaken at 2:00 AM and I am unable to get air into my lungs. I am gasping for air—deep gasps through my mouth. I become frightened. Still gasping for air, I tell Wayne, "I need to call 911."

Wayne says, "You don't need to call. You will be all right if you keep a wet washcloth on your face." He goes outside to smoke.

In the past, representatives from my insurance company have told me to always call "nurse call" first. I dial the number to "nurse call."

The person on call says, "Honey, you need to call 911."

"All right, but I was trying to save money."

Wayne returns from smoking his cigarette and sees me still gasping for air and fumbling with the phone.

Again he says, "Sarah, you will be all right if you keep the washcloth on your face."

Seventeen-year-old Kristen comes to my rescue and dials "911."

The operator hears a young girl, who is apparently distressed, and having trouble breathing. The operator asks, "Is anyone else present in the house?"

"Yes ma'am."

"Please give the phone to them. You need to be lying down."

Bonnie has awakened and says, "Mama, give me the phone."

Sarah returns and thinks, *I don't care if I die, so why should you? That wasn't me; it was someone else who dialed 911.*

NOTE: Kristen is a sweet little adolescent who rescues me or Susie when we can't take it anymore. All my strength and energy is centered in Kristen. When my spirits get low, and I begin listening to my abuser values and putting myself down, Kristen always comes back and talks to me, reminding me of positive affirmations I vaguely remember previous therapists telling me.
- ➤ You are not a bad person.
- ➤ It is not your fault.
- ➤ You were only a child.
- ➤ You are not stupid.
- ➤ Remember all the people you have helped.

The ambulance finally arrives. After placing an oxygen mask on me, the emergency medical technicians help me down Bonnie's long flight of stairs. Wayne rides with me and Bonnie drives her car. Oh, I finally have oxygen. I can't get enough of this oxygen. I wonder if these people can actually help me. Oh, dear God, is it possible? Will these people help me? I am tired, so tired. I surrender; I give up. I don't remember the rest of the ride or getting to the emergency room. I remember little of what happens for the next few days.

Later, my doctor tells me, on my admittance, my oxygen level was only eighty-one and my sodium level was extremely low, and could have possibly damaged brain cells. Either condition was serious enough to have caused me to go into a coma. Also, my liver was inflamed, and my chronic obstructive pulmonary disease was causing major respiratory problems. I stay in the hospital for five days. Well, so much for helping Bonnie, and attending my son's "Welcome Home" celebration.

My sister, Rebekah, calls me at the hospital on Saturday morning. She says she wants to come see me.

"No, I am too far away."

"Oh, that's all right, especially if I can get my youngest daughter, Adriana, to drive for me."

"Rebekah, please don't bother her. You and your girls have your hands full with your own families. Wayne is here with me. I'll be fine." I say good-bye and promise to let her know if anything gets worse. About five hours later, Rebekah and Adriana walk through the door. I can't believe it, because I didn't know for sure she was coming. I need someone to talk to so badly. Wayne is sleeping. I give both of them a big hug, and I begin crying. I barely let them get seated before I start pouring out my heart to Rebekah. I feel I *must* share my feelings with someone or I will die.

I know I am in a situation I cannot continue to live in. Wayne is nine years younger than me, and possessive about my being away from him, or having time alone. When I married him, I had been alone, doing whatever I wanted for many years. Wayne and I started out living the childhood we never had. It doesn't work too well with us trying to relive our childhoods, while he still has to raise his fourteen-year-old disrespectful-disobedient, spoiled child who now has his own child. Also, Wayne and I have taken in an eighteen-month-old little Black girl belonging to Wayne's stepdaughter. I am depressed, sick physically, and feel I have no escape except to die. At this point, dying would be a welcome relief.

A few weeks before, Mama had died. I hadn't visited her as often as I felt I should have, but it was a four-hour drive from where I lived in Alabama to where she lived in Georgia. Another reason for not visiting often was my depression, and the pneumonia I couldn't seem to get over. Earlier, I had fallen and broken a rib, and then pneumonia set in. I had run a low-grade temperature for almost three months. I had heard it called "walking pneumonia" when I was younger. I call it "ignoring body symptoms."

Wayne awakens from his deep sleep, surprised to see Rebekah and Adriana. I tell Wayne, Rebekah, and Adriana to go on to Nathan's party. Wayne says he is not going to leave me.

Rebekah says, "Oh, I'm going. Adriana and I both want to see Nathan. I want to see Noah too."

Rebekah and Adriana go to the party. When they return, Rebekah tells me she and Noah enjoyed seeing each other. They have not seen each other since our divorce in 1989. The two of them enjoyed many old tales and laughs, which were mostly about me. Adriana says she enjoyed seeing her three cousins again, and was sorry it had to be under these conditions—my being sick and in the hospital.

Noah and I are friends today for the benefit of our children. Unfortunately, for Nathan his party became a discussion about the physical and emotional condition of me. Since I am not yet getting any better, my children decide, without my knowledge, to arrange a meeting with the chaplain and my doctor early on Sunday morning. The five decide Wayne must be taken back to Alabama.

He is unshaven, and has not bathed since Thursday. He is having tremors from lack of alcohol.

Allen visits me first, and offers to take Wayne out for breakfast. While they are gone out for breakfast, Nathan and Bonnie come in to tell me Nathan has volunteered to take Wayne back to Alabama so he can get home and take care of the children. When Wayne returns, he is not too happy he has to leave without me. Now it is his responsibility to gather all the children again, and try to provide for them without my help.

After Wayne is gone, the chaplain comes to see me that afternoon. He tells me to call him Evan. I like him, and I share some of the problems which led up to my being admitted in the hospital.

At 6:00 on Monday morning, the Respiratory Therapist awakens me. She says, "Sarah, we are going to remove your oxygen. I need to teach you how to use this breather and your puffers."

I think, *"Oh no, please don't take away my oxygen."* I will never forget that horrible night at Bonnie's when I felt I would never again get enough oxygen into my lungs. Reluctantly, I cooperate and the therapist is pleased with my first effort to use the breather.

As she leaves, she says, "I'll be back about 3:00 this afternoon to practice with the breather again. You have a nice day."

When Doctor Vainer, the nephrologist, makes his rounds about 8:00 PM on the same day, he explains to me who he is, and tells me I cannot drink alcohol anymore. He further explains, when someone continues to have pneumonia over an extended period of time as I did, the kidneys fail to produce a hormone needed to keep the bladder from eliminating sodium. Dr. Vainer was called in to study my medical condition when the emergency room doctor received reports my sodium level was dangerously low. He restricts me to 1000 cc. fluid intake each day. While in my room, he says that Dr. Gudur, the general practitioner assigned to my case, has ordered glucose since I am too sick to eat.

On the third day I am in the hospital, Dr. Vainer writes an order for the lab to perform another test to find out my sodium level. He drops my fluid intake to 800 cc. a day. When he visits my room, he tells me to be sure the nurses measure my fluid intake and output.

My little protector Kristen thinks, "I believe your doctors have a conflict of interest. One in pushing fluids through your veins, and one is limiting the fluids by mouth."

A few hours later, Dr. Gudur comes to visit. First, he checks my blood pressure. It has skyrocketed. Thinking nicotine withdrawal could possibly have caused it, he orders nicotine patches and high blood pressure medication. He stops my glucose, but does not remove the IV needle, much to my sorrow. It is located in the fold of my arm, and sticks me every time I move. At least now I can sneak up, and go to the bathroom alone.

I am reminded by Kristen, "That is a no, no."

I go anyway. I despise being dependent on others. I remember to save the urine in the proper container for measuring.

Monday in the hospital is like the local burger joints on its busiest day. A staff comes and takes me to the X-ray department. Dr. Gudur orders a sonogram to check for gallstones and another test to check the condition of my esophagus and stomach. When the test results return, Dr. Gudur tells me I have no gallstones, my esophagus has cleared some since my last test, but now the lining of my stomach is covered with ulcers.

On Tuesday's visit, Dr. Gudur requests blood work for a CHEM-7 test. He says if this test comes back normal, he will allow me to go home tomorrow. My sodium has not risen to normal levels; however, another test reflects my liver is no longer inflamed, and the oxygen in my blood now checks out normal. He decides I can go home, but will need to stay in touch. I need to schedule an appointment with both him and Dr. Vainer for next week.

When I am dismissed from the hospital, Evan, the chaplain, visits me once at Bonnie's home where I now live, until I can regain more strength. I learn Evan has a private practice besides his work at the hospital and his church. I visit Evan's church at Birmingham United Methodist Church, which is twenty-two miles away. I can feel the Holy Spirit on entering the church where the chaplain is a member.

In the few months since I began attending this church, I have come to love the pastor, Reverend John Wolfe, and his wife, Reverend Judy C. Wolfe, Associate Pastor and Grief Counselor. I already cared for the chaplain, who first led me into the arms of these warm and loving people. He is Reverend Evan Bergwall, Minister of Pastoral Care and Counseling.

NOTE: Later, when I was admitted to the Women's Institute of Incorporation Therapy, this church I now attend regularly, kept me on their prayer list throughout my stay. This church has grown so fast, there are two services each Sunday morning, and soon there will be three.

Mary recently told me Adam said, "It is unfortunate Sarah would drive twenty-two miles to see a man instead of going to church to worship the Lord."

When I tell Evan what my brother said, he says, "Confront him. Ask him why he said that."

I do confront Adam and his reply is, "I hope that's the reason you went."

Evan tells me I should be angry with Adam.

I say, "I should?"

He tells me, "Definitely."

I tell him, "But, I don't know how to be angry. When I was a child, getting angry meant getting a whipping."

He says, "Maybe so, but you are not a child any longer, and your brother should be supporting you, and not discouraging you."

The storm in my head, the loyalty to my abusers, and the internal communication I have learned from my perpetrators have convinced Susie it was the beer, which hurt her, and a few mixed drinks won't damage her at all.

Susie says, "It will numb the pain. Go buy a bottle of Limon Rum and you will begin to feel like royalty again." In about four days the bottle is gone. My feet swell again and the emotional pain is no better.

Bonnie goes with me to Alabama to get some of my belongings. Wayne is angry because he feels my children abused him.

He states emphatically, "I married you, not your children."

Wayne's brother, Ed, comes out to the mobile home in the country to help Bonnie and I pack the utility trailer. So many people are here to help me—mostly members of Wayne's family. They are angry with Wayne for stopping work and allowing me to support him, Ray, Wayne's stepchildren, and step-grandchildren.

Wayne wanders around drinking one beer after another, while others are working. It takes most of the day to get the trailer and vehicles loaded. Faith, feeling empathy for Wayne, is concerned about how he will live without my money. Before leaving, she tells Wayne he can take $200 out of their savings account. This account has Wayne's name on it so he will have no problem getting the money.

Bonnie will drive the black jeep home and pull the red utility trailer, while I follow in her Suzuki and trailer. Bonnie and I leave. I cry most of the way back to Georgia. (Faith had bought Wayne another jeep—not as new or as nice as the first one.)

I later learn Wayne withdraws $400 out of our checking account without my permission. The United States President has passed a bill giving everyone claiming a child on their 2002 income tax report, a check for $400, thereby, helping to put money back into the economy. Wayne has received this check and cashed it. This should have been mine, since he had no income for the year 2002. I learn about it months after the fact and ask him what happened to the check.

He answers, "I used it."

I become deeply depressed after this trip. Two weeks later, I go alone to Wayne's home in Alexander City. We need to discuss the loan I have on his home. Mark wants me to force Wayne out of his own home by selling it. I have discussed this with friends and family. I believe it would be unfair because the house was his before I moved in; however, I cannot continue making the loan payment of $512 a month.

Rebekah calls the following Saturday to see how I am feeling. I tell her, "I am so tired and I don't feel well. I don't know what to do. I don't see any reason I should go on living." Rebekah calls Mary and tells her I said, "I don't see any reason I should go on living." Later, I don't remember saying these words. Possibly, it was Kristen who said these words to Rebekah.

Mary was diagnosed long ago with the chemical imbalance that runs in our family. She has been worried about me for a long time, and she knew this statement was a cry for help. It was a warning sign from a person who was deeply depressed and suicidal. Mary sends me an ad in a bipolar newsletter asking me to read it. She writes me in the email, to which she has attached the bipolar newsletter, "Sarah, this is the hospital you need to go in. You need to admit yourself into this hospital."

I read the entire newsletter. The experience of a woman named Julie is written into the advertisement. It tells of her experience with the Women's Institute for Incorporation Therapy in Hollywood, Florida.

This hospital offers treatment for the following psychiatric issues as well as other women's trauma issues: Depression, Bipolar Disorder, Borderline Personality, Child Abuse, Sexual Abuse, Post Traumatic Stress Disorder, Dissociative Disorders, D.I.D., Multiple Personality Disorder, Ritual Abuse, Incest, and other Women's Programs.

This hospital seems nothing like the hospital I admitted myself into in Columbus. This hospital sounds wonderful to me.

But, when Mary calls to ask what I think about going into this hospital, Susie answers, "It's in Florida and my insurance probably won't pay out-of-state."

Mary's response is, "We are talking about your life. Look how much money you have recently thrown away on men."

Kristen hears Susie, and she now holds the phone, "Yes, you are right. *We* have to go into the hospital or *we* will die."

Mary, not knowing about my DID (Dissociative Identity Disorder), hears her sister say "we" and is momentarily confused; however, she doesn't have time to dwell on it now. She can hear the childlike, willingness in Kristen's voice, and she thinks Sarah has finally humbly accepted she must have psychiatric intervention before she can begin the road to recovery.

Mary thinks, *"Before Sarah has time to change her mind, I will call the hospital to find out more about the hospital policies and admission procedures."*

I try to run from getting the psychiatric and medical help I need to survive. Again, Jesus is holding me tightly in his arms. He will not let me go. When he does allow me to walk alone, a few steps at a time, I often collapse.

When he trusts me to walk alone, I never make much progress. But, do you know what? He never leaves me lying by the wayside. He always picks me up and carries me again tightly in his arms. He never stumbles and falls while he is carrying me. I adore the poem, "Footprints in the Sand." Jesus has carried me so much of my life.

Mary calls a few days later and tells me, "Rebekah and I will drive you to Hollywood, Florida, next Wednesday, July 23. They have a bed available. Their hospital *is* included on your insurance plan."

I cry frantically. My mind is a crazy mixture of hope and anxiety. Here is God doing for me what I cannot do for myself. In these last few weeks there have been many similar occasions. Not only did Jesus carry me, he held me tightly, so I couldn't get away. Now is my chance to show gratefulness for his kindness by working as hard as I can to get well, or at least get better. Nathan, Bonnie, and Allen need their "real" mother back. Noah has been concerned for me because of our children.

Mary explains there may be one problem about my admission.

Then she tells me all about her conversation with Mel, the admissions clerk. I fell off a ladder while hanging pictures for Bonnie two weeks ago. I fractured two vertebrae in the center of my spine. My doctor decided it was better to use a brace than to operate.

When Mel heard this, he told Mary, "We are not equipped to handle this type medical problem."

Mary quickly told him, "Oh, she doesn't need special help. She takes care of her own personal needs."

Mel asked about alcohol. "Has she been sober for at least thirty days?"

Mary explained she hadn't; however, she told Mel she would tell Sarah she had to stop right now. She explained to Mel, Sarah is able to stop any time she wants, and never has tremors or any aftereffects from alcohol. She explained Sarah is not an alcoholic.

Mel explained to Mary, if alcohol becomes a problem for Sarah, she will be moved to another wing of the hospital.

Now, Mary tells Sarah, "Honey, do not drink any more between now and when you go in the hospital."

It is one week before we leave for South Florida. I use alcohol strictly to numb feelings. Thoughts of going into the hospital cause knots in my stomach, pain in my chest, and a dull ache of foreboding. I drink more this last week than I normally drink, trying to stay numbed out. I am afraid Susie might appear when it comes time to go and persuade me not to go into the hospital.

On July 23, Wayne is scheduled to be in court in Alabama for a second DUI he received since I left him. I can't worry about him. He must weather the storm alone. I have my own storm now.

July 22 finally arrives. I drive to Rebekah's home, having only a few clothes and gowns to take with me to the hospital, because those I have won't fit over my back brace. My little salad dressing bottle filled with the last of my rum will help to numb the pain and frustration I will feel tonight. When I arrive at Rebekah's home, I intend to have some time alone to fix a healthy mixed drink. Rebekah spoils that when she pulls out Mama's clothes. Rebekah is happy because she has tried to find someone who would appreciate Mama's clothes since she died earlier this year. Rebekah also gives me her lotion and some other personal items. I am thankful for these items. I wrap the salad bottle of rum in towel and hide it in one of the drawers, hoping Rebekah won't find it until I get back to claim it.

Rebekah and I leave early the morning of July 23 to pick up Mary and head south. I know for sure now I need to be in the hospital, because I see Rebekah's mouth moving as she talks to me but I can't hear her. Instead, I hear voices in my head. I can always recognize Susie's voice but I hear another voice too. I try to go inside myself; this pain is too great.

"You should never have agreed to go into the hospital, Sarah. They will find out all our secrets. They will stop us from having any fun in our lives. I tried to tell you. Why won't you listen?"

"Don't listen to Susie, Sarah. She always gets us into trouble. We are on the right road now. You almost died before you went to Bonnie's and I called 911. If you don't go in this hospital, Susie will cause us all to die."

I put my hands over my ears and lean forward in my seat. This mental skirmish is exhausting me.

"Sarah," Rebekah says as she touches me on the arm.

I jump and sit up straight, shaking my head to clear it.

"I'm sorry," she says. "I didn't mean to startle you. I wanted to ensure you were all right."

"I'm fine; just nervous, I guess." My heart is pounding like a bomb with a timer ready to explode. I believe Kristen is right; this is it—my last chance. I am reminded of one of my favorite songs, "It's Now or Never."

Rebekah and Mary are relaxed as we travel the long Interstate to Hollywood, Florida. They laugh about old childhood memories—the few enjoyable ones we had. Honestly, I had none except the time I spent with the cows at the barn, the trips I took through the 4-H Club, and once to FHA Camp when I paid my own way.

I am thinking, *how can Rebekah and Mary enjoy themselves, knowing they are taking me to be admitted to a psychiatric hospital?*

We finally arrive at our cousin's house. He has invited us to sleep at his home this evening. He knows the area well and does not want us traveling alone. The four of us leave early the next morning.

On arrival at the Pavilion, we learn that Mel, the intake person Mary had communicated with, is unavailable to do my evaluation. Sherri, a different intake person, meets with us to handle all the initial admission paperwork. She, my sisters, and Joe begin discussing the plans we have made for me to stay at Joe's house when I leave the hospital to change from the inpatient program to the outpatient program.

Joe says, "The tri-rail is near my house. I will carry you, Sarah, each morning to catch the train. You can ride it to a station, which is within a few blocks of the hospital."

Sherri replies, "Yes, and we have a van that will pick you up from the station and bring you here to the hospital."

I have no memory of what transpires next; however, several people have told me it was unbelievable how much my voice sounded like a three or four-year-old child's. I turn to Mary and hug her. "Y'all know I'm afraid of getting lost. I can't ride on a train by myself. What if I get on the wrong one? How will I know where to get off?"

Susie sniffles and wipes her nose, then continues, "Mama shouldn't have left me in that store. I thought I was holding her skirt, but I looked up and it was another lady. I ran all through the clothes racks, searching for Mama, and she wasn't there. She shouldn't have gone off and left me."

NOTE: Mama had gone upstairs to another level of the store. She had forgotten all about me. A sales clerk asked me for my mother's name and then she told me she would find my mother. She took me to the office and asked me to wait. I waited a long time before she found Mama.

Mary told me later, tears came into Rebekah's eyes. Rebekah is upset because I was so frightened, and because my voice changed to sound like a little child.

Sherri told Susie, "Sarah, where the tri-rail lets you off, that is where our van comes to pick you up. If you get afraid, there is a doughnut shop right there. Go inside and sit down in a booth. Wait a little while until you feel calmer, and then call the hospital, and we will come and pick you up."

Susie is upset, and she cannot stop crying. The outpatient therapist, Angie, comes to get her so they can start the intake evaluation. Rebekah is worried about her sister being upset, and she asks if she can go with her for the intake evaluation. Angie tells her she can't, but she reassures Rebekah that Sarah will be all right.

And…Susie is fine. Angie is gentle and kind with her intake evaluation questions. She causes Susie to feel special. In a short time, Angie gives Susie about ten compliments. Later, when Sarah goes to outpatient therapy, she is happy to learn Angie will be her therapist.

When the intake evaluation is complete, we go back to the front lobby to tell Joe, Rebekah, and Mary good-bye, because we brought in my luggage when we first arrived. After Mary, Rebekah, and Joe have left, and are about to get into their car, they look back at the hospital front door. They see Susie has run back out of the hospital after them. Rebekah goes back and takes her back inside the hospital. When she returns, she is crying so hard she is unable to drive her car. Joe takes the keys from her, and tells her he will drive.

I am back now, and one of the nurse technicians takes me to my room. She goes through all my belongings. The technician locks some items I may need later on the first floor. Others are locked up on the second floor—the ones I am not allowed to have until I am discharged from the hospital.

When my clothes are unpacked, the technician takes me and introduces me to the group in progress. The therapist seems to genuinely care about the patients. I believe I will like this place, and possibly, learn much about the issues specific to my problems.

I have learned more in this hospital in one and one-half days than I did in my entire stay of five days in the Columbus hospital. It is unbelievable what I'm hearing and learning. There are so many assignments. I feel like I'm in graduate school again. We are given a notebook containing a list of assignments, the assignment sheets, and the number of days before they are due. One important assignment is to write my autobiography. When I complete writing mine, it is twenty-nine pages long.

The most outstanding lesson taught—and I hear it from four different facilitators—is the "Dissociative Continuum." The first presenter I hear it from is Pat Richards, Clinical Director of the hospital. I never understood my problems until I heard this presentation, but now some of my behaviors are making sense. Memories that have returned since coming to the hospital are:

➤ Daddy forced me to sit on his lap. He may have done it before age four; however, that is the first time I remembered him slipping his finger under the leg of my panties and playing with my pee pee.

➤ I remember it felt good, so I began doing it to myself when no one was watching.

➤ When I was sitting on Daddy's lap, he moved me around over his erect penis, and sometimes he tried to put his finger in my vagina, but the opening was too small.

➤ After a while, I told other family members I was Susie—not Sarah.

➤ Daddy took the lock off the bathroom door and, when questioned, said no one was keeping him out of any room in his house. He stood at the lavatory looking in the mirror, watching me while I bathed. Sometimes he turned around and leaned against the laboratory, grinning at me.

> ➤ I began sticking objects up in my bottom.
> ➤ Daddy started touching me more often, and then he began touching me on my chest and butt. Looking back now, I can tell, as time went by, Daddy became more sexually aroused. The time we lived at the shack in Raccoon Valley and he took me to get a loaf of bread was the worst. He ejaculated during that incident.
> ➤ Mama forces me to move upstairs to sleep with my fourteen-year-old brother, when I am seven, because the bed downstairs is overcrowded with all three girls. Why? Didn't she know it wasn't a good idea to put a seven-year-old girl child in bed with a fourteen-year-old boy?

Ms. Richards continues with her presentation. "If the abuse begins before the age of seven, the child experiences one of three outcomes:

...they die,

...they go insane, or

...they survive, depending on their intelligence and creativity.

I think to myself, *I'm here, and I was four when my abuse began, so I must be intelligent and creative.* From all I have learned since coming here, I know it took creativity for me to learn to dissociate—separate my head from my body—in order to survive the horrible dysfunctional family I lived in. I know now learning to dissociate was not a bad reaction—it was a healthy response for a child in danger. It allowed me to go away until it was safe for me to return.

As Ms. Richards goes on, tears flood my eyes. No therapist, no spouse, no friend, no one has ever told me I was bipolar, much less that I had Dissociative Identity Disorder (DID). The presentation is slowly coming to an end. It is almost impossible to fool these therapists, but I have specialized in "hiding my feelings." Ms. Richards doesn't realize how upset I am. Now, I know what I have to deal with. I must learn the skills to deal with it.

After this presentation, I am called to the office. This scares me. I quickly switch to Kristen. She thinks for sure we are in trouble, but she doesn't know why. When she gets to the office, Jennifer, the regular inpatient group therapist, tells Kristen Sarah's insurance has approved her stay only through tomorrow and it may be her last day.

Only five minutes earlier, Kristen has understood and finally accepted the depth of Sarah's sickness. Now she thinks she will lie down and die...right here and now. She tells Jennifer, "We can't leave tomorrow."

"Why?" Jennifer asks.

Kristen cries, "Because...because I'm not able to save us anymore. Susie will kill us if we have to leave. We finally find a place where we can get the help we desperately need, and you all are going to kick us out after four days?"

Jennifer hears the desperation in Kristen's voice and she is sympathetic. She tells her, "I will see what I can do."

I later learn from my daughter, Bonnie, the insurance company only approves three to four days at a time the rest of my stay, but the office never again shares this with me. Emotionally, I couldn't handle it until I was stronger.

My stay in the hospital is twelve days inpatient and, thanks to the hard work of many employees there, my insurance approved me for another two weeks of outpatient treatment.

While inpatient, the first piece of mail I receive is a card from my dear sister, Rebekah. While on vacation, she notices the card, "Footprints in the Sand." The card has the bookmark shown in Figure 10.1. It is a benefit

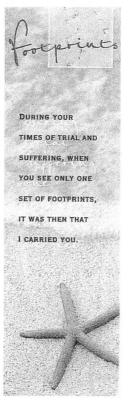

DURING YOUR TIMES OF TRIAL AND SUFFERING, WHEN YOU SEE ONLY ONE SET OF FOOTPRINTS, IT WAS THEN THAT I CARRIED YOU.

Figure 10.1
Footprints

to me in my assignment book as a constant reminder, when times get tough. Knowing how much I love this poem, Rebekah took time out on her vacation to buy it, write to me, and find a post office box to mail it. My first letter is from my dear sister, Mary. My dear son Allen, who lives in Charlotte, North Carolina, but travels doing audits for his company, volunteers to come to the Miami area while I'm in outpatient, to spend time with me in the evenings. While Allen is visiting with me, we reminisce about one of my visits with him when we went to Cheaha Mountain. I tell him I am beginning to have those same feelings of peace I had the day I was with him. I try to explain to him how sorry I am about hurting him and Nathan and Bonnie; however, the way I live my life from this day forward will be different from the past. I tell Allen I will not be hurting any of my children again. I never realized the love my children and my sisters had for me until now. There is nothing I wouldn't do for them, but I didn't realize it was the other way around as well.

While in outpatient therapy, I begin reading a book entitled, *God's Plan for Me*. After reading a chapter, I write in my journal the quote for the day, the Bible scripture the lesson is based on and God's purpose for me for the day. The Lord has been so good to me. He blesses me in many ways.

At WIIT hospital, the goal of treatment for multiple personality disorder is not the fusion or integration of the alter egos, but the harmonious cooperation between the ego states so the whole functions as an incorporated system.

During my outpatient care, I ask Dr. Tollefson for an incorporation and he grants my request. Dr. Tollefson is the founder of "incorporation therapy," and he is Director of Women's Institute for Incorporation Therapy. All the patients call him "Dr. Bill." Before Dr. Bill and I leave the outpatient room, he announces to the group, "I said a special prayer for Sarah last night asking for her incorporation to be successful."

Tears come to my eyes, because I have spent much time in prayer and meditation preparing for this incorporation. I am confident this will be the beginning of a new life in Christ. He has carried me so much when I was unable to walk alone. I can hardly wait for Dr. Bill to go with me so we can get the process started. We leave from the outpatient room and go directly to his office.

On entering Dr. Bill's office I ask him if I can say a personal prayer before we begin. He grants my wish.

> Dear Lord,
>   Thank you for watching over little Susie, age four; Faith, age eight; Kristen, age seventeen, and me, Sarah, a retired teacher of sixty. Susie was first abused by her father at age four and by her brother at age seven.
>   Faith became aware of how poor Sarah's mother and father were—so poor they didn't have enough food to feed five children and two adults. Kristen tried to take care of all the problems and protect herself and everyone else.
>   Since I have been here at WIIT, I have felt more peace, joy, and confidence than I have felt in my life. Many of my friends and loved ones' prayers have been heard. Dr. Bill's willingness to guide me through my incorporation is the answer to those prayers. I know something wonderful is about to happen. Heal my fractured mind, Lord, and I will dedicate the rest of my life to you. Amen

I tell Dr. Bill, "I wish I didn't have to take away Kristen. She has always protected me. I want to keep her."

Dr. Bill laughs and says, "We aren't going to get rid of any of your alters. We're going to give them new functions and a safe environment to grow."

"Oh, I didn't know that."

"Okay," Dr. Bill informs me. "Let's get started. This could take some time."

Dr. Bill asks me to get into a comfortable position in my chair, and then he places his thumb on my forehead. He asks me to close my eyes, and lay my hands in my lap.

As I close my eyes, I feel peace and contentment come over me. I feel the presence of angels around me. I feel safe when Dr.

Bill begins the incorporation. To try and explain the joyful, exhilarating, spiritual experience that happens to me in the next hour is impossible here. I had prayed so hard…I had longed so much for the time when I would not hear other voices talking in my head. I had felt splintered and fractured since early childhood. I don't know if I will know how to be one person—the same to everyone I meet every day. How will it be with no other alter making faraway noises in my head or coming to my rescue—or getting in trouble and causing me to get blamed for something I don't remember doing?

Dr. Bill continues… I must concentrate…

I undergo over an hour of beautiful healing and I leave feeling I am truly whole. As each alter is brought into my dome, my system becomes stronger. Kristen is first, then Faith, and finally Susie. I hug and love each one. They pass through my chest. After all are in, we join hands and agree to work together as a system, each with its own responsibilities. New functions designated are shown by each name in Sarah's complete system as designated in Figure 10.2:

NOTE: I want to cry each time I look at a picture of myself at age four or five. For some unknown reason, my family made more pictures of me at that age than at any other age, and in each of the pictures my hand is holding up my dress or it is under my dress. How could my mother look at all these pictures and not suspect a problem? I feel so sad, looking at all these pictures.

When I entered this hospital, I was aware hospital staff would be able to administer my medications. I hoped they could help me emotionally, but never once did I expect my stay here to be a spiritual experience as well.

I ask Dr. Bill, "How did you ever learn how to do an incorporation?"

His response is, "I didn't, God did."

I understand efforts to incorporate are not successful for

Sarah - 60
Facilitator, Loyalty to Self

Kristen - 17
Protector, Energizer,
Intelligence

Faith - 8
Spirituality, Strength

Susie - 4
Sexuality, Bravery,
Innocence

Figure 10.2 Sarah's complete system
Functions designated to self and alters at incorporation

everyone. For those patients who have a successful incorporation, Dr. Bill pins a set of wings on their shirt. I am so proud of my wings.

I believe it happened for me for several reasons. First, I had reached the bottom, and there was nowhere to go but up. My depression and my drinking led me to the point where I wanted to end it all. The second reason I believe the incorporation was successful for me is that mentally I was ready to receive it. I had complete faith Dr. Bill could guide me into the receptive state of mind needed to make the incorporation happen. And last, I had gone to God in prayer. I had asked him to make me whole, and I had faith he would answer not only *my* prayer, but those from my church members and other family members and friends.

I was once a victim. Most of my life I was a survivor, but now I am a recoverer, thanks to the staff of this hospital, whom Dr. Bill has trained to work with trauma victims like me. My aftercare notebook, *Continuing My Journey*, is filled with assignments, which will guide me through the next series of tools needed to complete my recovery journey. I have faith peaceful times are ahead. The storms are now calm. I have self-love, I say positive affirmations daily, and I journal with my *God's Plan for Me* book daily.

Because of Joe's mother-in-law's illness and her coming to stay with him and his wife Pat, I do not spend my outpatient therapy time with them. I stay in a small apartment close by the hospital where a shuttle bus picks me up daily. When I told Joe about my "Wings", he told Pat. She bought me the most beautiful plaque (See Figure 10.3) and presented it to me the last night I was in Florida. She said from now on we will call you "Ms. Wings".

I now have a solid foundation to stand on and my wings to fly if times get tough. In looking back at some of my journal notes from WIIT, I promised myself I would never cause myself shame or guilt again because of my past. I know now I was the victim and I *am* a worthwhile person.

Three of the most helpful lessons while at WIIT were "Self-

When you come to the very end of all the light you know,
and are about to step into the darkness;

Faith is knowing that one or two things will happen,
there will be something solid to stand on,
or you will be taught to fly.

Gay Lord
7/1950

Figure 10.3 Pat's gift

Sabotage," "Setting Boundaries," and "Internal Communication." I never knew how much I hurt myself until I studied the "Self-Sabotage" lesson. I don't cause those awful things to happen to me now. I have learned from the "Boundaries" lesson how to set up healthy boundaries. I learned from the "Internal Communication" lesson how to become stronger and how to help my entire system work more effectively.

I realize God has a purpose for my life. I had reached the point where I didn't want to live before I went to WIIT. Now I realize God's first purpose for me is to take care of myself and to love me as I am. I can't give love away until I love myself first. I am now active in my church for the first time in nine years.

Alas, the storm has lifted. The winds blowing around in my head have changed to the calm of the ocean breeze. I no longer blame myself for Susie's behavior; for I know in my heart she was born as a result of what my father did to me. I do good things for myself; those which a loving mother does for a little child—nurture, cuddle, love and provide for special needs—food, clothing, and shelter. Now I have balance in my life.

Through the continued support of my church, and especially Reverends John and Judy Wolfe, I learned to depend on Christ as my only true Father. He has cleansed me from all the shame and doubt. Prayer and spiritual readings are part of my daily life.

Luke 24:46-48 in the *Living New Testament* says, *"...the Messiah must suffer and die and rise again from the dead...that this message of salvation should be taken...to all the nations."*

On the day my pastor used that scripture as the text for his sermon, I sat in the pew with tears blinding my eyes. I swallowed hard, trying to choke back a sob. The tears spilled over and ran down my cheeks. I put my hands over my heart, because it was overflowing with joy, and I closed my eyes and said a silent prayer.

> Dear Lord,
> I understand that, without your suffering, there would have been no resurrection. I know that, if you hadn't risen again, you wouldn't have commanded your disciples to "go and spread the word of salvation." *[Suffering → Resurrection → Salvation]*
> Please help me, Lord, to be more like you. Help me to "rise again" as you did...to rise above my abusers and all those who would prefer to keep me chained to the past. Use my witness and the story of my life to give others courage to walk their own path toward healing and peace. Most of all, help me to proclaim the good news of Jesus Christ—the source of everlasting peace! Amen

You Love Your Daddy, Don't You?

Epilogue

I thank God that none of my alters appeared while I was teaching in the classroom for thirty years and I had a special place in my mind for my students. I treasured teaching children and each morning when I walked out the door of my home, everything left my mind except my plans for the day. My students were my top priority until I walked back into my home that afternoon. My alters had no place in my classroom.

Thank God for those counties across the nation who today have active CASA Programs (Court Appointed Special Advocates.) Oh, how I wish someone had helped Mary and me when we needed it so desperately. We would have been grateful had the welfare representatives exerted more authority on the first visit when someone reported Mama for not taking better care of her children. I had not yet been born the first visit and I was too young to remember the second visit. When they returned after the first warning, the family was gone to Grandmother's home in Alabama. What an injustice for Mary and me that no one was willing to help us.

I have memories of Daddy sexually arousing me at age four. It may have happened earlier but I have lost the memories. By age seven I was using anything I could find to arouse myself sexually. I prayed daily to Jesus to help me survive, to help me understand who I was, and why I existed in that life the way it was.

I constantly condemned myself; I could not forgive myself; I didn't know who to turn to for help. I tried to forgive myself; I thought I should have, but I couldn't. I tried hard to be a Christian. I was a victim trying to survive. I had *no* boundaries and I knew no way to set them up. I had never heard the term "boundaries." Even if I had, children living in my parents' household were not allowed to have boundaries. My only means of survival was to dissociate.

In becoming Susie at the age of four I didn't have to feel responsible for my sexual behavior.

Faith caused me to suffer, and I am still suffering financially because of all the money she gave to men. Faith surfaced during the nine months my father left the family stranded in an impoverished situation in the shack near the foothills of the Smoky Mountains of Tennessee. If Faith believes people are hungry, she gives them money. She doesn't want them to be hungry, as she remembers how it feels to be hungry and not know where the money will come from to buy more groceries. Faith's inclination to give was also born from our parents' Primitive Baptist teachings. We were taught to always share with those less fortunate and to put our elders before ourselves.

The staff at Women's Institute for Incorporation Therapy made three important suggestions for me to work toward when I left. The most important at the moment was filing a lawsuit against my brother, who owed me several thousand dollars. He was planning to file bankruptcy soon, and my lawyer said I needed to get my lawsuit filed before he filed bankruptcy. Therefore, if I were listed with the creditors, he would be admitting he *did* owe me the money. I filed the lawsuit and he added me to the list. My brother won his case; therefore he will never have to pay me the funds he owes.

It is important I focus on all I learned in the hospital: reinforce my boundaries, keep check on self-sabotage, and don't listen to abuser values. Even though I occasionally lose ground I immediately pull out my WIIT notebooks to get me back on track. I will never allow myself to be victimized again.

The WIIT staff encouraged me to work towards getting my divorce from Wayne. I had some financial matters to settle with him about the mortgage I had on his house, and I had to get his name off my property in Jackson Gap. These matters needed to be completed while we were still amicable with each other. Therefore, I postponed the divorce until I completed this other business. These matters were finalized about six months after leaving the hospital.

The last objective was for me to move out of the house I shared with my daughter, Bonnie. We were interfering with each other's lives. I learned she wanted to move closer to her job because she had a fifty minute commute in heavy traffic. Bonnie moved closer to her work and I stayed in her house and paid the mortgage until it sold. This arrangement worked well for both of us.

While living in Bonnie's home, I met and married a wonderful man. He loved me for what and who I am. I loved him as I never loved another man, and he felt the same way about me. We were married only eighteen months when he was diagnosed with stage IIIB lung cancer. It was the aggressive type, and I nursed him for the next ten months. He died January 2, 2006. I am lost without him, but am thankful for having had someone who truly loved me, even if it was for such a short time.

I have made the following commitment to my Inner Child.

My precious child, I promise to listen to your needs. Whenever I feel your distress, I will stop what I'm doing and put my arms around you and we will go to a place where it is safe. Maybe we will go in the sunshine, or in a meadow, or down by a stream of water. Perhaps we will curl up in a corner where it is quiet, but whatever we do, I will put my arms around you and I will listen...and I will kiss the tears from your cheeks for I know the depth of your wounds. You have a right to your feelings, and I promise I will never tire of listening to you. You are my precious child and I love you.

"If you are struggling with a broken heart or emotional distress, God wants to renew your mind, restore your soul, and give you a fresh start."
- By Joyce Meyer,
Ending Your Day Right, Devotions for Every Evening of the Year

May God bless you!
Sarah Harrison (sharr@comporium.net)

Printed in the USA
CPSIA information can be obtained
at www.ICGtesting.com
BVHW031127230823
668792BV00001B/14